EXCEPTIONAL CHILDREN IN FOCUS

Fourth Edition

James R. Patton, University of Hawaii
James S. Payne, University of Mississippi
James M. Kauffman, University of Virginia
Gweneth B. Brown, University of Delaware
Ruth A. Payne, Lafayette County Schools, Mississippi

SO-BZH-398

Merrill Publishing Company
A Bell & Howell Information Company
Columbus   Toronto   London   Melbourne

To Catie, Others Like Her, and Those Who Care So Much About Them

Cover Photo: Merrill publishing / Mary Hagler

Photo credits: All photos copyrighted by individuals or companies listed. Merrill Publishing/photographs by Larry Hamill, chapter 1; Mary Hagler, chapters 2 and 4; Jan Smyth, chapter 9; and Bruce Johnson, chapter 10. Mike Davis, Franklin County (Ohio) Board of Mental Retardation and Developmental Disabilities Respite Service, chapters 3 and 14; Luanne Voeltz, chapter 5; Joanne Kash, chapters 6 and 11; Vivienne Della Grotta, chapter 7; and Edgar Bernstein, chapters 8, 12, and 13.

Published by Merrill Publishing Company
A Bell & Howell Information Company
Columbus, Ohio 43216

This book was set in Bookman.

Administrative Editor: Vicki Knight
Production Coordinator: Rex Davidson
Cover Designer: Cathy Watterson

Library of Congress Catalog Card Number: 86-62083
International Standard Book Number: 0-675-20720-7
Printed in the United States of America
    2   3   4   5   6   7   8   9—91   90   89   88   87

Preface

While most special education texts are analogous to a full-course meal, this book is intended as a nutritious snack: a readable, compact, stimulating, fulfilling, but not overfilling, introduction that will give you some things about which to think seriously. If it serves its purpose well, it will whet your appetite for more.

This new edition, like the three preceding ones, includes anecdotes to give you a better idea of what it is like to work with exceptional individuals. We illustrate that retarded persons can learn, that emotionally disturbed kids are not completely crazy, that most blind people can actually see a little bit, that learning disabled students are brighter than they appear, that gifted youngsters may or may not be overly intelligent, and that hearing impaired persons can understand other people.

You'll find a new chapter in this edition entitled Adolescence and Adulthood, balancing the chapter on Early Childhood. We believe it is important to cover this topic because most exceptional children grow up to be exceptional adults. Over the course of the last few years, more attention has been directed to the needs of disabled adolescents and young adults. With the current emphasis on "transition from school to community," it becomes useful to highlight the major issues and efforts being undertaken with this older population.

We have made every effort to substantially revise and update all of the chapters with the latest information and developments. Within most chapters, you will find basic information (definition, prevalence, etiology), fundamental concepts, major issues, and current trends. Furthermore, in most chapters of this fourth edition, we have also added a "Working With . . ." section, which provides suggestions for working with individuals possessing a particular disability. We feel that this section provides readers with useful information that can be used in everyday situations. At the end of each chapter, except the first and last ones, there are sections entitled "Ponder These," which present exercises to help facilitate the integration of information, concepts, and issues.

Our overall goal for this book was simple. We hope that you will obtain not only a view of exceptional persons as individuals but also some useful descriptive information about exceptionalities.

We are grateful to Dr. Virgil S. Ward, who gave us helpful comments on Chapter 10, and to Ed Polloway and Dave Smith, who shared some of their experiences with us. We thank the following reviewers of the manuscript, who provided valuable comments: Cynthia Schloss, Williamsport Community College; Sally Todd, Brigham Young University; and Dr. Warren J. White, Kansas State University. Finally, Celeste Lehman and Gayle Tsukada receive our gratitude for their tireless, patient assistance with the preparation of the manuscript.

JRP

Contents

1 **Introduction to Exceptionality**   **1**

PART ONE
Learning and Behavioral Disorders   **7**

2 **Learning Disabilities**   **9**

Definition and Prevalence   13
Etiology   16
Learning Disabled or Learning Dyslabeled?   17
Current Developments   21
Suggestions for Working with Learning
    Disabled Children   23
References   25

3 **Emotional Disturbance/Behavioral**
Disorder   **27**

Terminology   32
Definition and Classification   33
Prevalence   35

Etiology   35
Issues in the Education of ED/BD Children   37
Conceptual Models   37
Suggestions for Working with ED/BD Children   41
References   44

4 Mental Retardation   47

Definition   52
Prevalence   54
Etiology   54
Realistic Expectations   55
Conclusions   63
Suggestions for Working with Mentally
  Retarded Persons   64
References   67

5 Severe and Profound Handicaps   69

Historical Perspective   74
Definition   75
Prevalence   77
Etiology   77
Administrative Concerns   79
Teacher Competencies and Preparation   80
Future Considerations   83
Suggestions for Working with
  Severely/Profoundly Retarded Persons   84
References   86

PART TWO
Physical, Sensory, and Communicative
  Impairments   89

6 Physical and Health Impairments   91

Definition and Classification   95
Specific Impairments   97
Behavioral Characteristics   101
Administrative and Educational Concerns   102
Prevalence   104
Trends and Issues   104

Conclusions   106
Suggestions for Working with Persons Who
   Have Physical and/or Health Impairments   106
References   109

7 Visual Impairments   111

Definition   114
Prevalence   115
Etiology   116
Visual Impairment in Perspective   117
Educational and Practical Concerns   119
Suggestions for Working with Persons Who
   Have Visual Impairments   121
References   124

8 Hearing Impairment   127

Definition   130
Prevalence   131
Etiology   131
Assessment   132
Impressions   133
Cognition and Communication   135
Postscript   137
Suggestions for Working with Persons Who
   Have Hearing Impairment   138
References   140

9 Communication Disorders   143

Definition   147
Etiology   148
Language Disorders   149
Speech Impairment   151
Multiple Disorders   153
Prevalence   155
Speech and Language Programs   155
Postscript   156
Suggestions for Working with Persons Who
   Have Speech/Language Disorders   157
References   159

PART THREE
Other Exceptional Areas 161

10 Giftedness 163

Definition 167
Prevalence 169
Characteristics 169
Etiology 170
Creativity 172
Differential Education 172
Conclusions 176
Suggestions for Working with Persons Who
  Are Gifted 177
References 180

11 Cultural Diversity 185

Introduction 187
The Nature of Cultural Diversity 188
Major Issues 190
Conclusions 196
Suggestions for Working with Persons Who
  Are Culturally Different 197
References 199

PART FOUR
Exceptional Perspectives 201

12 Early Childhood 203

Rationale for Early Childhood Education 206
Definition of Early Childhood Education 207
Prevalence of Young Handicapped Children 208
Etiology 209
Language Development 210
Early Intervention Projects 212
Recent Federal Initiatives Supporting
  Preschool Programs 215
Major Issues In Early Childhood Education 215
Suggestions for Working with Early
  Childhood Handicapped Children 219
References 222

13 **Adolescence and Adulthood**   **225**

Transition from School to Community
   Living   228
Adolescence   229
Adulthood   234
Conclusions   239
Suggestions for Working with Exceptional
   Adolescents and Adults   239
References   241

14 **Yesterday, Today, and Tomorrow**   **243**

The Development of a Field   248
Where Are We Headed?   264
Conclusions   266
References   269

1

Introduction to Exceptionality

The other day the little 4-year-old girl from next door came over and watched me rake leaves. For over 30 minutes she watched and then, out of the blue, said, "My daddy has a glass eye."

Well, how do you respond to that? Since I didn't know what to say or do, I just kept on raking the leaves and nonchalantly said, "Oh."

She continued, "Yeah, he really does, but I don't understand it. He can't see any better with it in than he can with it out."

Most people would agree that there's humor in the innocence of that four year old's statement. It's funny to me, it's probably funny to you, and it was certainly funny to my one-eyed neighbor. Thank goodness we can occasionally share a laugh about a circumstance which involves an unfortunate condition.

Students taking an introductory course in special education had just completed a class in tests and measurements and understood the normal curve better than their special education professor. It had been some time since the professor had thoroughly studied statistical distributions and, unfortunate-

ly, he was oblivious to the fact that his students had studied the curve very recently. With all the erudition that he could muster, the professor explained, "As you will observe, the normal curve is symmetrical, like a bell. Indeed, I'm sure you will find that this distribution is usually called the 'bell-shaped' curve."

Much sooner than the students would have preferred, final exam time rolled around. Lo and behold, not only was their professor a daring and dramatic lecturer, but he also had a talent for writing confusing test questions! One on the normal curve went as follows:

The normal curve is: (choose the best answer)
a. Symmetrical
b. Bell-shaped
c. Doesn't really matter
d. Who cares anyway

Most good students resist their impulse to circle d and fluctuate between a and b. The students in this class, however, had trouble deciding on their answer. Having just completed their tests and measurement course, they knew immediately that the correct answer must be a —symmetrical. But that was not the answer that the professor liked. "It's quite clear," he stated, "the answer is b because bells are symmetrical which includes a. Since there are many symmetrical things that are not bell-shaped, by the process of elimination, b is the best answer." After hearing this explanation, most of the students groaned, and some young rebels stormed out of the room. But no manner of protest or persuasion moved the steadfast professor. He loved his question and he loved his answer. He was even heard mumbling to himself, "I love it! I love it! I can tell the bright students from the not so bright just by this one question. The poor students think I'm just throwing them a curve, yuk, yuk, yuk!"

Not long after the course ended, a group of admiring students anonymously presented the professor with a token of their appreciation. Hanging on his office door one morning were three bells—a trapezoidal cowbell, a round sleigh bell, and a square bell. The thank-you note that was attached to the bells read, "Take these bells and. . . ."

People who work with exceptional individuals sometimes convey the impression that life is always serious and tragic. Stressing the sorrows that arise for handicapped individuals, these people tend to overlook the joys and rewards in the field of human services. Moreover, professors in teacher training institutions so often preoccupy themselves with statistical data that they neglect to give students a "feel" for exceptional people and what it is like to work with them. Thus, the unknowing may get the erroneous impression that working in human services will be dry and tedious, or even worse, full of sadness.

We have found that working with exceptional children, youths, and adults is exciting, engaging, and uniquely rewarding. Despite occasional "down" moments, it is a world of joy and delightful communication. When working with exceptional persons, one's perspective becomes very important. We can mourn because a rosebush has thorns or rejoice because a thornbush has roses. Those who cannot see the joy and humor in life's struggles will soon find that the thorns drain their enthusiasm and strength to endure the difficult periods.

Shortly after undertaking the writing of this book, we looked up from our professional journals full of confusing definitions, elaborate theories, conflicting results, and current controversies. We suddenly realized we had fallen into the same trap as many others in attempting to teach students about exceptional individuals. We had blindly missed the essence of our field. Our preoccupation with academic analysis had distracted us from viewing the emotional side of our work. We had forgotten the joy of watching a physically disabled child take her first steps, a retarded child finally learn to write his name, or an emotionally disturbed child bring his temper under control. We had even forgotten about the bad times—our disappointment when a retarded child returned from vacation having lost all that he had worked so hard to learn; our agony when we held down a self-destructive, emotionally disturbed child; and our anxiety as we told desperate parents about the lack of local services for their child.

If we, as professionals in special education and human services, don't project the joys as well as the pains of working with exceptional people, we are not projecting reality. If students enroll in an introductory course about exceptional people and they only learn how many times a Down syndrome child rocks during lunchtime, the frequency of thumbsucks of a severely handicapped student, the number of head-bangs exhibited by a severely emotionally disturbed child, then it is no wonder that handicapped individuals are thought to be odd. And it is no wonder that those of us working with disabled people are also considered a little crazy.

Many professors, in trying to help students grasp essential but often confusing information, forget to communicate the emotionally appealing aspects of special education. These professors also frequently entangle students in complicated details of very simple concepts. Consider the following brief lecture on the exogenous-endogenous concept.

Almost every introductory text about exceptional children will mention the terms "exogenous" and "endogenous" in relation to mental retardation. Most of these survey texts mention that the terms are used differently by different authorities in the field, but go on to say that usually exogenous is a term referring to causes of mental retardation which originate outside or external to the body and which are synonymous with pathological causes. Endogenous usually refers to causes of mental retardation that originate within the body or central nervous system and are synonymous with nonpathological causes or psychosocial (cultural-familial) mental retardation. Examples of exogenous causes of mental retardation include chromosomal anomalies, metabolic disorders, blood type incompatability, hypoxia (anoxia), prematurity of birth, etc.—all of which, at first glance, seem to be causes occurring inside rather than outside of the body. The majority of endogenous, or cultural-familial cases of mental retardation are caused by a combination of biological and environmental factors. Of course, the big emphasis should be on the environment which, it seems to me, is on the outside of the body rather than on the inside. Most dictionaries define the terms as they relate to plants. Large and more expensive dictionaries do define exogenous as "having its origin external" while endogenous refers to "originating within." It seems that exogenous means outside, but when it is related to causes of mental retardation it means inside, and endogenous means inside, but when it is related to mental retardation it means outside.

Now, the simple truth about these two terms is this. When someone uses the term *endogenous*, consider child-rearing practices, lack of educational opportunity, and inheritance as possible factors contributing to the retardation. When someone uses the term *exogenous*, consider genetic abnormalities, physical trauma, disease, prematurity, and metabolic disorders as possible factors contributing to the retardation.

Of course, once you finish your introductory course you probably will never hear these terms used again. While few professors who teach introductory courses overlook the opportunity to test students on the concept, in all our years working in the field of special education, we have never heard a teacher, counselor, principal, parent, or retarded child utter either "exogenous" or "endogenous."

In fact, the American Association on Mental Deficiency, an organization of professionals interested in mental retardation, regards these terms as obsolete.

Our message is simple: Special education is exciting and vibrantly alive. Rather than permitting dry academic commentary, nit-picking detail, and only sorrowful emotional experiences to dominate introductions to exceptionality, basic courses should impart a flavor of the personal joy of dealing with exceptional people.

However, we are worried about misinformation and misconceptions concerning exceptional individuals. Please note that we consider exceptionality to apply to people whose physical traits, mental characteristics, psychological abilities, and/or observable behaviors are significantly different from the majority of any given population. This deviation can be in either direction, including giftedness. Our concern derives from the fact that the misinformation and misconceptions can have a profound effect on the attitudes of the general public and therefore influence interpersonal relations and public policy.

With these ideas in mind, we have pushed aside traditional academic format and customary formalities in an attempt to provide you with a light, enjoyable reading experience. You needn't take copious notes or scrutinize the print; just sit back, gather a little basic information, and share with us the simple joys of working with exceptional people.

ONE
Learning and Behavioral Disorders

2

Learning Disabilities

Anna was in the sixth grade. She was a good student in most respects. She tried hard and did acceptable work in most areas. She was easy to get along with and related well to her peers, but she just couldn't spell.

Most sixth-grade classes love art projects and mine was no exception. I had acquired a kiln and some clay discarded by another school in the district, and we were having a really great time making all kinds of things. Anna brought me a beautiful slab pot that she had just finished. It was about 2 inches high and 6 inches in diameter, and I commented on its nice form and proportion in addition to the quality of construction. Obviously elated, Anna said that she was going to label her bowl so that everyone would know what it was (she didn't like having it called a "pot") and hurried off to do the job. About 20 minutes later she was back with her bowl. In perfectly formed, 2-inch letters, she had written on the side of her treasure, BOWEL.

I worked with Josh for 8 months on penmanship. I felt he was really making progress. His writing was more legible, he reversed fewer letters, and he could now mark within the lines. On the last day of the school year, a small box was left *anonymously on my desk. Inside was a small figurine of an owl with the following note:*

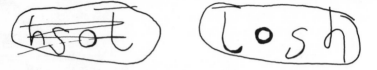

Now that I think about it, it really wasn't bad when you realize that at the beginning of the year, he couldn't even hold a pencil.

Eddie could count and add. If you showed him 3 dots plus 5 dots, he would say 8. However, when presented with any numeral, he experienced difficulty identifying it. After one year, I was exhausted and frustrated with the entire process of teaching him the identification of numbers. As he arrived for the first day of school for the second year, he dropped by my resource room and asked, "Am I going to learn the names of my numbers this year?"

I responded, "I sure hope so."

He quickly replied, "Don't worry about it, there is always another year."

Dr. Fonerden:

I wish to explain to you a strange mental weakness, to which I have all my life been a victim. At the age of seven or eight, I could read quite well, but shut the book and I could not spell the smallest words. My aunt who instructed me, beleeveing that it was obstinacy on my part, turn me over to my grandfather, and he having punished me severely gave me a collum of words to commit by a certain time; but alas, when the time had expired, I could not spell the first word, which was urn. Hour after hour and day after day was I compeled to study over this word; but let me shut the book for ten minutes and I could not spell it right, except by chance, and to my utter mortification a little collored boy was called up to spell it for me, he having lurned it from hearing it repeated to me so often. At last to such an extent was I persicuted on account of this word that I deturmined to run away. . . Now this peculiarity of my youth sticks by me still. When I went to sea, I toodk a dictionary, with the determination never to return home until I had lurned to spell; but it was no use. If I had kept my resolve I should never have returned. The hours of study I have wasted in endeavoring to become a good speller would have given me a profession. For that which I read, if it excite any interest, becomes stamped upon my memory indelibly, with this single exception, that which I wonce lurne I never forget. When I left school I wrote a very good hand, but spoilt it in endeavoring so to disguise the letters, that they might pass for what they should be, instead of what they were. I had occasion very recently, to direct a letter to my sister, but could not do so untill I had looked over many books to find the name Rachal, which I could not spell. I have been puzzled to distinguish between the agative too and preposition to, and between the article the and the pronoun thee. Were I to write this over from memory a great majority of the words would be spelled differently.

. . .The chief difficulty that I have to contend with is this; that when I write the most familiar words, and then ask myself are they spelt right, some jugling friend whispers in my ear many ways of spelling them, and I became lost in a maze of doubt and conjecture. To no other than yourself would I make this humuliating confession; and only to you in the faint hope that you may suggest a remedy. If you can, all that you have done to develope my mind, and to strengthen my character, will be as nothing in comparison.

Yours, truly_____[1]

Patrick Milton Wills frowned as he closed the file folders containing the information presented at the eligibility meeting for Edwin and J. C. Fifteen years ago, when he first became director of special education for the Marion County Schools, he had anticipated that his job would become easier as the years rolled by. Instead, it seemed to him that the decisions he faced were getting tougher all the time. True, the decisions about Edwin and J. C. were not his alone. He was only one member of the eligibility committee that was to decide whether these students were handicapped under PL 94-142 and, therefore, eligible for special education. But that didn't make it any easier for him to decide how he felt about these boys' education. "Fact is,"

---

[1]*Note. From American Journal of Insanity (pp. 61–63) author unknown, 1850.*

he thought to himself, "I have my hunches about them both. But if I were cross-examined in court, I'd have an awfully hard time defending any decision on either of them with hard facts and figures that make sense."

Mr. Wills let his mind drift back to the state's adoption of the LD definition under which Edwin and J. C. were being considered for special education. After seemingly interminable wrangling among state officials and LD experts, the state education department decided that the proposed federal formula for defining LD was too complicated and unreliable. Learning disability, the state decided, meant a difference of 20 or more points between WISC-R Full-Scale IQ and standard scores for the Woodcock-Johnson achievement test in written language or mathematics, or the Peabody Individual Achievement Test in math or reading. Seemed simple enough, he thought at the time. He remembered how the superintendent had slapped him on the back and said, "Well, P.M., I think we've finally got us a definition that'll cut out a lot of this needless haggling about who belongs in our LD classes."

Only it hadn't proved to be so simple. Take Edwin, for example. He was a third grader with a WISC-R Full-Scale IQ of 74. His W-J standard scores were lower than his IQ, 19 points in written language and 17 in mathematics. He didn't quite qualify for LD services under the definition, but he was certainly having lots of trouble in school. His teacher was at his wit's end to know what to do with Edwin. He was a constant behavior problem, according to the teacher—nearly always out of his seat, taunting and teasing his classmates, bullying smaller children on the playground, making life miserable for everyone. This was not a teacher whose class was generally disorderly or who had difficulty managing and teaching most children. Obviously, Edwin was not a bright child, though he didn't quite qualify as mentally retarded. And he was having more academic difficulty than one would expect based on his IQ. A lot more difficulty, in fact. His parents were extremely concerned and wanted him placed in one of the county's self-contained LD classes. But the classes were already filled. Besides, nearly 4% of the county's students were already identified as LD, many of them with test score discrepancies smaller than Edwin's.

Then there was the case of J. C., a bright and talented sixth grader. J. C. had a Full-Scale WISC-R score of 129. Here was a highly motivated, well adjusted boy who was well-liked by his peers, well-liked by his teachers, and well-read on nearly every topic. But he had only third grade math skills. On all achievement tests, he scored about two standard deviations above the mean in written language; but his math scores were consistently 40 or more standard points below his IQ. He seemed not to care; his peers seemed not to notice; his parents were convinced that the problem was simply poor teaching and strongly resisted the notion of his being identified as LD. They gave permission for J. C.'s formal evaluation for special education only with great reluctance. And, to make matters worse, P. M. Wills knew that J. C.'s math instruction had been, for the past three years, anything but exemplary. "Perhaps," he thought, "J. C. does not belong in an LD program even though he does technically fit the definition. I think his problems could quickly be resolved by a skilled tutor. And if he were my son, I don't think I'd want him in special education either."

P. M. Wills sighed. "Where are all those nice, neat cases I was taught about in graduate school?" he asked himself.²

DEFINITION AND PREVALENCE

The idea that some people have specific disabilities in learning is not new. The term *learning disability*, however, is only about 25 years old. Besides being the most recently labeled, learning disability (LD) is certainly the most controversial and least understood special education category. Ironically, nearly everyone has heard the term *learning disability*—and most people who talk about LD use the term *as if* they understand it. Recent estimates indicate that perhaps 1,000 people *per day* in the U. S. alone are newly and officially classified as learning disabled (Reeve & Kauffman, in press). And LD is now by far the largest category of special education in terms of the number of children and amount of money involved. Yet the definition of learning disability is still being debated. As one leading scholar and his colleagues put it, "though even the most illiterate student of education is likely to know the term, even the most literate scholar is likely to have

---

²*Note.* From *Introduction to Learning Disabilities* (pp. 293–294) by D. P. Hallahan, J. M. Kauffman, and J. W. Lloyd, 1985, Englewood Cliffs, NJ: Prentice-Hall. Copyright 1985 by Prentice-Hall. Reprinted by permission.

difficulty explaining exactly what a learning disability is"
(Hallahan, Kauffman, & Lloyd, 1985, p. 2).

Why do we have so much difficulty defining a problem that
is so widely recognized and deciding the precise meaning of such
a popularly applied label? Probably we find the definition difficult because the *idea* of a learning disability is pretty straightforward but application of the concept to real people is extremely complex. The same is likely true for the difficulty we have in
trying to decide how many children have a learning disability:
The abstract formula is a neat gadget, but it doesn't work very
well in the real world of schools and children. As Hallahan et al.
explain:

> Learning disability is easy to define as an abstraction.
> When we consider flesh and blood children, however, our
> abstract definition that seemed so adequate, or even
> elegant, on paper becomes a house of cards. The moment
> we try to apply our neatly written criteria to an actual
> child, our definition collapses around us, a casualty of
> the child's living, breathing individuality. Naturally, if
> we have difficulty deciding that any given child fits our
> definition, then we have little basis for stating how many
> children are LD. Our estimation of the prevalence of
> learning disability often is based on a statistical prob-
> ability that, like our definition, is attractive in the
> abstract but unworkable in practice. (1985, pp. 292–293)

In the abstract, experts estimate that 1–3% of the school-
aged population has a learning disability. In the real world of the
mid-1980s about 4% of the U. S. public school population has
been identified as LD (Hallahan et al., 1985; Reeve & Kauffman,
in press). Meanwhile, controversy about definition continues. The
current federal definition of LD, which is included in PL 94–142,
reads as follows:

> *Specific learning disability* means a disorder of one or
> more of the basic psychological processes involved in
> understanding or in using language, spoken or written,
> which may manifest itself in an imperfect ability to listen,
> think, speak, read, write, spell, or do arithmetic calcula-
> tions. The term includes such conditions as perceptual
> handicaps, brain injury, minimal brain damage,
> dyslexia, and developmental aphasia. The term does not

include children who have learning problems which are primarily the result of visual, hearing, or motor handicaps, of mental retardation, or environmental, cultural, or economic disadvantage. (USOE, 1977, p. 42478.)

In essence, children with learning disabilities have been defined by exclusion—they are not emotionally disturbed, culturally disadvantaged, retarded, visibly crippled (although the term "invisibly crippled" has been used), deaf, or blind—they simply do not learn some specific, basic developmental and academic tasks as most children do. And nobody knows why for sure. This line of thinking, however, precludes the possibility of a learning-disabled person being multiply handicapped. Hammill and colleagues (1981) offer a good example of why this interpretation is not accurate. "Take for example a blind 14-year-old child who lost spoken language as a consequence of a brain tumor. This would be a clear-cut case of a multiply handicapped LD child" (p. 338).

Because learning disabilities is a relatively new area of study, service, and research, definitions must be considered in an experimental, developmental stage. Other attempts at definition have been offered as well. Hallahan and Kauffman (1977) suggested that much more specificity is needed in labeling each person's particular problem, for example, "specific learning disability in remembering the spelling of words" (p. 29).

Of particular note to anyone interested in learning disabilities is the emergence of a new definition. Representatives from major professional and parent organizations forming the National Joint Committee on Learning Disabilities (NJCLD) were motivated by displeasure with the definition used in PL 94-142 and, as a result, have proposed the following definition:

Learning disabilities is a generic term that refers to a heterogeneous group of disorders manifested by significant difficulties in the acquisition and use of listening, speaking, reading, writing, or mathematical abilities. These disorders are intrinsic to the individual and presumed to be due to central nervous system dysfunction. Even though a learning disability may occur concomitantly with other handicapping conditions (e.g., sensory impairment, mental retardation, social and emotional disturbance) or environmental influences (e.g., cultural differences, insufficient/inappropriate instruction, psychogenic factors), it is not the direct result of those conditions or influences. (Hammill, Leigh, McNutt, & Larsen, 1981, p. 336)

ETIOLOGY

As mentioned previously, learning disabilities have traditio_ally been defined by exclusion. Consequently, it has been denied that children became learning disabled because of mental retardation, emotional disturbance, visual or hearing impairment, crippling conditions, or environmental disadvantage (lack of appropriate stimulation or opportunity to learn). What is left? As the argument goes, if the child is not learning and the lack of achievement cannot be explained in any other way, there must be something wrong in the child's head—there must be brain dysfunction.

As will be mentioned in the discussion of the etiologies of other exceptionalities, brain damage can result from a very large number of factors. But knowing that brains *can* be injured by many factors does not prove that a given child's brain *has* been injured. It is also extremely difficult to provide conclusive evidence that a child's learning disability is the direct *result* of brain injury, even if it is *known* that the brain has been damaged. Consequently, it is only safe to say that brain injury is a suspected etiological factor in many cases of learning disability.

By most definitions, seriously emotionally disturbed children are excluded from the learning disabled population; however, there is little doubt that emotional factors are involved in learning disabilities. Mildly emotionally disturbed and learning disabled children do exhibit many similar characteristics, but it is not clear whether emotional disturbance is an etiological factor in or a consequence of a learning disability (Hallahan et al., 1985; Kauffman, 1985).

There is a third possible etiological factor in learning disabilities that special educators are only now beginning to face squarely—instructionally related problems such as inadequate teaching (Wallace & Kauffman, 1986). While it would be ridiculous to suggest that *all* learning disabled children have been poorly taught, it seems likely that in a significant number of cases the problem is as much one of providing appropriate instruction as of finding the child's disability. This line of thought places a lot of responsibility on the teacher, but that is where it should be. If a child is not learning, it may be concluded that the teacher has not found an effective way of teaching. The malady may be as much in the teacher's lack of instructional prowess as in the child's lack of ability to perform (see Engelmann & Carnine, 1982).

LEARNING DISABLED OR LEARNING DYSLABELED?

Given the ambiguities and controversy surrounding the definition of learning disabilities, it is not surprising that there are arguments about what the children in question should be called. Concern for the label to be attached to those who have only recently been recognized as a distinct group of handicapped individuals is heightened by the realization that other special education labels seem to have a deleterious effect on children. It is no secret that "retarded" can be a bad name, and it does not take a Rhodes Scholar to recognize that "emotionally disturbed," "autistic," "stutterer," "crippled," "hyperactive," or any other special term used to describe a handicapped individual can likewise become an epithet designed to hurt or degrade the person. Many of the people who were instrumental in developing the "new" field of learning disabilities in the 1960s were also determined to avoid stigmatizing still another group of children. In a frantic effort to foil the pernicious influence of labels known to carry negative connotations, these people thought up a wide variety of new ones, all of them used at some time or other, to refer to essentially the same type of child or condition. Moreover, many of the terms used to describe individuals who experience difficulty in learning-related endeavors reflect a given professional orientation or affiliation. A sample of such terms follows:

Attentional Deficit Disorder	Dyslexia
Atypical Child	Dyssychronous Child
Brain Damaged	Educationally Handicapped
Brain Injured	Educationally Maladjusted
Choreiform Child	Hyperactive Behavior Disorder
Developmental Aphasia	Hyperkinetic Child
Developmentally Imbalanced	Interjacent Child
Driven Child	Invisibly Crippled Child
	Language Disordered

Learning Disabled	Psycholinguistic Disability
Learning Disordered	Psychoneurological
Learning Impaired	Disorder
Minimal Brain Dysfunction	Psychoneurological
Minimal Cerebral	Learning Disability
Dysfunction	Reading Disability
Organic Brain Syndrome	Remedial Education Case
Performance Deviation	Special Learning Disability
Performance Disabled	Specific Learning
Performance Handicapped	Disability
Problem Learner	Strauss Syndrome
Problem Reader	Underachiever

Predictably, as soon as people found out what these labels really meant, the names became noxious. Of course, what's derogatory in a name is the social role, quality, deviancy, or conformity it suggests. In our society the imagery conjured up by *any* label for a handicapping condition tends to be stigmatizing, not because of the label itself, but because of our archaic attitudes toward handicaps. The stigma of being exceptional will not go away, no matter what the label, until a handicap is no longer the reason for pity, mourning, disgust, humor, segregation, or reverence. When we can laugh, cry, teach, learn, struggle, and enjoy life with handicapped people as we do with other individuals who share our human limitations, there will be no pain in labels (see Burbach, 1981).

But stigma is not the only problem with labeling. We need to classify people in order to avoid total confusion and miscommunication. The real issues in labeling are: "Labeled according to what criteria?" "Labeled by whom?" and "Labeled for what purpose?" When labels are based on objective and relevant criteria, are applied by responsible professionals, and are used to communicate essential information about an individual, they can even be helpful to the individuals involved.

Numerous factors are known to influence how a child is perceived and categorized including: *(a)* the social role and cultural context of children's behavior, *(b)* the fads and predispositions of labelers, *(c)* the legislation and legal rules regarding exceptional children, and *(d)* the awareness or unawareness of environmental cues for children's behavior on the part of diagnosticians. Some of these factors inevitably contribute to "dyslabelia."

Social and cultural contexts

These vary from location to location and change over time. In our country, attitudes toward the behavior of children in school have changed dramatically over the last century. Gnagey (1968) reports that S. L. Pressey found a list of misbehaviors and recommended punishments published in North Carolina in 1848. Among them were:

Playing cards at school (10 lashes)
Swearing at school (8 lashes)
Drinking liquor at school (8 lashes)
Telling lies (7 lashes)
Boys and girls playing together (4 lashes)
Quarreling (4 lashes)
Wearing long fingernails (2 lashes)
Blotting one's copybook (2 lashes)
Neglecting to bow when going home (2 lashes)

Today, many Americans would be more likely to recommend lashes for playing too many video games or for a student's *insistence* on bowing when going home. The important thing to remember is that whether or not a child is considered disturbed, retarded, learning disabled, speech handicapped, gifted, and so forth, depends to a significant degree on when, where, and with whom the individual lives and works (i.e., on the demands and expectations of the environment). A case in point is that most mildly retarded children are not considered retarded until they enter school and are not thought of as retarded by most people after they leave the school environment.

Fads and predispositions

Like clothes and furniture, labels for exceptional children become fashionable and go out of style. People who label children—physicians, psychologists, educators—are influenced by "in" terms. A child may receive a certain label because it "sounds right" or because it is more acceptable to parents than another term that seems to be more denigrating. White and Charry (1966) studied approximately 3,000 referrals to school psychologists. They found a significant relationship between the child's socioeconomic level and IQ and the label given. Children low in IQ and socioeconomic level more often were labeled "culturally disadvantaged" or "educationally inadequate," while children high in IQ and socioeconomic level were more often labeled "brain injured" or "emotionally disturbed." It seemed clear to these investigators that the labelers had definite biases or expectations that influenced how they chose to interpret and label children's behavior.

Legislation and legal rules

It is not a complete distortion of reality to say that legislation and school codes sometimes "make" children exceptional. It is obvious to most of us which children need help, but what to call them is a problem. Now, if a state legislature decides that money and services will be available for "educationally handicapped" children, then "educationally handicapped" children will be identified and served in the schools of that state, regardless of the fact that in another state they would be labeled "learning disabled," "maladjusted," or "Type 600." For example, for a number of years the state of Illinois decided that "maladjusted children. . .means children between the ages of 5 and 21 years who, because of social and emotional problems, are unable to make constructive use of their school experience and require the provisions of special services designed to promote their educational growth and development" (The School Code of Illinois, 14–1, par. 2). Children who in most states would be considered "learning disabled" were considered, in Illinois, to be "maladjusted" because "social problems" was interpreted as "serious educational maladjustment resulting from extreme discrepancy between ability and school achievement associated with such factors as perceptual impairment, severe learning disorders, and neurological disorders" (Article VII, Rule 7.01b). One is tempted to speculate that if funds were provided for "sinful" children, wickedness would abound among our youngsters.

Environmental cues

No one likes to take the rap for children's educational deficiencies—not parents, and certainly not teachers who are always tempted to look outside the classroom for the reasons for the child's lack of success. The mind, the intelligence, the culture, the emotions, the family, the brain—certainly, somehow, somewhere, teachers hope to find the locus of the problem and avoid having the buck stop with them. How often have children been labeled mentally retarded, learning disabled, or emotionally disturbed primarily because teachers did not recognize their own ineptitude? It is clear that many times teachers inadvertently reinforce the very behavior they want to stop (Smith, 1984; Wallace & Kauffman, 1986) or simply do not know how to teach effectively (Engelmann & Carnine, 1982).

Furthermore, we want to emphasize the point that labels themselves do not add any information to our store of knowledge, offer any explanation of what is observed, or provide new insights. Labels are only succinct ways of communicating a concept or set of expectations. There is danger in thinking that once a problem is classified or labeled a solution has been found and appropriate intervention will automatically follow. There is also danger in using labels as explanations for behavior, a type of circular reasoning known as reification.

"Why isn't this child, who appears to be of normal intelligence, learning to read?"

"Well, because he has a learning disability."

"But how do you know that he is learning disabled?"

"Because he appears to have normal intelligence but he isn't learning to read."

The danger in reification or in labeling for its own sake is that sloppy thinking will prevent children from being helped. Exceptional children have suffered too many indignities and have waited too long for effective education for us to play word games.

CURRENT DEVELOPMENTS

Within the last few years, a number of important events have occurred that have influenced the field of learning disabilities. Services to LD students have expanded to include children at a preschool level as well as college students. Although there is still a paucity of information about the corresponding services for LD adults, some attention is beginning to be directed in this area (Patton & Polloway, 1982).

The sophistication of various organizations concerned with learning disabilities has also been witnessed. The Association for Children and Adults with Learning Disabilities (ACALD) has continued to be concerned with the problems faced by LD citizens. The Council for Learning Disabilities (CLD) and the Division for Learning Disabilities (DLD), of the Council for Exceptional Children, also have continued to be professionally involved with encouraging research, sharing information, and furthering the development of the field. In addition, in various locations throughout the nation, other organizations are forming. These groups, however, differ from the two previously mentioned ones in that they are composed of LD adults themselves (e.g., groups such as Time Out to Enjoy).

There also have been some major research efforts conducted with LD students. In 1977, the federal government funded five major research projects specifically focusing on LD students. The five institutes were located at the University of Illinois at Chicago Circle, University of Kansas, University of Minnesota, University of Virginia, and Columbia Teachers College in New York. All of these LD institutes developed multifaceted research programs, the results of which are having a major impact on the field of learning disabilities (Kneedler & Hallahan, 1983). By no means do we want to imply that the only notable research is emanating from these sources. On the contrary, many other significant research efforts have also been conducted by various research groups and other individuals as well.

At the present time, professionals and nonprofessionals alike are tackling some major questions confronting the field. Some of these issues are listed below:

How are services best delivered to LD students?

Which model of intervention (remedial, compensatory, vocational, functional skills, or learning strategy) is most appropriate for LD students?

How should persons with learning disabilities be identified?

Are various intervention techniques and therapies (e.g., pharmacological, dietary, megavitamin) effective or warranted?

How do LD students process information?

What impact and implication does the competency movement have on LD students?

How should we prepare professionals to work with LD students?

Attempts to ameliorate the confusion and indefiniteness of the concept of learning disabilities and efforts to research the nature of this handicapping condition must be encouraged, supported, and continued. Yet we must always be mindful of the specific individuals for whom such endeavors are directed. The problems that they faced daily can have profound social, academic, and vocational repercussions. Let us not fail to realize a learning disability is not something that a person merely outgrows.

SUGGESTIONS FOR WORKING WITH LEARNING DISABLED CHILDREN

1. Always remember the major purpose or objective of the child's effort. It's easy to lose sight of the relative unimportance of some of the things we expect from nonLD children. For example, if the goal is to have the child write a composition, don't be obsessive about neatness and spelling; rather focus on the expression and flow of ideas.

2. Be sure you don't expect the child to perform beyond his or her capacity. A child cannot be expected to perform tasks *just because he or she is intellectually bright.* Some individuals have specific learning problems even though they are generally bright. Expect the child to try and make a little improvement in the area where you're offering instruction.

3. Realize that working in the area of disability is frustrating. Remember that some things are very hard for you to do, and you probably have found successful ways of avoiding them. When you are pushed to do things you find very difficult (singing, swimming, reading, math, or whatever), you probably tend to become emotional about it rather quickly. It shouldn't surprise you if the child responds in the same way.

4. Try another way. See if you can find a different method of teaching the skill, one that might be simpler or easier for the child. Or try to substitute a slightly different skill for the one that seems so difficult to learn. For example, if the child has great difficulty in writing things by hand, try letting the child type or use a word processor.

5. Be sure the environment is conducive to learning and successful performance. Give clear instructions. Comment positively on the child's efforts. Eliminate distractions by working in a quiet, uncluttered place.

6. Try to figure out what strategies the child is using to learn or perform. If he or she doesn't appear to be using a strategy or is using one that is ineffective, try to think through and teach the child a new and more effective approach to the task. For example, the child may not be aware that there are common strategies that people use to try to remember things, like saying things to themselves and making associations between what they can and are trying to remember.

PONDER THESE

If you were in Patrick Milton Wills' shoes, how would you handle the cases of Edwin and J. C. (see pp. 11–13)?

When teaching the
l_ _ _ _ _ _ _ _ d_ _ _ _ _ _ _ _
Behavior is often mislabeled
When a kid doesn't learn
To his b_ _ _ n people turn
And that's why we say he's dys_ _ _ _ _ _ _ _ .

Experts often have difficulty deciding whether a child is LD, disturbed, or retarded. What would be the advantages and disadvantages of using the LD label for all children with mild handicaps?

Federal and some state governments are considering putting a "cap" on the LD category—passing laws or regulations that would prohibit school districts from receiving funding for services to more than a certain percentage of students placed in LD programs. For example, a district might receive special education funding for LD programs for no more than 2% of its enrollment. Debate the merits of such a cap.

REFERENCES

Burbach, H. J. (1981). The labeling process: A sociological analysis. In J. M. Kauffman & D. P. Hallahan (Eds.), *Handbook of special education* (pp. 361–377). Englewood Cliffs, NJ: Prentice-Hall.

Engelmann, S., & Carnine, D. (1982). *Theory of instruction: Principles and applications.* New York: Irvington.

Gnagey, W. J. (1968). *The psychology of discipline in the classroom.* New York: Macmillan.

Hallahan, D. P., & Kauffman, J. M. (1977). Categories, labels, behavioral characteristics: ED, LD, and EMR reconsidered. *Journal of Special Education, 11*, 139–149.

Hallahan, D. P., Kauffman, J. M., & Lloyd, J. W. (1985). *Introduction to learning disabilities.* Englewood Cliffs, NJ: Prentice-Hall.

Hammill, D. D., Leigh, J. E., McNutt, G., & Larsen, S. C. (1981). A new definition of learning disabilities. *Learning Disability Quarterly, 4,* 336-342.

Kauffman, J. M. (1985). *Characteristics of children's behavior disorders* (3rd ed.). Columbus, OH: Merrill.

Kneedler, R. D., & Hallahan, D. P. (Eds.). (1983). Research in learning disabilities: Summaries of the institutes. *Exceptional Education Quarterly, 4*(1).

Patton, J. R., & Polloway, E. A. (1982). The learning disabled: The adult years. *Topics in Learning and Learning Disabilities, 2*(3), 79-88.

Reeve, R. E., & Kauffman, J. M. (in press). Learning disabilities. In V. B. Van Hasselt, P. S. Strain, & M. Hersen (Eds.), *Handbook of developmental and physical disabilities.* New York: Plenum.

Smith, D. D. (1984). *Effective discipline.* Austin, TX: Pro-Ed.

U. S. Office of Education. (1977). Education of all handicapped children: Implementation of Part B of the Education of the Handicapped Act. *Federal Register, 42,* 42474-42518.

Wallace, G., & Kauffman, J. M. (1986). *Teaching students with learning and behavior problems* (3rd ed.). Columbus, OH: Merrill.

White, M. A., & Charry, J. (Eds.). (1966). *School disorder, intelligence, and social class.* New York: Teachers College Press.

3

Emotional Disturbance/Behavioral Disorder

I was aware, of course, that emotionally disturbed children sometimes have wild fantasies, but I was not prepared for Wanda. Wanda was 11 years old when I met her. She had a tested IQ of about 160, but it didn't do her much good except, perhaps, to enrich her fantasy life. I was never able to find a topic of conversation, an area of the curriculum, a place, or a time that was free of her bizarre imaginings. She had fantasies about jeans— she "wore" special 40-pocket and 100-pocket jeans with zippers in the front and drew stylized pictures of them. She had fantasies about the president and the governor and crucifixes and The Pit and the Pendulum, doctors, nurses, swimming pools, toilets, injections, physical examinations, Project Mercury (this was in 1962), moles (she had one on her arm that was a microphone into which she talked and one on her leg that was a thermostat controlling her body temperature). . .there was no end.

When she engaged in her fantasies, Wanda got a peculiar, fixed grin on her face, her eyes became glazed, she giggled, and she talked (often apparently to herself) in a high-pitched, squeaky voice. Frequently, she drew pictures with captions representing the fantasied objects and activities. Sometimes she engaged in other bizarre behaviors, such as flattening her-

self on the floor or wall, kissing it, caressing it, and talking to it. It was impossible to teach Wanda or to have a rational conversation with her while she was fantasizing, and she was "in" fantasy most of the time. It was impossible to predict when, during times of lucidity and reality-oriented behavior, she would suddenly enter her fantasy world again.

Mostly, Wanda had fantasies about buildings. She carried on conversations with them, and they took on human characteristics. Certain parts of buildings—doors, floors, windows, chimneys, porches, and the like—sometimes became separate entities with lives of their own. At other times, these parts of buildings were body parts to be physically examined, injected, or manipulated. Custodians and engineers were to Wanda, "building doctors." "Dr. Brady just sprayed some white stuff in Bonnie's ass" could be translated to mean that the chief building engineer had just sprayed some lubricant in the door locks in the residence hall.

Wanda had some very special building acquaintances: Elmer (the school building), the governor's mansion (it actually had a name—Cedar Crest), capitol buildings (it didn't really matter which one—they were all prized for their domes), certain churches (those with more than one steeple were special), and the White House (even though it had a peculiar and irreverent habit of "passing gas from under the South Portico"). Wanda also had some favorite building parts. A dome or cupola was, in her terms, a "Beulah Murphy." And a "Beulah Murphy" was a breast. A church steeple represented a penis. Buildings always cried from their windows and talked out of their doors.

I worked with Wanda as a teacher in an institutional school for two years. By the time she was thirteen, she had made some academic progress and seemed to have her fantasy under a little better control, but her imagination still ran very wild.

Six years later, when she was 19, I saw her again. I had, meanwhile, moved to another state and had not seen her for at least 3 years. She was, I had heard, now living in a boarding home and bussing tables in the restaurant in the motel where I happened to be staying while attending a conference. Much to my dismay, I learned that the windows from the old governor's mansion (a new mansion had been built) were used in the construction of the restaurant and the old mansion's "Beulah Murphy" had been transplanted to the top of the motel.

When I met Wanda in the restaurant she recognized me almost immediately and we talked for a few minutes about how things were going with her—quite well, apparently.

Then suddenly she said, "You know, I don't have those old fantasies about buildings any more. Only, now these dishes talk to me."

One of the most interesting and beautiful children I have ever taught is Barry—blond hair, large blue eyes, eye lashes that curl above his eyebrows. His delicate features have earned him the label "pretty" since he entered kindergarten. Now, at age 9, he shows promise of becoming an exquisitely handsome young man. Achievement and ability testing shows that his skills and abilities range from slightly above average to the moderately mentally retarded range. He has such serious problems paying attention, however, that it is almost impossible to obtain valid test scores.

Barry struggles to pay attention. He'll turn his head toward the book or my face but his eyes turn later. I have to wait for them to catch up before I begin instructing. His eyes catching up with his head always makes me think of the pictures of fruit spinning in a slot machine, one stopping in position in the window after another. Sometimes Barry refuses to even try to pay attention and becomes defiant or disruptive. He is outrageously unpredictable and often gets into trouble with other children in my class. One day he threw the school into a panic by disappearing with another child—and during a time when his mother was visiting the class! We found them, 30 minutes later, trying to start a car in the parking lot. A few days later he stripped himself naked in the bathroom and put all his clothes in the toilet, including shoes and socks.

If Barry has one particular behavioral characteristic it is a sense of the dramatic. This might be, partly at least, a result of the fact that his mother was a drama major and often plays with her children by altering her voice and speaking for objects. Barry talks to magic markers and other objects as if they were people or pets, and he carries on extensive "conversations" with his mother and father when they are not present, speaking their parts (questioning and reprimanding himself, for example) with great authority. Some days he has laughed maniacally or *screamed for hours. Occasionally he has thrown himself on the floor with a sickening thud.*

Perhaps my most frustrating and surprising experience with Barry involved an attempt to reinforce him with praise for appropriate behavior. One day as I was working with another group of children across the room I observed him playing quietly and appropriately with a classmate. Because this was something he seldom did that I wanted to encourage, I decided to do what I'd been taught will "reinforce" good behavior. I walked over to Barry, knelt beside him, gave him a hug, and commented, "Barry, I really like the way you're playing quietly with the blocks and having fun with Susie." He looked at me strangely, jumped to his feet, and screamed at me, "Well, fuck you, shitload!"

Reinforcement doesn't work every time.[1]

Rodney's personal care habits were atrocious. He seemed to attract dirt, grease, and filth. His vocabulary was also foul, and he was generally just plain obnoxious. Not always, though—for he could be very likeable. However, most of the time he found ways of making people want to get away from him as fast as possible and stay away for as long as possible. It is hard to imagine a more repulsive 12-year-old, and it is no wonder that he found his way into the psychiatric hospital where I was teaching.

In school, the work Rodney handed in reflected his personality. He picked his nose until it bled and wiped the blood and mucus on his papers. He picked his ears and wiped the wax on his papers. He picked his acne and wiped the blood and pus on his papers. He spit on his papers and smeared the saliva over his answers to try to erase them. When he did use an eraser, he made holes. He wrote answers at the wrong place and then circled them and drew arrows, often to another wrong place. He wrote four-letter words and drew lewd pictures and swastikas on his papers. He punched holes in his papers, tore them, wadded them, taped them together, ripped them apart again, and retaped them. All the while, he muttered curses— he couldn't do the damned work because it was too babyish or too hard or too stupid or too crazy and "what kind of a stupid goddamned bastard was I to give him such crap?"

[1]The authors are grateful to Patricia L. Pullen for contributing this anecdote.

Rodney made himself the bane of everyone's existence. He teased and bullied smaller children unmercifully. He baited teachers and threatened other adults. Cleanliness and pleasantness seemed completely foreign to him. He referred to his former teacher most often as "fuckstick."

My first confrontation with Rodney was the first minute of the first day I tried to teach him. He sauntered into the classroom, took one look at me, and said, "If you're going to be in here, then I'm getting the hell out!" In an instant, he was out the door, and around the corner, up two flights of stairs, and out of the building. It did not take me long to realize that I had to go after him and bring him back, even if it meant dragging him. I caught up with him about 20 feet outside the building. I fully expected that we would have a physical struggle, and I would end up dragging him back to the classroom. Instead, when I reached out to grab him he stopped, looked at me for a moment, and said, "Well, hell! I guess I might as well go back." He got back to the classroom before I did and never tried to run again.

But that was not our last confrontation. Rodney did not like homework. We teachers assigned homework as a policy, and we expected that it would be done. Rodney said that if I gave him homework he would burn it. I replied matter-of-factly that I didn't think he would since he wasn't allowed to have matches and that even if he did, it wouldn't get him anywhere because I had duplicate assignments I would give him. "Well, you son-of-a-bitch, just wait and see," he said. The next morning he was brought to the classroom by a child care worker (attendant). Triumphantly, he threw a tin can on my desk and sneered, "Here's your goddamned homework!" I opened the can. It was full of ashes.

John was almost 14. Academically, he was at a low, second grade level. He had been expelled from a special public school class for children with brain damage, because he threatened the teacher and other children and had actually beaten another child with a chain. He was on the waiting list to be admitted to the state mental hospital, but he was to be enrolled in my public school class for emotionally disturbed children because there was nowhere else for him to go.

When his mother brought him to school the first day, he refused to get out of the car. She coaxed and pleaded, but he *refused to budge. She got the principal, and he coaxed and pleaded, but John would not talk to him. John's mother and the principal came to me. I went out to the car and coaxed and pleaded, but he would not even look at me. Now what? We decided that we would tell him it was time to come in and that he was going to come into the building now. He could choose the way he was going to come in—he could walk or we would carry him. Once he had come in and looked over the classroom, he would have another choice—to stay or to go home, and the decision would be his alone. We told him, but he did not appear to listen, and he did not budge. We pulled him out of the car, and he stood up and walked into the building. Five minutes later we were showing him the classroom—he was smiling and talking and decided to stay.*

John tested me out in several other ways, and I was beginning to wonder if I was getting anywhere with him. About a month later a new boy entered the class and began the usual testing. Did I mean what I said and would I level appropriate consequences for behavior? At a beautifully timed moment, John went over to the new boy and said, "Look, you might as well do what Mr. _____ tells you to, because it's for your own good. Besides, he means what he says, and if you don't do it you'll only be hurting yourself."

TERMINOLOGY

To us, emotional disturbance or behavioral disorder means getting lost in a tangle of irrelevancies, distortions, unpleasantness, disorganization, and nonproductive activity. Teaching such children means helping them find their way out of the mess.

A confusing array of terms is used to designate children who have special difficulty relating to others or behaving acceptably. *Seriously emotionally disturbed* is the term used in federal laws and regulations governing special education. Some states also use that term. But *behaviorally disordered* is preferred by many special educators (Huntze, 1985), and some states use *behaviorally disordered, socially and emotionally disturbed, personal and social adjustment problem, emotionally handicapped,* or a wide variety of other terms to refer to this group of children. The terminology for this category of special education is in transition, and *emotionally disturbed* (ED) seems to be giving way gradually to *behaviorally disordered* (BD) as the preferred term. Consequently, we have chosen to use *emotionally disturbed/behaviorally disordered* (ED/BD) in this chapter. We do not think ED and BD children are two distinctly different groups, and we sometimes refer to these children simply as *disturbed.*

DEFINITION AND CLASSIFICATION

There is no commonly accepted definition of ED/BD children. Many of the terms and concepts in this area (indeed, the term *emotionally disturbed* itself) have their origins in psychiatry and psychology. Educators have had to make up their own definitions to fit children's behavior in school. Essentially, teachers have defined ED/BD children as those who behave in ways that are considered harmful or inappropriate. The children do things teachers want them to stop or, on the other hand, fail to do things teachers think they ought. This would mean, of course, that *all* children are disturbed, and in a way that is true—all children do most of the things ED/BD children do. The difference is that ED/BD children exhibit behavior that goes to an extreme: they are too aggressive or too withdrawn, too loud or too quiet, too euphoric or too depressed. Furthermore, they exhibit these extreme behaviors over a long period of time, not just for a short while. In addition, they tend to exhibit behaviors in strange contexts—there is often nothing wrong with what they are doing, only with when and where they are doing it. In short, *ED/BD children behave in ways their teachers consider undesirable or inappropriate, and their behavior differs from that of normal children along several crucial dimensions: (a) severity—* the extremes to which their behavior goes; *(b) chronicity—*the period of time over which they exhibit inappropriate behavior; and *(c) context—*when and where they do certain things.

The specific behaviors that ED/BD children exhibit are enough to fill a dictionary. However, Bower (1981) has grouped these behaviors into five classes or types that are relevant to teachers: *(a)* inability to achieve in school that cannot be explained by sensory or health factors; *(b)* inability to establish and maintain satisfactory interpersonal relations with peers and adults; *(c)* demonstration of inappropriate feelings or affect under normal conditions (e.g., laughing when someone is hurt); *(d)* a pervasive mood of unhappiness or depression; and *(e)* a tendency to develop physical symptoms such as pains or fears associated with their problems.

Bower's five point definition provided the basis for the federal definition of *serious emotional disturbance* included in the rules and regulations for PL 94–142. But, unfortunately, the federal definition has several clauses added to it that make it so vague and confusing that it is of little help in deciding who is and who is not disturbed (Kauffman, 1982, 1985). For example, it excludes "socially maladjusted" children, unless they are also emotionally disturbed. Yet the difference between social maladjustment and emotional disturbance is not clear; and it is common sense that a "socially maladjusted" child will exhibit some of the characteristics that are used to define emotional disturbance (especially items *b* and *c* in Bower's list; see Bower, 1982). Thus the federal definition is almost nonsensical. And its flaws seem to allow many ED/BD children to go unserved (Kauffman, in press).

Classification of ED/BD children has not been very meaningful for special educators. The traditional psychiatric categories have been of almost no value whatsoever in teaching. Factor analytic studies of children's behavior (see Achenbach & Edelbrock, 1983; Quay, 1979) have shown that some children are aggressive, rude, attention-seeking, and hyperactive, and that others are anxious, hypersensitive, fearful, and withdrawn. Others are primarily delinquent, truant, or antisocial according to middle-class standards. The simplest and most productive classification system for *educators* involves two categories: mild or moderate and severe. Children with mild or moderate problems can be taught in regular public school classs, where the teacher gets some advice and consultation in behavior management, or in resource rooms, where the child spends only part of the day with a specially trained teacher. Occasionally, these children, who are often labeled neurotic, personality disordered, behavior disordered, and the like, must be taught in segregated special classes, but they are ordinarily returned to a regular class in 2 years or less. Children with severe problems, often classified as psychotic, frequently must be educated in special classes in public schools or sometimes in special schools or in institutions. Some severely ED/BD children never enter the educational mainstream.

PREVALANCE

For over 20 years the federal estimate of the prevalence of serious emotional disturbance among school-aged children and youth was 2%. Many authorities in the field, however, believe that this is an extremely conservative estimate and that a figure of 6–10% is much more realistic (see Graham, 1979; Grosenick & Huntze, 1979; Kauffman, in press; Kauffman & Kneedler, 1981). But the number of ED/BD children actually identified does not come anywhere close to 2% of the school-aged population. In fact, a recent report of the U.S. Department of Education (1984) stated that only about 0.9% of school children nationwide have been identified as seriously emotionally disturbed and are being served by any form of special education. The fact that less than half the number of children *conservatively* estimated to fall into this category are receiving services means that ED/BD children are one of the most neglected, underserved groups of exceptional children in American schools today.

It is not difficult to guess why estimates of the prevalence of ED/BD vary so greatly and why so few of the estimated number of disturbed children receive special education. When you have a very vague, jumbled, and subjective definition, it is next to impossible to make an accurate count of the number of children who fit it. And if there is a lot of room for argument about whether or not a child is disturbed, then the school officials responsible for special education can avoid identifying and serving many children who probably are (Kauffman, 1982). Sometimes school officials probably feel justified in ignoring the needs of children who are arguably not handicapped because they simply do not have the money or the personnel (nor any idea where they'd get either) to provide special education. The question of prevalence of ED/BD sometimes seems in practice to be less "How many ED/BD children are there?" than "How many ED/BD children can we afford?"

ETIOLOGY

The causes of erratic, disturbing, debilitating human behavior have always been a puzzle, which now seems insoluble. All that is clear is that such behavior stems from a complex interaction of many factors. These factors have long been known, but the exact role of each has never been fully understood.

The devil made him do it has always been, especially until the twentieth century, a very popular explanation. The idea that God and the devil battle for control of the mind and body dies slowly, and it is not uncommon, even today, to hear spiritual explanations of and cures for troublesome behavior. There simply is no scientific evidence that divine or demonic powers control the way people behave, but people's belief in such powers is a reality that teachers do sometimes have to contend with.

Something just snapped in his head is another popular explanation of deviant behavior. The belief is that something is biologically wrong with the person—his brain, blood, nerves, and so forth, are said to be damaged, diseased, or dysfunctioning. Medical science has discovered that biological factors such as malnutrition, disease, fatigue, trauma, and brain damage can cause aberrant behavior. Yet, in the vast majority of cases, even those involving severe disorders, there is no clear evidence of a specific biological etiology. The search for medical explanations and cures remains, to this day, mostly a matter of speculation.

It runs in the family, the genetic explanation, has never been confirmed. It is known that for some types of severe disorders (psychoses) the more blood relatives one has who are extremely disturbed, and the closer the blood relationship, the greater is one's chance of developing such a disorder. However, this relationship could result from child-rearing practices as well as from genetic factors. The search for genetic contributions to the development of disordered behavior, like the search for other biological causes, is still going on.

He has a sick mind is often the ultimate explanation of those who approach behavior from a psychoanalytic perspective. A person's mind is thought to get "sick" because of early experiences that cause the person to become anxious and because of his subsequent attempts to defind himself against anxiety. Many experiences and thoughts related to his anxiety are repressed and kept unconscious. There is hardly more scientific evidence for this point of view than for the religious or spiritual explanation, but the notion is deeply entrenched in our culture and because of its pervasive influence it is not easily dismissed.

He just can't seem to find himself suggests that a person does not know or understand his own feelings or perceptions, or has not developed an adequate self-concept. Deviant behavior supposedly arises because the person has not learned introspection, self-awareness, self-regard, sensitivity, and the like. The role of one's feelings and lack of self-awareness *as a cause* of emotional/behavioral disorders has not been demonstrated in any scientific manner.

He never learned how to get along connotes that deviant patterns of behavior are learned and that appropriate behavior can be taught. A body of scientific evidence indicates that this is correct, particularly for mild disorders, but it cannot be said that there is conclusive evidence that the explanation is totally correct, especially for more severe problems. It is of primary importance to educators, however, because they are in the business of teaching children new patterns of behavior. Inappropriate learning is the only etiological factor that educators are specifically trained to do something about.

In summary, it seems highly probable that most problem behavior is the result of many interacting factors, some of which (such as genetics and disease) give children a predisposition to develop disordered behavior and some of which (such as child rearing and schooling) trigger or precipitate behavior problems (Kauffman, 1985; Quay & Werry, 1979).

ISSUES IN THE EDUCATION OF ED/BD CHILDREN

How to help troubled children has been nearly as perplexing a problem as how they got that way. Until recently, it was thought that psychotherapists, usually psychiatrists (medical doctors with training in psychiatry) or psychoanalysts (psychiatrists with a special training in psychoanalysis) or clinical psychologists (nonphysicians with advanced graduate training in psychology), were best equipped (if not the *only* people equipped) to help ED/BD children. Fortunately, most psychotherapists now readily admit that teachers are also equipped to offer extremely significant help to the child. But the critical issue today is the question of exactly *how* teachers can best go about helping (See Kerr & Nelson, 1983; Paul, 1985).

CONCEPTUAL MODELS

There are different conceptual models—sets of assumptions about what the problem is, how it came about, and what can be done about it—that can be adopted in working with ED/BD children (see Hallahan & Kauffman, 1986; Kauffman & Kneedler, 1981, for more detailed descriptions of some of these models). In fact, there are so many different models, each having proponents who claim their ideas are best and that the advocates of other models are ignorant or malicious, that the field is confusing for a beginning student. We will try to guide you through this array of models.

You should keep three things in mind. First, there are many ways to group models that conceptually "slice" the field. Ours is not the only way to do it; other sources may give descriptions of more or fewer models or use different terminology. Second, relatively few professionals let themselves become the prisoners of a single model even though they think one model is better. Most thoughtful people realize that each model has its limitations and that it is an attempt to impose a useful order on information and events, but that it is not a full and complete description of reality. Third, you can get into trouble by being mindlessly eclectic. Many students and some professionals try to take the position that they see merit in *every* conceptual model. And because they want to maintain a friendly neutrality on all issues, they fail to make necessary judgments on the basis of research evidence *or* common sense. Our contention is that if you are going to help ED/BD children most effectively, you have to have your feet on the ground *and* be guided by the findings of research.

Psychoanalytic model

This model, based on the ideas of Freud and other psychoanalysts, has its biggest appeal for psychotherapists and social workers. Educators who respond to this model tend to advocate a permissive classroom in which the child can "work through" or express his underlying problems freely. A premium is placed on two things: *(a)* an accepting attitude of the teacher toward the child's feelings and *(b)* an understanding of the unconscious motivation of the child's behavior. What do we think of this model? Not much. The reason is because there is very little empirical research showing that it works. You may find anecdotal reports of successes, or cases reporting favorable results, and these outcomes are said to prove the value of psychoanalytic concepts. However, such reports are not based on scientific research in which the effects of "treatment" are clearly and reliably measured and demonstrated.

Psychoeducational model

Psychoeducation is not well defined, even by the people who are identified with it. Implying a combination of psychological and educational concepts, this model includes psychoanalytic ideas about unconscious motivation and puts a premium on the teacher-pupil relationship. In addition, the concern for "surface behavior" (what children do) and for academic progress puts the emphasis on talking to children and on getting them to achieve insight into their problems. This model offers most of its teaching through projects and creative arts. Although we think the psychoeducational approach is far more sensible than the psychoanalytic model, it still suffers from the same flaw—little or no supporting data from empirical research. However, it represents a commonsense approach to talking to children about their behavior (sometimes called a *Life-Space Interview*). Furthermore, some psychoeducational techniques help children learn strategies for dealing with their problems similar to techniques known as *cognitive behavior modification*. And cognitive behavior modification *is* supported by scientific research data.

Humanistic model

"Nonauthoritarian," "self-directed," "self-evaluative," "affective," "open," "personal"—these words are often used to describe the humanistic model. This model grew out of humanistic psychology and the development of open schools, alternative schools, and other nontraditional practices of the late 1960s and early 1970s. These approaches represent an attempt to give more attention to the affective side of education and to get children more involved in their own education. In our opinion, humanistic educators made important contributions to society by highlighting how it feels to learn, succeed, fail, be a pupil, be a teacher—in other words, how it feels to be human. Unfortunately, the proponents of this model seem too often satisifed with merely developing a nontraditional educational setting without documenting its effectiveness in helping children improve their academic learning and behavior.

Ecological model

Many concepts of the ecological model were adapted from research in biological ecology and ecological psychology. Every child is enmeshed in a complex social system. Consequently, one has to consider the entire social system, not just the child in isolation. Therefore, educators are concerned with the child in the classroom, the family, the neighborhood, and all other aspects of the social environment. The value we see in this model is not in the specific tactics it offers for teaching or managing behavior, but in its overall approach or strategy for dealing with the child's problems. For example, one might use behavior modification tactics for teaching and managing the child, but use an ecological strategy that involves the child's family and community. While being eminently sensible, the ecological view is also supported by research.

Behavioral model

The behavioral model includes these fundamental ideas: *(a)* behavior can be observed and directly and reliably measured; *(b)* behavioral excesses and deficits *are* the problem, not underlying or unconscious feelings; and *(c)* behavior is a function of its consequences and, therefore, can be modified by changing the consequences. If it is assumed that children's behavior is learned, then the problem with ED/BD children must be that they have learned the wrong behaviors. The solution is to teach them new, more appropriate ones. In classrooms operated according to a behavioral model, specific behavioral goals are achieved by using specific teaching and management techniques. Also, a careful daily measurement of behavior is designed to tell the teacher to what extent the techniques are leading to an achievement of the goals. In our opinion, the behavioral model is the most valuable for two reasons: *(a)* it is supported by more scientific research than any of the others; and *(b)* it is compatible with certain sensible, research-supported aspects of other models. One can talk meaningfully with children about their behavior (psychoeducational), care about their feelings and individuality (humanistic), deal with all aspects of their social environment (ecological), and still be a good behaviorist. *But without the behavioral model as a basis, the components of the other models are relatively meaningless.*

In conclusion, we want to point out that ED/BD children come to the attention of teachers, parents, peers, and others because of their behavioral excesses and deficiencies. Kauffman (1985) wrote that:

Not to define precisely and measure these behavioral excesses and deficiencies, then, is a fundamental error: it is akin to the malpractice of a nurse who decides not to measure vital signs (heart rate, respiration rate, temperature, and blood pressure), perhaps arguing that he/she is too busy, that subjective estimates of vital signs are quite adequate, that vital signs are only superficial estimates of the patient's health, or that the vital signs do not signify the nature of the underlying pathology. The teaching profession is dedicated to the task of changing behavior demonstrably for the better. What can one say, then, of educational practice that does not include reliable and forthright measurement of the behavior change induced by the teacher's methodology? I believe simply this: *It is indefensible.* (pp. 339–340)

SUGGESTIONS FOR WORKING WITH ED/BD CHILDREN

1. ED/BD children are masters at making their problems yours. Make sure you do not let yourself get caught up in their "pathology." For example, such children may try to drag you into senseless arguments or make you feel that their problems in following classroom rules are your fault. You must emotionally distance yourself from interactions with children to be able to tell their difficulties from yours.

2. Children should know what you expect from them. ED/BD children especially need to know what is and is not OK. Don't keep them guessing.

3. When you make a rule or give an instruction, make it stick. By this we mean *(a)* think through the rule or instruction before you give it, *(b)* tell the child the consequences of meeting or not meeting your expectation, and *(c)* be consistent in applying the consequences. Before you tell the child what to do, you must consider whether doing it is appropriate and important, whether the consequences are reasonable and desirable, and whether or not you can follow through with the consequences.

4. Don't expect love and affection in return. If all ED/BD children needed was someone to love them we could cure most of them next year (maybe even this year!). If you

want to help them you must be willing to extend love, affection, and *structure*—appropriate rules, clear expectations, and consistent consequences—without the expectation that you'll receive respect, love, or gratitude in return.

5. Don't demand perfection or steady progress; do expect gradual improvement. Remember that we all have our quirks and our bad days. Life for most ED/BD kids is especially rocky. The goal is to help them get their behavior smoothed out enough to live happily and independently in the mainstream of society. The goal can't be reached overnight, and it leaves a lot of room for imperfection by most people's standards.

PONDER THESE

Study the following behaviors according to your interpretation of emotional disturbance or behavioral disorder and rank these behaviors from most serious to least serious. Under what conditions would you consider the behaviors normal?

Interrupting conversations
Banging head against the wall
Screaming
Killing another person
Scratching oneself
Masturbating
Eating paper
Swearing
Saying, "I'm no good. I hate myself."
Reading

Elmer has a pair of scissors. He is making deep scratches on the wall of the classroom. You tell him to stop, but he pays no attention. You go to him and take hold of his arm and matter-of-factly say, "No, Elmer, you can't do that."

He flies at you, tries to scratch you with the scissors, and screams, "Let me go, you bastard!"

You loosen your grip on Elmer and he runs out of the room. You follow, but lose sight of him as he rounds the corner at the end of the hall. You suspect that he has gone into the boys' restroom. As you enter the restroom you see Elmer perched on top of the stall partition. He has taken off one shoe and is about to throw it at you.

As you approach him he shouts, "Get away from me—you can't make me come down. I'll kill you, you bastard. I'll break my leg, and then my dad will sue you. You come any closer and I'll knock your teeth out."

Describe alternative ways you could respond to this situation.

ED/BD children have a way of forcing other people to make decisions for them or about their behavior. Much of the controversy in the field concerns the child's right to make his own decisions versus the teacher's responsibility to make decisions for the child. For each of the following problems, specify the decisions you would be willing to make *for* a child and those you believe should be left to him:

The child is not coming to class on time.

The child refuses to read.

The child hits others.

The child makes loud animal noises in class.

The child takes things that are not his.

REFERENCES

Achenbach, T. M., & Edelbrock, C. S. (1983). Taxonomic issues in child psychopathology. In T. H. Ollendick & M. Hersen (Eds.), *Handbook of child psychopathology* (pp. 65–93). New York: Plenum.

Bower, E. M. (1982). Defining emotional disturbance: Public policy and research. *Psychology in the Schools, 19,* 55–60.

Graham, P. J. (1979). Epidemiological studies. In H. C. Quay & J. S. Werry (Eds.), *Psychopathological disorders of childhood* (2nd ed., pp. 189–209). New York: Wiley.

Grosenick, J. K., & Huntze, S. L. (1979). *National needs analysis in behavior disorders.* Columbia: University of Missouri, Department of Special Education.

Hallahan, D. P., & Kauffman, J. M. (1986). *Exceptional children: Introduction to special education* (3rd ed.). Englewood Cliffs, NJ: Prentice-Hall.

Huntze, S. L. (1985). A position paper of the Council for Children with Behavioral Disorders. *Behavioral Disorders, 10,* 167–174.

Kauffman, J. M. (1982). Social policy issues in special education and related services for emotionally disturbed children and youth. In M. M. Noel & N. G. Haring (Eds.), *Progress and change: Issues in educating the emotionally disturbed. Vol. 1. Identification and program planning* (pp. 1–10). Seattle: Program Development Assistance Systems, University of Washington.

Kauffman, J. M. (1985). *Characteristics of children's behavior disorders* (3rd ed.). Columbus, OH: Merrill.

Kauffman, J. M. (in press). Educating children with behavior disorders. In R. J. Morris & B. Blatt (Eds.), *Special education: Research and trends.* New York: Pergamon.

Kauffman, J. M., & Kneedler, R. D. (1981). Behavior disorders. In J. M. Kauffman & D. P. Hallahan (Eds.), *Handbook of special education* (pp. 165–194). Englewood Cliffs, NJ: Prentice-Hall.

Kerr, M. M., & Nelson, C. M. (1983). *Strategies for managing behavior problems in the classroom.* Columbus, OH: Merrill.

Paul, J. L. (1985). Behavioral disorders in the 1980s: Ethical and ideological issues. *Behavioral Disorders, 11,* 66–72.

Quay, H. C. (1979). Classification. In H. C. Quay & J. S. Werry (Eds.), *Psychopathological disorders of childhood* (2nd ed., pp. 1–42). New York: Wiley.

Quay, H. C., & Werry, J. S. (Eds.). (1979). *Psychopathological disorders of children* (2nd ed.). New York: Wiley.

U. S. Department of Education. (1984). *Sixth annual report on the implementation of PL 94–142.* Washington, DC: Author.

4

Mental Retardation

What does mental retardation mean? At times it can be clever perceptiveness, a happy grin, a belly laugh, an openness, or a blissful naivete. At other times it can be an embarrassed struggle to free oneself from a stigmatizing label, to pass as normal, to appear bright, or to dig out of the entanglement of a confusing problem that everyone else seems to overcome with ease. To us, mental retardation means going on a camping trip with Gerald:

After I set up the tent, the rain began to fall. It rained and it rained; it came in buckets, then barrels. We frantically dug trenches around our tent, and the holes began to overflow with water. I was disgusted, upset, frustrated, and depressed. I felt that the whole trip had been ruined. Gerald looked like a drowned rat, but he was fascinated by the squishiness in his shoes. He laughed as he stepped into puddles, and it was getting to the point where the puddles were becoming pools. I sat disgruntled on a stump, with elbows on my knees and my head in my hands. I began to shiver in the cool breeze. Gerald saw that I was upset. He came over, touched me with a wet, muddy hand and smiled. He sat next to me and tossed a stone in a nearby puddle. Then he looked up at me and said, "Do you think the rain will settle the dust?"

*I took a job as a counselor with the Division of Vocational Re-
habilitation and was assigned a caseload of clients diagnosed
as mentally retarded. During the first week, I was escorted by
Jim, a fellow counselor, to various job locations where my
clients were employed. My most vivid recollection is of my ini-
tial meeting with Elmer. The file on Elmer informed me that
he was 56 years old, that he had been institutionalized until
he was past 40, and that he had been castrated. Later, Jim explained that most, if not all, male retarded patients in this particular state were sterilized (castrated) by law. The law is still
on the books, but it is no longer enforced, and has not been for
over 10 years. Jim said that all castrates looked the same—
pear-shaped, gaining a great deal of weight around the hips
just like castrated hogs. He said Elmer was an excellent worker,
but that on previous jobs he always ate too much and gained
weight so fast that they had to terminate his employment and
return him to the institution to get his weight down for health
reasons. He also informed me that Elmer was basically an hon-
est sort although he was known to stretch the truth a little.*

*When we arrived at Elmer's place of employment, we found
him finishing a day's work and getting on his bike to go home.
He was a pear-shaped old man, with hips and waist much too
large for his height. When Jim introduced us, Elmer was shy,
very polite, and quite pleasant to be around. Then Jim began
questioning him about his weight. Elmer replied that he did not
think he had gained any, whereupon Jim pulled a bathroom
scale from the trunk of the state car. We found that within the
last 2 weeks Elmer had gained over 30 pounds. Jim immediately got upset and began talking to Elmer about his eating
problem, warning him that it he was not careful he would eat
himself to death. He asked Elmer what he had eaten for breakfast. Calmly, Elmer replied that he had only had eggs and toast.
After a thorough investigation, we found that Elmer had, in fact,
eaten at least six eggs and a half a loaf of bread. When asked
what he had to drink, Elmer quickly said, "Milk, yes sir, one
glass of milk—only one glass of milk. One glass of milk is all
I had."*

*Jim retorted, "And how many times did you fill that one
glass?"*

*Elmer looked down at his feet. "Four," he replied. Then he
got on his bike and started home.*

Jim looked at me, shrugged his shoulders and said, "Now

you tell me—how do you stop a guy from eating himself to death?"

I worked with Allen every day for 6 months teaching him how to garnish sandwiches in a high-volume restaurant. He learned very slowly, but he was fun and interesting to work with. We always joked with one another. Not even I would ever have guessed that he had a tested IQ of 52.

By about the sixth month, Allen was doing his job without my assistance, except during the rush periods. Over the next 3 months, Allen became very skillful and could garnish at an impressive rate—except during the very busy times when it was sometimes too hectic, even for me.

Slowly, day by day, pressure began to build. One night when tempers were short at cleanup time, Allen started yelling, "Don't touch me! Push, push, push, that's all you do. Don't come close to me. I hate this place! I hate hamburgers! I hate salads! I hate mustard!" With this outcry, he flung the mustard container against the kitchen wall and ran out the back door. Impulsively, I took off after him. Finally, I caught him by the incinerator on the back lot. He yelled, his voice shaking and hands trembling, "You'd better leave me alone!" Fearing that he might run in front of a car, I stepped closer to reach him. He pulled a kitchen knife about 10 inches long from his pocket and said, "Don't come near me, I hate you; take another step and I'll kill you!" Then he dropped the knife to the ground, fell to his knees and wept. He pulled me close to him, held my legs, and murmured, "I'm sorry. I love you. I'm sorry." Before the night was over, we had talked it out and could complete our cleanup duties together. That was over 5 years ago. Today, he is still garnishing sandwiches at the same high-volume restaurant, and we are still the closest of friends.

John had worked for 2 years as a dishwasher and had saved over $2,000 for a motor scooter. I was his employer and had talked with him on many occasions about types, sizes, and colors of motor scooters. One day I took him to several places that sold scooters, and he was surprised to find that he had enough money to buy any one he wanted. Within the week, he had bought a red scooter from a reliable dealer who agreed to teach him how to drive. When arrangements were made to begin lessons, we were suddenly faced with the cold reality that John could not read—he was totally illiterate.

I contacted the motor vehicle department and was informed of the types of driver's tests John needed to pass for his license. The written test could be read to him. I began to teach him lessons from the driver's handbook every day after work. He studied hard, and after 6 weeks I felt he was ready. He reported for the test and unfortunately failed it. I was sure he knew the answers, and, through further investigation, I found that he understood the material very well but was unfamiliar with the procedure of selecting the correct answer from among several choices. I must admit that when the questions and multiple choices were read to me, I also became confused.

So we worked harder. How frustrating for John to own a $2,000 motor scooter and know how to drive it, but be unable to ride it because he couldn't get a driver's license! Three weeks later John took the test again, and this time he only missed two questions. The license was his. He bought some insurance and rode to work every day on his proud possession. But I could not help wondering what would happen if he ever had an accident.

About 2 years after John got his license, he was involved in an accident—a car hit him at an intersection. He was skinned and shaken up but luckily not seriously injured. The driver of the car said that John had handled himself extremely well. John had remembered what to do from the driver's manual and he had followed each step to the letter.

After everything had been taken care of, John called me to come and get the scooter. When I arrived at the intersection, he was sitting alone, bruised and somewhat bloody. His scooter was really a mess. It was twisted and crumpled. As we began to slide it carefully in the back of the station wagon, John looked at me with concern and a tear in his eye. "Watch out, don't scratch it," he moaned.

Most people are aware of the Special Olympics—although some people may not realize that there is more to it than just track and field events. Other sports (e.g., skiing, soccer, and basketball) are also part of this program. Nevertheless, this story concerns the track and field competition. For months, a friend of mine, a teacher of trainable mentally retarded students, had

*been preparing them for the district-level meet. They practiced
every day. As every track runner knows, "getting out of the
blocks" is a critical part of any running event. This teacher consistently worked on this aspect with her students. She would
yell, "Get on your mark, get set, GO." After months of training, her students were ready. The district meet approached.*

*On the day of the meet, her students were ready in-
deed—they were "psyched"—they wanted to do well so they
could go to the state meet. Although they had entered a number
of different events, they were most excited about the running.
The truth of truths—athlete versus athlete—had arrived. The
officials lined up the runners in their appropriate positions. The
adrenaline was flowing; the excitement was building to a
climax. The official starter asked if the runners were ready.
They or their sponsors indicated that they were. The starter
then began the countdown: "Get on your mark, get set, BLAM!*

*The race had begun! Unfortunately, the participants from
my friend's class were still at the starting line—startled by the
loud sounds that had just thundered from the starter's gun to
be sure—but still waiting anxiously for him to say, "GO!"*

Sometimes people find themselves in situations where they are
not adequately prepared for dealing with mentally retarded individuals. The following example illustrates this:

*Every spring our college sponsors a camp for retarded per-
sons of all ages. The camp facility is provided by the state
JayCee organization. One spring, a nature study program was
included to enhance the campers' stay. One of the topics discussed had to do with snakes in the local environment. Who
better could cover this subject than a representative from the
state herpetology society?*

*Unfortunately, the herpetologist had never lectured to a
group of retarded children and adults. He started on a positive
note by showing the campers cages with examples of various
snakes; however, he then proceded to launch into a very detailed description far beyond the conceptual abilities of these
campers. No one knew what he was talking about.*

*One of the campers, a moderately retarded man in his late
twenties, raised his hand. Pleased by this interest in his presentation, the herpetologist stopped in mid-discourse to invite
the camper's question. "Do nakes bite?" the camper asked.*

Rather than address the question directly, the herpetologist continued with his detailed discussion about snakes. A few minutes later, the same camper again raised his hand and upon being acknowledged asked once again, "Do nakes bite?" As before, his question was not answered to his satisfaction. Five minutes later, his hand went up for a third time. As you might guess, he asked, "Do nakes bite?"

The state expert finally responded with perhaps the most understandable and useful information the campers learned that day: "Only if you step on them."

The camper acknowledged the answer by saying: "Now that makes sense." The campers may not have learned much about snakes, but perhaps the herpetologist learned something about tailoring his presentation to his audience. [1]

DEFINITION

A series of definitions of mental retardation have been used in the past. Today's most widely accepted definition was developed by the American Association on Mental Deficiency (AAMD). An earlier version of the AAMD definition was incorporated into PL 94-142, The Education for All Handicapped Children Act of 1975 (U.S. Office of Education, 1977). The most recent AAMD definition describes *mental retardation* as "significantly subaverage general intellectual functioning resulting in or associated with concurrent impairments in adaptive behavior and manifested during the development period." (Grossman, 1983, p. 11). *Subaverage intellectual functioning* refers to earning a score on an intelligence test that is approximately 2 or more standard deviations below the mean. *Adaptive behavior* refers to one's ability to cope with any demands of daily life and is manifested in such things as sensory-motor, communicational, self-help, socialization, academic, and vocational skills. The *development period* consists of the time span between conception and the nineteenth birthday.

Before a consideration of adaptive behavior was included in the definition, emphasis was placed solely on the intelligence test score for classifying a person as mentally retarded. If an individ-

---

[1]Our thanks to Dave Smith and Ed Polloway (Lynchburg College) for sharing this story with us.

ual scored in the retarded range on an IQ test, he was classified as mentally retarded even if he functioned adequately in the community, at school, on the job, or with his peers. In other words, once a person scored in the retarded range it was highly probable that he would be considered retarded for the rest of his life. It is important to accent the fact that equal weight should be given to both the intellectual functioning and the adaptive behavior dimensions. In other words, to be classified as mentally retarded, a person must show deficits in both areas.

In the past, children were placed in special classes for the mentally retarded simply because they scored in the retarded range on standardized tests and had troubled with academic learning. Many of these children have gotten along well in their community and with their peers. After leaving school, they have functioned successfully in their jobs, and in some cases have married and raised fine families. For these individuals, being labeled mentally retarded served no constructive purpose. According to the AAMD definition, they really were not mentally retarded since they were functioning within the normal range in life situations (i.e., they were not deficient in adaptive behavior).

With the current definition, those individuals who experience difficulty with school subjects and score low on tests, yet after completing school can get along well on a job in the community, may shed their classification of mental retardation (Patton & Payne, 1986).

The American Association on Mental Deficiency classifies mentally retarded persons by levels or degrees of severity: mild, moderate, severe, and profound retardation. The following translates the levels into approximate IQ values (Grossman, 1983):

Level	IQ Range
Mild	50–55 to approximately 70
Moderate	35–40 to 50–55
Severe	20–25 to 35–40
Profound	Below 20 or 25

Three terms frequently used in educational settings to refer to certain levels of mental retardation are *educable mentally retarded* (classified in the AAMD system as mildly retarded), *trainable mentally retarded* (AAMD: moderately retarded), and *severely handicapped* (AAMD: severely mentally retarded). Students labeled "severe" are most often placed in special classes designated for the severely mentally retarded or for the severely multiply handicapped. This latter situation occurs because often as the level of retardation becomes more severe, the chance of multiple problems being present increases as well.

PREVALENCE

Estimates of what percentage of the population is mentally retarded vary from one source to another. Prevalence figures ranging from 2–3% have been widely cited but also systematically criticized (Patton & Payne, 1986). A 3% figure would indicate that there are more than 6 million retarded citizens in the United States. The United States Office of Education estimates that 2.3% of the school-age population is mentally retarded. These figures are broken down into approximately 2% educable mentally retarded and approximately 0.3% trainable mentally retarded. Other professionals such as Mercer (1973) have argued for more conservative figures that approximate 1% of the population. According to the National Advisory Committee on the Handicapped (1976), an estimated 90% of those children identified as mentally retarded were receiving special educational services, leaving only 10% unserved.

   Some interesting trends have occurred since the initiation of PL 94-142 and the resulting compilation of data on the number of children designated by category served under this law. The number of school-age children classified as mentally retarded in the public schools between the years 1976–77 and 1984–85 has decreased by almost 36%. This change in population may be due to a number of reasons such as decertification, reclassification, or more conservative identification procedures. For whatever reasons, the mildly retarded group is most affected by this change (Polloway & Smith, 1983). One hypothesis is that students now found in classes for the mildly retarded may display functional levels much lower than those of students found in these same types of classes 10 years ago. If research confirms this, the implications for programming and mainstreaming are significant.

ETIOLOGY

Two general categorical schemes can be used to describe the many causes of mental retardation: biological/organic causes and psychosocial causes (Patton, Payne, & Beirne-Smith, 1986). Retardation can occur from infectious disease, physical trauma, chromosomal anomalies, abnormalities of gestation, dietary deficiencies, metabolic disorders, blood-type incompatability, poisoning, environmental influence, and many other factors including alcohol, drugs, and smoking.

Interestingly, most people classified as mentally retarded are mildly retarded; in fact, it has been estimated that the vast majority of the mentally retarded fall within the mildly retarded range. Although there is no conclusive evidence as to the causation, it is believed that the majority of those at this level are retarded due primarily not to organic causes, but to early environmental and social inadequacies. Recently, the term "psychosocial causes" has been applied to this group. These individuals have also been referred to as the *cultural-familial mentally retarded*. Both terms imply that the causation is a complex interaction of both environmental and hereditary factors.

REALISTIC EXPECTATIONS

Background information

When mentally retarded individuals are properly trained and given carefully planned assistance, their potential for achieving, learning, and living is enhanced. In this section realistic expectations for mildly and moderately retarded persons will be described, along with the types of treatment and care that are essential for furthering their cognitive, affective, social, motor, and vocational development.[2]

Chapter 5 elaborates on the problems and needs of the severely and profoundly handicapped. Because of the passage of recent legislation and the impact of landmark court cases, the entire area of the severely and profoundly handicapped, which includes the severely and profoundly retarded, merits a more extensive discussion.

Before proceeding, it is important to emphasize that regardless of the severity of retardation, an individual can be helped and can develop new skills. The mentally retarded child is not

---

[2]The expectations have been adapted in part from the adaptive behavior levels cited by Grossman, H.J. (Ed.). (1973). *Manual on terminology and classification in mental retardation*. Washington, DC: American Association on Mental Deficiency.

likely to blossom or intellectually unfold without special help. Undesirable behaviors can be ameliorated and desirable behaviors can be taught with proper intervention. And the earlier we get involved, the greater our chance of witnessing improvement.

At this point, we would like to review two investigations that demonstrate the effects of intervention. In the 1930s, it was believed that IQs were unalterable. Two researchers, Skodak and Skeels, set out to challenge the concept of the fixed IQ and to demonstrate the effects of environment on the cognitive growth of young mentally retarded children. They selected 13 children under 3 years of age for their study. This group was composed of 10 girls and 3 boys with an average IQ of 64. All were judged by the state law as unsuitable for adoption, although two were classified as nonretarded. Another group of 12 children under 3 years of age was selected for comparative purposes. The control group was composed of 4 girls and 8 boys with an average IQ of 86. All but two were classified as intellectually normal.

The control group, for the most part, remained in an orphanage and received adequate health and nutritional services. The environment was far from stimulating, being described as meager and desolate. On the other hand, the 13 experimental subjects were transferred to Glenwood State School and received care on a one-to-one basis from *adolescent retarded patients*. Each adolescent retarded "mother" was given instructions on how to care for her child. These mothers were instructed and trained on how to hold, feed, change, talk to, and stimulate the young children. "In addition to the opportunities afforded on the wards, the children attended the school kindergarten. They were sent to school as soon as they could walk . . . Activities carried on in the kindergarten were more in the nature of a preschool than the more formal type of kindergarten."[3]

Two years later, when the groups were retested, the 13 retarded children showed a mean gain of 27.5 IQ points, while the control group showed a mean loss of 26.2 IQ points. Approximately 4½ years from the origin of the study, 11 of the 13 experimental children had IQs high enough to be selected for adoption and were thus placed into good homes. In 1965 a follow-up study reported that 11 of the 13 had married and only 1 of the 11 marriages had ended in divorce. A total of 9 children, all of normal intelligence, were produced from these adults. Of the 12 contrast children,

---

[3]Brown and Edwards. (1972). *History and theory of childhood education.* Belmont, CA.: Wadsworth, p. 216.

1 was deceased, 2 had married, and 1 of the 2 marriages had ended in divorce. Five children were produced from these control-group adults, 1 of whom was diagnosed as mentally retarded with an IQ of 66. An investigation of educational levels showed that the experimental group had completed a median of 12 grades while the control group had completed a median of less than 3. In the experimental group, 4 of the subjects had one or more years of college work. One had received a B.A. degree and had taken some graduate training. Difference in occupational levels was also great. In the experimental group all subjects were self-supporting or married and functioning as housewives. The experimental-group occupations ranged from professional and business to domestic service (for the 2 girls never placed in adoptive homes). The control group ended with 4 of the subjects institutionalized and unemployed. Those who were employed, with one exception, were categorized as "hewers of wood and drawers of water."

Skeels (1966) concluded:

> It seems obvious that under present-day conditions there are still countless infants with sound biological constitutions and potentialities for development well within the normal range who will become mentally retarded and noncontributing members of society unless appropriate intervention occurs. It is suggested by the findings of this study and others published in the past 20 years that sufficient knowledge is available to design programs of intervention to counteract the devastating effects of poverty, socio-cultural, and maternal deprivations. . . . The unanswered questions of this study could form the basis for many life-long research projects. If the tragic fate of the 12 contrast group children provokes even a single crucial study that will help prevent such a fate for others, their lives will not have been in vain. (pp. 54–55)

The creative and partially successful attempts of Jean-Marc-Gaspard Itard to educate a 12-year-old *"homme savage"* deserve mention in any discussion of mental retardation. In 1799, a wild boy was captured in the forest of Aveyron, France. The boy, later named Victor, behaved in many ways like a wild animal. Victor did not speak or respond to the sound of gunfire, yet he quickly startled at the sound of a cracking nut. Victor did not seem to feel differences between hot and cold, or smell differences between foul and pleasant odors. His moods swung from deep depression to hyperexcitement. Itard believed that with proper education Victor could be cured. For 5 years, he worked intensively with Victor and then abandoned his goals, concluding that he had failed. Later, the French Academy of Science recognized Itard's significant accomplishments and requested that he publish a report of his work. The result was a classic for the field of education, *The Wild Boy of Aveyron.*

Although Itard had failed to "cure" Victor, many very dramatic changes in the boy were evidenced. Victor's behavior was greatly changed and after much training he was taught to identify various vowel sounds. Ultimately, he learned even to read and write a few words; however, he remained mute.

Itard also concerned himself with the teaching and evaluations of difficult social concepts. He described one of his lessons on justice as follows:

> I thought I ought to test my pupil's moral reactions to submitting him to another species of injustice, which, because it had no connection with the nature of the fault, did not appear to merit punishment and was consequently as odious as it was revolting. I chose for this really painful experience a day when after keeping Victor occupied for over two hours with our instructional procedures I was satisfied both with his obedience and his intelligence, and had only praises and rewards to lavish upon him. He doubtless expected them, to judge from the air of pleasure which spread over his whole face and bodily attitude. But what was his astonishment, instead of receiving the accustomed rewards, instead of the treatment which he had so much right to expect and which he never received without the liveliest demonstration of joy, to see me suddenly assume a severe menacing expression, rub out with all the outward signs of displeasure what I had just praised and applauded, scatter his books and cards into all corners of the room and finally seize him by the arm and drag him violently towards a dark closet which had sometimes been used as his prison at the beginning of his stay in Paris. He allowed himself to be taken along quietly until he almost reached the threshold of the door. There suddenly abandoning his usual attitude of obedience he arched himself by his feet and hands against the door posts, and set up a vigorous resistance against me, which delighted me so

much the more because it was entirely new to him, and because, always ready to submit to a similar punishment when it was merited, he had never before, by the slightest hesitation, refused for a single moment to submit. I insisted, nevertheless, in order to see how far he would carry his resistance, and using all my force I tried to lift him from the ground in order to drag him into the room. This last attempt excited all his fury. Outraged with indignation and red with anger, he struggled in my arms with a violence which for some moments rendered my efforts fruitless; but finally, feeling himself giving way to the power of might, he fell back upon the last resource of the weak, and flew at my hand, leaving there the deep trace of his teeth. It would have been sweet to me at that moment could I have spoken to my pupil to make him understand how the pain of his bite filled my heart with satisfaction and made amends for all my labor. How could I be other than delighted? It was a very legitimate act of justice and injustice, that eternal basis of the social order, was no longer foreign to the heart of my pupil. In giving him this feeling, or rather in provoking its development, I had succeeded in raising primitive man to the full stature of moral man by means of the most pronounced of his characteristics and the most noble of his attributes. (pp. 94–96)[4]

In presenting some of the characteristics and behaviors exhibited by retarded persons, we will discuss some objectives which we believe to be representative of realistic expectations for many of them. Realizing that the retarded differ from one another as much as normal persons differ among themselves, it is essential to recognize that the discussion will not apply to *all* individuals classified as retarded. The behaviors described are typically displayed at some age level by all children; retarded people just develop at a slower rate or later than do most children.

Mild retardation

A terminal goal for expectation for mildly retarded individuals should be employment and successful adjustment to community

---

[4]From Itard, JMG, *The Wild Boy of Aveyron* copyright © 1932 The Century Co. and 1962 Meredith Publishing Co., pp. 94–96. Reprinted by permission of Appleton-Century-Crofts, New York.

living upon the completion of formal schooling. People with mild retardation are usually quite capable of caring for their own personal needs. Overall, they should be able to carry out everyday activities without the assistance of family, friends, or benefactors.

In addition to the obvious problems in cognitive ability that characterize those with mental retardation, certain other areas have been identified as problematic for mildly retarded persons (Patton, Payne, & Beirne-Smith, 1986). These include possible difficulty in the following areas: personal/motivational (e.g., self-concept, dependency, failure syndrome); social/behavioral skills (e.g., self-direction, responsibility, social relationships); learning problems (e.g., attentional variables, mediational strategies, memory, generalization); speech/language skills (e.g., articulation, receptive and expressive language ability); physical/health dimensions (e.g., body measurements, motor skills); and academic behaviors (e.g., underachievement).

One problem area for many retarded adults is their inability to handle leisure time. Although they may be able to dance or bowl, they often spend their days watching television or riding buses. Thus, developing interests and actively participating in recreational programs is very important. With proper training, mildly retarded adults can learn appropriate leisure skills as well as good health habits (keeping clean, eating balanced meals, getting dental and physical checkups), money management, and banking.

Most mildly retarded persons are unrecognized until they confront what soon becomes a nemesis to them—school. The demands of school create a situation whereby a mildly retarded student becomes what the President's Committee on Mental Retardation (PCMR) called "the six-hour retarded child" (1970). Essentially, being classified as mentally retarded may only be appropriate when these students are attending school.

What does become important is the fact that mildly retarded children can be effectively educated in a public school system. In the elementary grades, many mildly retarded students can be fully or partially *mainstreamed* (integrated) into regular classrooms when these settings are determined appropriate. In a partial arrangement, students spend some of their instructional day in the regular education setting with the remainder of their time spent in a special setting with a trained special education teacher. The special education time is usually devoted to helping the student with language, reading, math, or social skill development.

During the latter elementary grades, and certainly by the junior high level, special provisions must be made for teaching the essential and practical academic subjects. Students should remain with their normal peers as much as possible, but they may require special programs in language arts, reading, and math.

Career education is essential and should begin in the elementary grades and continue throughout the students' schooling and through life. Attention to prevocational and vocational skill development should be programmed into the students' academic plan. Instruction in the areas of general job skills and specific vocational training are essential. By high school, they may remain with their peers in all subjects in which they can successfully compete, and vocational training should be a major concern. They should be given an opportunity to learn various types of job skills and be allowed to realistically demonstrate their competence by working on various jobs in the community (e.g., community-based training). Job training can be accomplished through programs that allow students to attend school for part of the day and for the remainder of the day to be placed on a job for training and evaluation.

Postsecondary programs and continuing educational opportunities are also important (Patton & Payne, 1986). These programs should supply the necessary guidance for helping the mildly retarded person with personal problems, and should provide opportunities for socialization and recreation. Programs for the mildly retarded must be comprehensive (cover social, motor, cognitive, and academic skills) and continuous (begin early and continue well into adulthood).

Moderately retarded

Moderately retarded persons can be viewed developmentally as usually being 3 or more years behind those who are mildly retarded. We typically think of the moderately retarded adult as working in a sheltered workshop[5] although more are becoming capable of holding unskilled jobs in competitive employment settings. Nevertheless, even into adulthood, these individuals may need supervision in carrying out routine daily activities. Many

---

[5]A sheltered workshop is usually a civic-sponsored project that hires handicapped workers who are unable to compete in industry. Pressure is reduced by allowing the handicapped worker to work at his own rate. The type of work is usually repetitive and menial.

moderately retarded adults are able to recognize written words and may even be able to read a simple sentence, but for all practical purposes they will be viewed as illiterate. They can carry on simple conversations and can perform such household chores as dusting, mopping, and cleaning. They can feed, bathe, and dress themselves, but will probably need help in selection of clothes. Although they can cook simple foods and make sandwiches, most of their meals will need to be prepared for them. By adulthood their gross and fine motor coordination will be developed to the point where they will have good body control. However, social life will be a constant problem and, if left alone, moderately retarded adults will sit idly in a chair, possibly watch television, or ride a bus for hours on end. Although moderately retarded individuals are limited in many respects, they may be interesting, challenging, and, in most cases, enjoyable company.

At age 3, moderately retarded children are so significantly delayed in their development that most are already diagnosed as retarded. At this age, such children are usually not toilet trained, but may indicate when their pants are wet and may be ready to cooperate in attempts to teach toileting skills. Self-feeding is messy, but they may become somewhat proficient with a spoon. They can stand and walk alone but will need help in climbing steps. They have a vocabulary of from four to six words, recognize others, play for short periods of time with others, and communicate many needs with gestures. By age 6, moderately retarded children begin to exhibit the same characteristics that mildly retarded persons do at age 3. For instance, they can feed themselves with a spoon (although this may still be messy), and can drink unassisted. They can climb up and down stairs, but still not with alternating feet. They can speak two- or three-word sentences and name simple common objects. Moderately retarded individuals remain 3 or more years behind the mildly retarded right on into adult life.

Moderately retarded individuals are so intellectually limited and developmentally slow that it is not to their advantage to be placed in regular school classrooms for instructional purposes. More likely, they will need highly specialized programs to assist them in developing to their maximum potential. Usually, a moderately retarded student will be educated in a self-contained classroom; that is, one room in which all school work and personal needs are attended to. This may even include lunch, since feeding must be considered an integral part of the curriculum.

However, interaction with other nonhandicapped students in the school should be encouraged and programmed. Benefits of such interaction accrue for both the retarded and nonretarded children. In general, the emphasis of the educational program must be on "functionality"—the ability to take care of oneself, to get along with others, and to display other requisite community living and vocational skills. Moreover, the program should strive to get the students or clients to feel good about themselves and ultimately to enjoy their lives.

As one can see, mildly retarded persons are much closer to normal people in what they can accomplish than are moderately retarded individuals. Also, a mildly retarded individual usually looks normal. That is, you probably would not be able to tell that someone you have merely seen on the street is mildly retarded. This is not the case with moderately retarded individuals, who frequently look like something is different about them; they usually have one or many observable, distinctive features (e.g., language problems, motor incoordination, physical characteristics as with Down syndrome persons, or inappropriate behaviors).

The distinctive physical characteristics become more prevalent the more severe and profound the retardation. In addition, as mentioned earlier, the severely and profoundly retarded are usually multiply handicapped.

CONCLUSIONS

The characteristics and behaviors that we have reported for the mildly and moderately retarded represent the upper limits of the continuum. For instance, it is not unusual to find a mildly retarded individual who is incapable of holding a job and who may even experience a great deal of difficulty remaining employed in a sheltered workshop. The important thing to remember is that retarded individuals can acquire new skills, learn, and grow intellectually, and that the facilitation of this developmental process is greatly enhanced when adequate services can be provided at the earliest possible time and continue to be offered into adulthood.

It is obvious that being retarded is no prize. Having a retarded child is something parents neither hope nor strive for. The difficulties that parents continually encounter are sometimes compounded not so much by poor services as by a total absence of services for their retarded children. Initially, parents are often given the "runaround," because no one feels comfortable telling them that their child is retarded and what they should expect. Many physicians, who are often the first to notice that a child is retarded, state that parents, once told of their child's developmental lag, are likely to seek other services in the hope that someone will tell them that their child is not really retarded after all. The point is that living and working with retarded people is not easy for anyone—parents, siblings, teachers, or physicians.

In ancient times of kings and castles, the retarded were often used as court jesters, but their condition is nothing to be laughed at. We hope to convey the idea that retarded individuals are people, who are much more like than unlike the rest of us. Although they often get caught in life's absurdities and amusing circumstances, they can lead successful and rewarding lives. Because retarded people themselves do not enjoy strong political clout, it is important that we sometimes act as advocates for them. We must ensure that the public in general and legislators, policy makers, and judges in particular realize that mentally retarded people are entitled *(a)* to the same rights that every citizen enjoys and *(b)* to the same human dignity that you and I continually demand.

SUGGESTIONS FOR WORKING WITH MENTALLY RETARDED PERSONS

1. Set goals that are realistic for the individual and the community in which the individual lives.
2. Assign tasks that *(a)* are personally relevant, *(b)* are carefully sequenced from easy to difficult, and *(c)* allow the learner to be highly and frequently successful.
3. Recognize the individual's strengths and weaknesses, provide incentives for performance, and establish necessary rules for behavior.
4. Explain required tasks in terms of concrete concepts.
5. When giving instructions be specific:
   John, go to the principal's office, give Mrs. Smith the absentee sheet, and come back here.
6. When giving instructions briefly summarize:
   Remember, John: *(a)* Go to principal's office, *(b)* Give the sheet to Mrs. Smith, and *(c)* Come back.

7. When giving instructions ask what is to be done:
   John, tell me what you are to do.

8. When praising be specific not general:
   John, you did a good job taking the absentee sheet
   to Mrs. Smith. You went directly to the office and you
   came straight back.
   Don't just say you did a good job or thanks for taking
   the absentee sheet.

9. When praising emphasize 'you' rather than 'I':
   John, you got 9 out of 10 math problems correct.
   That took a lot of effort, keep up the good work.
   Try not to use "I," as in, "I like the way you correctly
   completed 9 of the 10 problems, keep up the good work."
   The use of "I" encourages dependency on the teacher,
   away from the learner; while the use of "you" en-
   courages self-direction and enhances self-esteem.

10. Give constant praise and feedback especially when the
    retarded individual is just learning the task.

11. Don't give something for nothing:
    John comes to your class and states he doesn't have
    a pencil. Explain you will loan him a pencil for his
    shoe.

PONDER THESE

What are the arguments for and against the following
actions:

Sterilizing retarded adults

Encouraging matrimony among retarded individuals

Advocating for a community home for retarded adults
in your neighborhood

Allowing the initiation of a retarded child into your
son's or daughter's Cub Scout or Brownie troop

Think about how you could convince a businessperson to
hire a retarded adult. For example, how would you:

Request cooperation (phone or personal contact)

Describe your client; i.e., would you use the term *retarded?*

Ask questions about the job description

Describe the competencies of your client

Guarantee success

Would you take your client with you?

You are a first-grade teacher in a public school. Your classroom is next to one for trainable mentally retarded children. Your class and the trainable children go to recess together. Ted, a trainable child, frequently soils his pants and your children are beginning to make fun of him, tease him, and laugh at him. How will you deal with this situation?

What are some everyday living skills necessary for successful functioning in your community?

REFERENCES

Brown & Edwards (1972). *History and theory of childhood education.* Belmont, CA: Wadsworth.

Grossman, H.J. (Ed.). (1983). *Classification in mental retardation.* Washington, DC: American Association on Mental Deficiency.

Itard, J.M.G. (1962). *The wild boy of Aveyron.* New York: Appleton-Century-Crofts.

Mercer, J.R. (1973). *Labeling the mentally retarded.* Berkeley: University of California Press.

Patton, J.R., & Payne, J.S. (1986). Mild mental retardation. In N.G. Haring & L. McCormick (Eds.), *Exceptional children and youth* (4th ed., pp. 233–269). Columbus, OH: Merrill.

Patton, J.R., Payne, J.S., & Beirne-Smith, M. (1986). *Mental retardation* (2nd ed.). Columbus, OH: Merrill.

Polloway, E.A., & Smith, J.D. (1983). Changes in mild mental retardation: Population, programs and perspectives. *Exceptional Children, 50,* 149–159.

President's Committee on Mental Retardation. (1970). *The six-hour retarded child.* Washington, DC: U.S. Government Printing Office.

Skeels, H.M. (1966). Adult status of children with contrasting early life experiences: A follow-up study. *Monographs of the Society for Research in Child Development, 31,* No. 3. (Whole No. 105).

U.S. Office of Education. (1977). Education of all handicapped children: Implementation of Part B of the Education of the Handicapped Act. *Federal Register, 42,* 42474–42518.

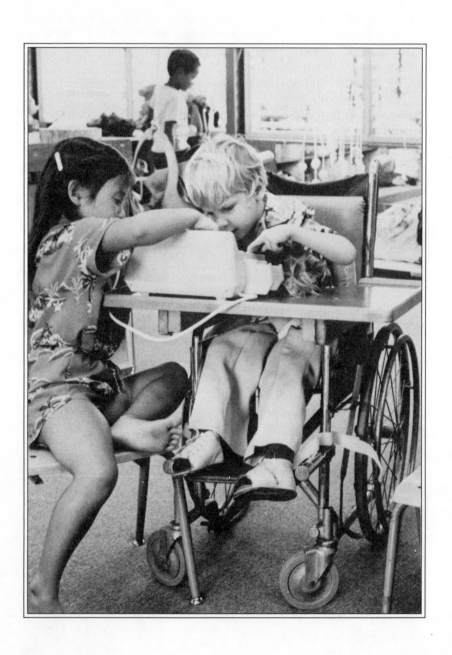

5

Severe and Profound Handicaps

For many institutionalized individuals with severe or profound handicaps the most important persons in their lives are the direct care staff who tend to their daily needs. These employees typically have more physical contact with these residents than any other human being. Heidi, a member of the direct care staff of a large residential facility for mentally retarded people, depicts the importance of this type of employee. Most importantly, she demonstrates what we think is a healthy attitude toward her charges.

Heidi is an older woman of German background who works in a unit of very low functioning residents. Every day she wakes up her assigned group, attends to their immediate needs, cleans their beds, bathes, dresses, and feeds them. While she is doing the tasks most of us would find less than enjoyable, she is talking to these uncommunicative and mostly unresponsive persons, as if they were her best friends or close relatives, about all sorts of topics. The fact that none of them ever contributes to the conversation does not seem to affect her at all.

After witnessing these events on more than one occasion, I asked her why she carried on the way she did with people who probably don't understand a word she was saying. She looked at me strangely and said, "Got to be a person in there somewhere."

I left that particular unit very humbled but with a renewed respect for those who mean so much to those we actually know so little about. I was particularly struck by the idea that we don't know what is going on inside these individuals who perform so low on our existing measures of ability. Perhaps they hear and understand everything that is said to them but just can't communicate their feelings to us. (For a related example, read the book Johnny Got His Gun, *by D. Trumbo [1959, Bantam Books]). On this particular day, I was also reminded of something that I tell students every time we visit such residential facilities: these individuals are much more like us than unlike us.*

I also realized one other thing—to a small number of people, Heidi is more important than the President, the governor, Elizabeth Taylor, Don Johnson, or Eddie Van Halen.

I worked with Albert every day for 3 years in Allen's Restaurant. He was the 57-year-old dishwasher and, while washing dishes, loved to listen to baseball games on the radio. It didn't make any difference what teams were playing, he just enjoyed listening to the play-by-play action while he worked. Before coming to Allen's, he lived his entire life in the state institution. He couldn't read or write, couldn't make change, and didn't talk very much, although, he did know about baseball. He knew most of the famous ballplayer's batting averages, and he knew what place each team was in on a particular day. He was diagnosed as severely mentally retarded, but I didn't think much about it until I left for a three-week vacation. When I returned, Albert didn't recognize me. I don't mean he didn't remember my name; I mean he didn't remember me at all. At first my feelings were hurt; later I just figured he had a short memory.

When he was 6, Johnny was still in diapers. He was able to say four or five words, and could barely walk. All day long for 6 years he had stared at the blank walls of a crowded ward of a state school, where he had been brought shortly after he was born.

Severely retarded, he faced only the bleak prospect of eventually moving into another ward where the residents were older. That was all.

*But one day Johnny was taken out of the back ward and
into a hostel where five other severely retarded youngsters were
living.*

*Johnny now is a lively little boy who goes to special educa-
tion classes; he talks and sings, goes down the sliding board,
dresses himself, and, of course, is toilet trained. Five days a
week he, along with the others of the "family," is bused to
their special classes, physical therapy, and recreation
programs.*

*Perhaps more important, he is being introduced to normal
living, in a real home, on a real street, and living with a real
couple who are taking on the role of parents (Weinberger, 1972,
pp. 42–43).*

---

*Charles was 24 years old and worked for me as a sander of
furniture that was to be refinished. He was severely retarded
and lived in a halfway house about four blocks away. At first
he had trouble walking to and from work. He seemed to always
get lost. He was clumsy, but he could sand furniture pretty well.
Charles loved to talk. Although it was difficult to understand
what he was saying, he nevertheless talked from the time he
entered the shop until he left. If no one was around, he talked
or hummed to himself. One day I was working on an old spinning wheel that had just come in. Charles came in jabbering
away, but, when he saw the spinning wheel, he immediately
quit talking. He just stared at the spinning wheel. He walked
around it at least three times and finally asked, "How do you
ride it?"*

The first retarded and disturbed children to catch the attention
of special educators were the most severely handicapped, the
"hopeless," "bottom-of-the-barrel" cases. We are apt today to
think that the needs of the severely and profoundly handicapped
are just now being recognized for the first time in special education's history because of a recent reawakening of interest. But
as the following descriptions show, the severely or profoundly
handicapped child was an object of concern in the early part of
the nineteenth century as well as in the last half of the twentieth:

*The age of Charles Emile is fifteen: he was admitted to the
school in June, 1843. He is described as being of a nervous and
sanguine temperament, and in an almost complete state of*

idiocy: the faculties which remain being in a state of extraordinary activity, and rendering him dangerous to himself and to others: but still idiotic in his inclinations, sentiments, perceptions, faculties of perception and understanding, and also of his senses, of which some were obtuse, and others too excitable. He was consequently unfit, to use the words of M. Voisin, "to harmonise with the world without." As regards his inclinations, he was signalized by a voracious, indiscriminate, gluttonous appetite, un erotisme hideux, and a blind and terrible instinct of destruction. He was wholly an animal. He was without attachment; overturned everything in his way, but without courage or intent; possessed no tact, intelligence, power of dissimulation, or sense of propriety; and was awkward to excess. His moral sentiments are described as null, except the love of approbation, and a noisy instinctive gaiety, independent of the external world. As to his senses, his eyes were never fixed, and seemed to act without his will; his taste was depraved; his touch obtuse; his ear recognized sounds, but was not attracted by any sound in particular; and he scarcely seemed to be possessed of the sense of smell. Devouring everything, however disgusting; brutally sensual; passionate,—breaking, tearing, and burning whatever he could lay his hand upon; and if prevented from doing so, pinching, biting, scratching, and tearing himself, until he was covered with blood. He had the particularity of being so attracted by the eyes of his brothers, sisters, and playfellows, as to make the most persevering efforts to push them out with his fingers. He walked very imperfectly, and could neither run, leap, nor exert the act of throwing; sometimes he sprang like a leopard, and his delight was to strike one sonorous body against another. When any attempt was made to associate him with the other patients, he would start away with a sharp cry, and then come back to them hastily. M. Voisin's description concludes with these expressions: "All the faculties of perception in this youth are in a rudimentary state; and if I may venture so to express myself, it is incredibly difficult to draw him out of his individuality, to place him before exterior objects, and to make him take any notice of them. It would not be far from the truth to say, that for him all nature is almost completely veiled." (American Journal of Insanity, 1845, 1, 335–336)

Jose was four years old at the start of treatment. His extreme negativism was reflected in tantrums, biting, and extreme stubbornness. He did not play with peers. He did not respond to his name or any commands. He had no speech, could not dress himself, was not toilet-trained, nor did he have any other self-help behaviors. Appropriate play was essentially absent. He was found to be untestable on intelligence tests. He had a social quotient of 59. In short, he was extremely behaviorally retarded.

He was treated as an inpatient at the UCLA Neuropsychiatric Institute for one year. His mother was given some limited training in how to continue therapy with him as described above. His treatment was primarily designed to overcome his negativism and to build some basic language skills. The latter included simple labeling, color discrimination, response to simple commands, and form discriminations. Some work was also done on the reinforcement of spontaneous babbling. (Lovaas, Koegel, Simmons & Long, 1973, 6, 158)

Who are the severely and profoundly handicapped? They are individuals who, in the past, were largely excluded from public education and denied social acceptance. More specifically, however, the severely and profoundly handicapped (SPH) comprise a rather heterogeneous population with extreme or multiple disabilities, or both. Many professionals refrain from considering this population as a separate category of special education; rather, they view this group as differing from other exceptional individuals in terms of the degree of handicap (Sontag, Certo, & Button, 1979). The SPH population may include individuals who are seriously emotionally disturbed, mentally retarded, or physically handicapped. For instance many SPH persons have multiple handicaps such as visual impairment, hearing impairment, or physical disabilities in addition to severe mental retardation or emotional disturbance. The common feature eminently apparent in all these individuals is that they are "functionally impaired."

Whatever handicap or handicaps an individual possesses, the person is impaired to the degree that the very basic self-help skills or behaviors necessary for everyday normal living have not been learned or cannot be performed. With the current rapid development of technology, teaching methodology, and specially trained personnel, expectations for individuals with severe and profound handicaps have risen significantly.

HISTORICAL PERSPECTIVE

In the early history, the SPH were usually cared for by placing them in monasteries or institutions. Some were even tortured or even killed (Scheerenberger, 1982). During the second quarter of the nineteenth century, attempts were initiated to educate, train, and reintegrate the more severely handicapped. Unfortunately, the public attitude toward the efforts of zealous educators became sharply critical. As a result, severely or profoundly handicapped individuals became institutional prisoners who were kept away from society. This regressive social attitude of separation and confinement persisted for many years.

For a long time, professionals did not have an adequate understanding of the educational potential of the SPH population, nor did they have the methodology to effect change. Until the advent of behavioral research and other technological advances involving the severely and profoundly handicapped population, this situation remained unchanged. However, behavior modification researchers revealed that these extremely handicapped people could acquire skills such as toileting, self-feeding, dressing, language, mobility, and socialization. They demonstrated that these SPH individuals could learn many useful skills when a systematic and intensive teaching program was employed.

The impetus provided by the gains of behavioral research in itself was not enough to assure educational services. However, the movement to establish services finally was rewarded by a number of legal decisions occurring in the early 1970s. In 1972, a parent organization in Pennsylvania won a lawsuit in the case of the *Pennsylvania Association for Retarded Children v. Commonwealth of Pennsylvania State Board of Education* that granted the right to education for all mentally retarded children. In addition, provisions for locating retarded individuals, due process, and reevaluation were mandated. Also in 1972, the *Mills v. Board of Education of the District of Columbia* decision extended the right of a free, public education, regardless of the degree of handicap, to all exceptionalities. Confusion regarding what constitutes a suitable education was clarified in a lawsuit brought to court by the *Maryland Association for Retarded Citizens v. State of Maryland* (1974). An equally important lawsuit furthering the rights of the SPH was the *Wyatt v. Stickney* (1971) decision that guaranteed the right to appropriate treatment while in a residential facility.

With the passage of Public Law 94–142 in 1975 (amended in 1983 as PL 98–199 and, in 1986, as PL 99–457), the favorable culmination of many years of lobbying and excruciating legal battles was realized. This law mandates as a top priority the free, public education of the most neglected individuals. As a result of this action, many administrative problems have been created that have a major impact on public school programs.

What constitutes an appropriate education for this group remains a matter of controversy and continuing discussion. The U.S. Court of Appeals rendered a significant decision favorable to the education of the handicapped in the *Armstrong v. Kline* case. In their decision, the judges struck down the 180-day school-year rule of the Pennsylvania Department of Education on the basis that some individuals, as a result of their handicaps, learn very slowly and are negatively affected when their educational programs are interrupted (Stotland & Mancuso, 1981). This decision opened the doors for many parents seeking to obtain extended school-year programming for their severely handicapped children.

Parent and professional organizations are largely responsible for achieving services for the SPH. The efforts of various state associations for retarded citizens can be seen in the litigation already mentioned. National Association for Retarded Citizens-U.S. has also been effective in its lobbying and informational functions. In 1974, the American Association for the Education of the Severely/Profoundly Handicapped (now known as the Association for Persons with Severe Handicaps) was established, reflecting the increasing professional interest in the education of these exceptional individuals.

DEFINITION

As yet a single statement that accurately and succinctly defines the SPH population does not exist. Earlier in this chapter, the concept of "functional impairment" was presented, and the explanation that accompanied this terminology can serve as a generalized definition. That is, SPH individuals do not have the ability to function independently in a normal living environment. The emergence of the concept of "developmental disabilities" and its emphasis on "substantial functional limitations" vis-á-vis major life activities further illustrates this point (cf., Developmental Disabilities Assistance and Bill of Rights Act of 1978, PL 95–602). Other more specific definitions usually reflect the various orientations of the defining agents.

Haring (1978) believes that the SPH "should be defined by their actual characteristics and potentials" (p. 196). While advocating an education-oriented definition, Haring acknowledges four additional perspectives that have been used to define the SPH: (a) social deviance, (b) medical, (c) intellectual, and (d) administrative.

In the past, a definition of social deviancy measured a person's difference according to his or her deviation from the normative order. The resulting treatment usually was isolation from society. The institutions of the early 1900s reflected the social ostracism of that time by performing a custodial rather than a teaching function. Although the concept of social deviancy does have a certain appropriateness to the SPH population, social stigma can be greatly minimized by emphasizing their learning potential and by educating society.

The frequent use of medical definitions reflects the fact that many SPH individuals have definite medical problems responsible for their condition. Thus, as with any medical model, these definitions are actually etiological explanations of a given problem. These medical definitions incorporate etiological descriptions that will be elaborated on in the etiology section of this chapter.

An intellectually-oriented definition of the SPH is based on classifying individuals on an intellectual measure such as the intelligence quotient (IQ). The most notable problem with this type of definition is that it attempts to classify individuals into a generalized category. Because even the SPH individuals who fall within a narrow IQ range are vastly different from one another, the IQ-based system is awkward to implement for purposes of understanding this population and programming for their educational needs.

Administratively-oriented definitions serve the purpose of meeting bureaucratic guidelines that demand precise accounting procedures and provide some consistency in the placing of students, determining teacher quotas, and ordering materials. Administrative definitions are predicated mainly on the salient characteristics that the individuals display.

PREVALENCE

The Association for Retarded Citizens–U.S. estimates that there are approximately 120,000 severely and profoundly retarded individuals under the age of 21 in the United States. Other sources estimate that 0.2–0.5% of the school-aged population can be classified as SPH (Schmid, Moneypenny, & Johnston, 1977). While the percentage of SPH individuals is low, the optimal teacher-student ratio also is low.

Recent medical achievements have had paradoxical effects on the prevalence figures. On the one hand, medical technology now has the capacity to keep alive many severely and profoundly handicapped individuals who would probably have died in the past, thus increasing the number of SPH individuals. On the other hand, medical developments such as amniocentesis, chorion biopsy, and fetal monitoring,[1] along with the proliferation of genetic counseling centers, will have a deflating effect on the prevalence rates, providing these procedures lead to abortion or corrective surgical or medical measures (e.g., embryonics) before the child is born.

ETIOLOGY

Etiological factors, as viewed from a medical standpoint, can be seen in the following categorical areas that are primarily based on an organizational structure presented by Haring (1978):

1. Chromosomal abnormality
2. Genetic disorders
3. Metabolic disorders
4. Infection and intoxicants
5. Neural tube closure (i.e., maldevelopment of the brain and/or spinal cord)

---

[1]Amniocentesis, chorion biopsy, and fetal monitoring are medical techniques which can be used during gestation to detect abnormalities in the developing fetus.

6. Gestational factors (e.g., prematurity, postmaturity, Rh incompatibility)

7. Perinatal difficulties (e.g., lack of oxygen or physical injury during birth)

8. Postnatal difficulties (e.g., physical trauma to the head, infection, disease)

9. Other environmental factors (e.g., extreme sensory deprivation, radiation)

All of the above causes can lead to conditions characterized as severe or profound handicaps. In addition, the conditions of deafness, blindness, severe orthopedic problems, and multiple disorders can also be major factors associated with a severe or profound handicap. Many causal factors produce more than one effect. For example, oxygen deprivation or head injury may result in blindness *and* mental retardation *and* a crippling physical disability.

Sontag and his associates describe a number of behaviors exhibited by some SPH children upon entry into the public school system:

> Students . . . are not toilet trained; aggress toward others; do not attend to even the most pronounced social stimuli; self mutilate; ruminate; self stimulate; do not walk, speak, hear, or see; manifest durable and intense temper tantrums; are not under even the most rudimentary forms of verbal control; do not imitate; manifest minimally controlled seizures; and/or have extremely brittle medical existences. (Sontag, Burke, & York, 1973, p. 2)

While this list of characteristics is extensive, it is not exhaustive. In addition to the characteristics mentioned, SPH persons may show poor discrimination abilities, slow motoric behaviors, poor perceptual abilities, and poor health. It is interesting to note that, unlike mild retardation, severe and profound retardation does not seem to be associated with socioeconomic status. Occurrence of SPH tends to be random rather than associated with any particular environmental variable (Stark, 1983).

Because learning will occur within a very systematic, task-analyzed program, the administrative problems associated with educating these individuals are monumental. The competencies and skills required of a teacher who works with SPH students are vast in number. In order for the teacher-to-be to possess requisite, instructionally-related skills, the program that prepares these teachers must be very comprehensive.

ADMINISTRATIVE CONCERNS

Since the passage of PL 94–142, school administrators have been quite aware of the time deadlines mandated by this law. By September 1, 1978, services had to be provided for *all* handicapped individuals between the ages of 3 and 18. By September 1, 1980, these services had to be extended to cover all exceptional people between the ages of 3 and 21. Now all school-aged handicapped children must be educated in the "least restrictive environment" at no cost to the parent. As a result of these legal requirements, school districts have experienced an influx of SPH children and adolescents into their schools from special day schools and institutions. The logistical problems associated with the change are extensive.

Prior to programming services for the SPH, a philosophy of education for these individuals had to be established. For many SPH, education often implies the learning of basic self-help behaviors or daily living skills (toileting, self-feeding, etc.). Therefore, the education of these people primarily involves the learning of behaviors which assist them in coping better with demands of their immediate environment. Efforts should be directed toward helping these individuals progress to a less dependent state of functioning. Programming should be age-appropriate and training should utilize natural settings, thus providing the best likelihood for skill acquisition and maintenance over time (Brown et al., 1979).

Two alternatives for the location of classes exist for SPH children: *(a)* classes located at one specific site in a school district, or *(b)* classes distributed throughout a school system (Sontag et al., 1973). From an administrative point of view, the former choice is usually most appealing; while, from the individual's perspective, the latter alternative may be most favorable. Arguments pro and con can be given for both choices; however, according to the law, the ultimate administrative decision must be guided by the principle of "least restrictive environment." Furthermore, integrated settings can produce benefits for both

SPH and their nonhandicapped peers as well as for teachers, administrators, and staff.

Regardless of where the class is located, the individual's mobility usually poses a major problem. In order to attend public school, transportation services must be provided, and many of these individuals require special features or modifications on the transporting vehicle. In addition, specially trained attendants are needed to assist in the children's travel. Within the various school buildings, specific changes must also be effected to allow mobility within the school. Therefore, with the increasing numbers of SPH in the school systems, various building and transportation modifications, both specific and general, must be made to assure appropriate educational services.

To maximize the learning potential of the SPH, professionals who make administrative decisions must establish a modus operandi that effectively uses the talents and skills of various ancillary personnel. Related service personnel who are extremely important in the education of SPH students include: occupational and physical therapists, speech/language therapists, audiologists, vision and hearing specialists, medical specialists (doctors, nurses, and nutritionists), psychologists, social workers, administrators, and paraprofessionals. Effective use of paraprofessionals is warranted with children who display extremes of behavior and who require much attention. Sontag, Smith, and Sailor (1977) eloquently stated that it is important to consider paraprofessionals as effective and bona fide members of this multidisciplinary team:

> The paraprofessional has been viewed as an assistant, rather than as a therapist or educator in his own right. However, programming for the severely/profoundly handicapped population engenders a teaching situation in which the ratio of professionals to children is optimally around one to three. To help meet this requirement and fulfill a greatly expanded role, paraprofessionals must be trained or retrained, must have professional status as teaching associates, and must be paid in accordance with their contributions, which are often considerable. (p. 208)

TEACHER COMPETENCIES AND PREPARATION

The one individual ultimately responsible for the education of SPH children is the teacher. Good teaching comprises a series of interrelated steps (Hasazi & York, 1978; Strain, McConnell & Cordisco, 1983) requiring considerable organization and planning to be carried out successfully. In order for SPH children to learn new behaviors, they must be instructed in a sequential, systematic manner, with appropriate behavioral strategies in operation. Appropriate learning opportunities will occur if the teacher entrusted with this task possesses certain competencies. Although many of the skills required to be competent may already exist in a person's repertoire before embarking in a training program, there are many specialized skills that must be developed. Teacher training programs of any type, but very notably of the SPH, have a three-fold obligation: *(a)* such programs must further develop the existing skills and knowledge-base of the teacher-to-be; *(b)* they must establish those skills that do not presently exist but are necessary for successful teaching; and *(c)* these programs should be accountable for the existence of various skills or competencies that they say a teacher has when they grant that teacher a degree.

Teacher competencies

What competencies are needed for the successful teaching of the SPH? We want to discuss the characteristics of the professionally competent teacher with the emphasis on *professional.* This latter distinction demands certain personal integrities such as sound ethical standards, an analytical awareness of various influences on the child, a conscientiousness, and a profusive enthusiasm for exceptional people. If these teachers are to be accepted as true "professionals," then these personal factors should be considered as competencies of significance for teachers. The impasse that teacher trainers experience is in answering the question: "How does one assess and train these required personal qualities?" Whether a teacher has these characteristics or not, at minimum a competent teacher must have a knowledge of and a demonstrated proficiency in a number of teaching skills. Among these skills are the ability to use evaluation procedures; to set goals; to analyze tasks; to operationalize various curricula such as self-help, affective, recreational, social and mobility; to use various methodological and instructional techniques; to effectively manage behaviors; to be familiar with a variety of prosthetic aids; and to work within a multidisciplinary context. Obviously, these skills are directly related to teaching the SPH student; however, other nonclassroom abilities are also essential.

The overall curriculum plan for SPH students can be divided into at least the following four domains: (a) vocational, (b) domestic, (c) recreation/leisure, and (d) community functioning (Brown, Branston, Hamre-Nietupski, Pumpian, Certo, & Gruenewald, 1979). Brown et al. (1981) maintain that the curriculum provided to severely handicapped students should be designed to provide direct training in a wide variety of school and nonschool environments. Severely handicapped children trained to successfully perform a task in school probably may not successfully generalize the skill to the nonschool environment unless direct training is given.

The well-trained teacher also will display abilities that indirectly affect students. Teachers must act as parent-trainers because the educational needs of SPH children certainly extend into the home. Parents are in great need of behavior management skills; they can also be used to reinforce learning that occurs in the schools. The skillful teacher must also be able to function and to communicate easily with parents and with the many supportive personnel who are involved with SPH children, especially paraprofessionals.

Another personal skill that teachers must exercise is the tolerance for risk-taking with SPH children. Often, a pattern of parental over-protection severely limits the activities of these children. While being mindful of the child's limitations, the competent teacher must allow the child to experience everyday situations which involve a certain degree of risk. Perske (1972) poignantly states:

> Overprotection endangers the . . . person's human dignity and tends to keep him from experiencing the normal taking of risks in life which is necessary for normal human growth and development. (p. 24)

Teacher preparation

It is the responsibility of institutions that train teachers of the SPH to provide relevant coursework and experiences that will either elaborate on or establish those skills necessary for successful teaching. Most of these professional competencies can be introduced in an academic setting, but maximal acquisition can only be achieved if a variety of field experiences also becomes an integral part of the program.

Institutions of higher learning also have the opportunity to provide important in-service programs to the school systems and community. The value of such programs for the professional in the field, and more importantly for the SPH students themselves, cannot be overemphasized. Especially after their professional schooling is over, competent professionals must continue to be well-informed of advances in their field. Another role that departments of special education can take is that of lobbying agent, one of whose purposes is to provide input on certification issues.

Finally, teacher training institutions can assist in developing community services for the older handicapped individuals who need continuing services after their school years. Together with the problems of reintegration of the SPH into the community, the need for a model for continued training must be explored. The numerous community agencies in most areas should be structured to enable them to deliver services to the SPH.

FUTURE CONSIDERATIONS

Since it seems that our knowledge in behavioral science and technology will keep increasing, it is not difficult to imagine that our knowledge about the learning potential of the SPH will also grow. As SPH individuals demonstrate the attainment of various behaviors, new goals that indicate higher levels of functioning or coping can be set.

Appropriate lifelong planning for these individuals is needed. It is not out of the question to hope for the development of a comprehensive lifelong curriculum for the vocational and personal development of SPH people.

Continued research must be encouraged, supported, and adequately funded in order to accelerate the pace of development now being experienced. Behavioral technology, which works particularly well with SPH students, needs to be refined. Efforts to enhance the maintenance and generalization of learned behaviors and to identify alternative reinforcement strategies must continue. Medical research into the etiology, assessment, and prevention of various pathological conditions must also continue.

Major issues related to the lives of persons with severe/profound handicaps remain controversial to this day. Serious questions concerning prenatal screening/intervention and the withholding of treatment postnatally are only a few of the volatile issues yet to be resolved. Other questions related to cost, efficacy, and even the educability of this population have also arisen. How these issues will be decided remains to be seen; however, we can be sure of one reality: Resolution and the subsequent treatment of SPH individuals will reflect the prevailing social, political, and economic climate of the times.

SUGGESTIONS FOR WORKING WITH SEVERELY/PROFOUNDLY RETARDED PERSONS

1. Make sure you have their attention before beginning any teaching activity.
2. Use age-appropriate materials regardless of the severity of the handicap.
3. Set clear goals—have a plan and stick with it.
4. Use teaching methods that minimize errors.
5. When errors occur, provide corrective feedback.
6. Be consistent. It also helps to follow a planned schedule throughout the day at home as well as at school.
7. Use activities and tasks that are relevant to the child.
8. Teach and assess in natural settings and at natural times whenever possible.
9. In order to promote skill generalization, teach a given skill across a variety of settings, trainers, and materials.
10. After a skill is mastered, plan opportunities for its use on a regular basis.

PONDER THESE

You are a parent and you have a one-week-old infant who has been diagnosed as severely handicapped. What are your reactions when you receive a sympathy card from friends saying that their thoughts are with you in your time of grief?

Suppose that you have a 4-year-old severely handicapped child, but this child is not receiving any educational services. What methods and arguments would you use to correct this situation?

Some people believe that profoundly handicapped newborns who cannot survive without life-sustaining equipment should not be allowed to live. Provide a list of arguments you could use to defend the profoundly handicapped child's right to life.

Would you consider an intellectually bright adult with a severe form of cerebral palsy (i.e., substantial motoric and communicative impairments) to be severely handicapped?

REFERENCES

Brown, L., Branston, M. B., Hamre-Nietupski, S., Pumpian, I., Certo, N., & Gruenewald, L. (1979). A strategy for developing chronological age appropriate and functional curricular content for severely handicapped adolescents and young adults. *Journal of Special Education, 13*, 81–90.

Brown, L., Pumpian, I., Baumgart, D., Vandventor, P., Ford, A., Nisbet, J., Schroeder, J., & Gruenewald, L. (1981). Longitudinal transition plans in programs for severely handicapped students. *Exceptional Children, 47*, 624–630.

Haring, N. G. (1978). The severely handicapped. In N. G. Haring (Ed.), *Behavior of exceptional children* (2nd ed., pp. 195–229). Columbus, OH: Merrill.

Hasazi, S., & York, R. (1978). Eleven steps to good teaching. *Teaching Exceptional Children, 10*(3), 63–66.

Lovaas, O. I., Koegel, R., Simmons, J. Q., & Long, J. S. (1973) Some generalizations and follow-up measures on autistic children in behavior therapy. *Journal of Applied Behavior Analysis, 6*, 158.

Perske, R. (1972). The dignity of risk and the mentally retarded. *Mentally Retardation, 10*(1), 24–27.

Scheerenberger, R. C. (1982). Treatment from ancient times to the present. In P. T. Cegelka & H. J. Prehn (Eds.), *Mental retardation: From categories to people* (pp. 44–75). Columbus, OH: Merrill.

Schmid, R. E., Moneypenny, J., & Johnston, R. (Eds.). (1977). *Contemporary issues in special education*. New York: McGraw-Hill.

Sontag, E., Burke, P. J., & York, R. (1973). Considerations for serving the severely handicapped in the public schools. *Education and Training of the Mentally Retarded, 8*, 20–26.

Sontag, E., Certo, N., & Button, J. E. (1979). On a distinction between the education of the severely and profoundly handicapped and a doctrine of limitations. *Exceptional Children, 45*, 604–616.

Sontag, E., Smith, J., & Sailor, W. (1977). The severely/profoundly handicapped: Who are they? Where are they? *Journal of Special Education, 11*, 5–11.

Stark, J. A. (1983). The search for cures of mental retardation. In J. J. Menolascino, R. Neman, & J. A. Stark (Eds.), *Curative aspects of mental retardation: Biomedical and behavioral advances* (pp. 1–11). Baltimore: Paul H. Brookes.

Stotland, J. F., & Mancuso, E. (1981). U.S. Court of Appeals decision regarding Armstrong v. Kline: The 180 day rule. *Exceptional Children, 47*, 266–270.

Strain, P., McConnell, S., & Cordisco, L. (1983). Special educators as single-subject researchers. *Exceptional Education Quarterly, 4*(3), 40–51.

Weinberger, C. W. (1972). MR 72: Islands of excellence. *Report of the President's Committee on Mental Retardation.* Washington, DC: U.S. Government Printing Office.

TWO

Physical, Sensory, and Communicative Impairments

6

Physical and Health Impairments

Handicapped people are not to be abused, talked down to, or pitied. They are people just like you and me. There is a film called Leo Beuerman, *about a man so handicapped he was described sometimes as "grotesque," or "too horrible to look at."*[1] *He was small, weighed less than 90 pounds, and his legs were bent out of shape so he couldn't walk. He also had poor eyesight and was hard of hearing. Leo lived on a farm in Kansas. Somehow, he learned to drive a tractor, and later he invented a hoist that allowed him to raise himself onto the tractor. He also invented and built a pushcart that enabled him to get around from place to place. Using a hoist to get his cart on the tractor, he would then get on the tractor and drive to town. In town Leo would park his tractor, lower himself and his cart down to the street, get in the cart, and propel himself down the sidewalk to the store front where he repaired watches and sold pencils. The reason the movie about Leo had such an impact on me is that I can remember buying pencils from him as a kid in school. At that time, I didn't realize how remarkable Leo really was. He just wanted to talk to people, work, and do his own thing. He wanted to be self-sufficient and independent. Here*

---

[1]*Leo Beuerman*, Centron Educational Films, 1621 West 9th St., Lawrence, Kansas 66044 (13 minutes—color).

was a man, deformed to the point that, for most people, he was a repulsive sight. However, he was more individual, more free, and more alive than most people.

I have a friend, Bobby, who has epilepsy. The medication he takes regularly seems to control the seizures to a great extent; however, he still experiences grand mal episodes once in a while (approximately once a year).

Bobby is athletic and enjoys sports. Interestingly, his favorite leisure time activity is surfing. Now, around here that is not too unusual; but for someone who is not completely seizure-free it is a bit risky, especially when surfing by oneself. Bobby is not about to let his epilepsy control his life, so his frequent trips by surfboard through the breaking waves do not surprise me a bit.

Nevertheless, one day when Bobby was talking to my introductory class in special education, I asked him about the danger in going surfing alone and possibly having a grand mal seizure. After a brief hesitation, Bobby replied that he had thought about it and that if he did have a seizure he would probably drown unless someone else could pull him to safety. The class was confused by his matter of fact attitude, but understood his strong feelings about doing what he wanted to do. Then Bobby made everyone sit back and reflect when he concluded his response to my question with this quip: "But at least I'd die happy!"

Terry Haffner (1976) was born with incomplete arms and legs. His parents treated him with affection and respect, making life as similar as possible to that of his twin brother Tom, who was born without any serious physical anomalies. Terry described one of his more interesting Halloween experiences.

"My childhood was probably not that much zanier than yours or your children's. My neighborhood activities included cops and robbers. (My siren was authentic and loud.) I wore a mean set of guns and holsters when we played cowboys and Indians. There was a lemonade stand with competition one house away, sportscasting at garage basketball games, slinging apples at cars and camping out in the back yard—you name it. Birthdays counted; as children, Tom and I had to have the

same presents or we would fight. Trick or treating—I did both. In fact, for my first Halloween I wore a pirate costume, and I remember one guileless lady saying, My, what an authentic looking costume, with the hooks and all! I thought that was funny" (pp. 15–16).

A few summers ago, our university hosted the National Wheelchair Games by providing facilities, lodging, and assistance to the athletes and to the games. I gave students in my class the option of volunteering to help with the games or to complete another assignment for the course. Some of the students chose to spend a few afternoons being involved with the wheelchair games. After the games were over, we discussed their experiences in class. One of them noted that she had learned much through this experience but was a little confused by a term the wheelchair athletes used to describe nondisabled persons. She pointed out that they kept referring to us as "TABs". Her observation had the entire class very interested in finding out what this was all about. She continued by explaining that TAB stood for Temporarily Abled Bodied. After further discussion, we decided that this was an acceptable, healthy, although unusual way to be perceived.

Bonnie Consolo was born with no arms, yet she learned to use her feet as most people use their hands.[2] She learned to cook, sew, write, feed, groom, and dress herself, drive a car, take care of her children—almost everything people with hands do. She tells the story of walking down a street when a small child popped his head up and down from behind a hedge and shouted, "Hello, hello, hello."

After this had happened several times, she finally asked him, "What are you doing?"

He replied, "I'm yelling at all the 'no armed' ladies that come by."

She followed with, "How many have been by?"

He replied with a big smile, "Not many, not many." She laughs when she tells this story and then comments that that

---

[2] *A Day in the Life of Bonnie Consolo*, Barr Films, P.O. Box 5667, Pasadena, CA 91107 (17 minutes—color).

was a healthy response for him to make; he accepted her as a person.

Every once in awhile, a singular statement from someone says more than a whole book on a particular topic. Such is the case with a quote by Kathleen Barrett, a young woman with cerebral palsy. Kathleen is a glider plane pilot and has received national attention for her achievements. Her poignant observation holds not only for her but for many other disabled people as well. Kathleen once remarked that, "I don't mind having cerebral palsy as much as society minds my having cerebral palsy."

Since the Vietnam War, various skiing schools have been developed to teach handicapped individuals how to ski. In the film, A Matter of Inconvenience, a skier with an amputated leg explains how difficult it was for him to make the adjustment from skiing with two legs to skiing with just one leg.[3]. As he mentions the problems of this transition, you can tell from his face and eyes that he is in deep thought. Slowly he looks up and with a grin says, "One thing though, you don't have to worry about crossing tips."

Sign on the back of a wheelchair: "I may not be totally perfect, but parts of me are excellent."[4]

American society, perhaps more than any other society, puts a premium on strong, healthy-looking bodies. This attitude is espoused in most media advertisements and conveyed to every person who comes into contact with Madison Avenue tactics. The fact that people in this country spend so much money each year on beauty aids, cosmetics, tanning lotions, dietary products, running shoes, and memberships to health spas supports the thesis that we are indeed striving to enhance our appearance and physical condition. Therefore, it is not too difficult to understand why

---

[3]*A Matter of Inconvenience*, Stanfield House, 900 Euclid Avenue, P.O. Box 3208, Santa Monica, CA 90403 (10 minutes—color).

[4]Slides accompanying *Science Activities for the Visually Impaired* (SAVI) Program. Berkeley, CA: Lawrence Hall of Science.

our society looks so aghast at a person with a physical or health impairment; these people just don't measure up to our ideal. They don't even come close. As a result, physically or health-impaired persons must grapple with two opponents: the impairment itself and the social attitudes toward it. A formidible task, indeed!

DEFINITION AND CLASSIFICATION

Many terms are used interchangeably to describe individuals with physical or health problems. Several of the terms are: *physically handicapped, physically disabled, physically impaired, orthopedically handicapped,* or *crippled.* Some of these terms have very definite negative connotations; others lead to confusion.

The terms *disabled* and *handicapped* are good examples of those that have different meanings but are used interchangeably in popular and professional literature. According to Smith and Neisworth (1975), a disability refers to "an objectively defined deviation in physique or functioning that, through interaction with a specified environment, results in behavioral inadequacies or restrictions for the person" (p. 169). The key feature in this definition is the interaction of the deviation with the environment.

Smith and Neisworth define a handicap as "the burden imposed upon the individual by the unfortunate product of deviation and environment" (p. 169). This "product" includes various social and emotional facets the physically impaired individual experiences. It is due to the confusion related to these differences, however subtle or moot they appear, that we will use the term *impairment* in this chapter to describe the physical conditions of these exceptional people.

Physically and health impaired (PHI) persons may be defined as individuals who have functional disabilities related to physical skills (e.g., hand use, body control, mobility) and/or medical conditions (e.g., loss of strength or stamina) (Sirvis, 1982). Hallahan and Kauffman (1986) extend the principles of this definition to special education by stating that these conditions also are of such magnitude that they "interfere with [children's] school attendance or learning to such an extent that special services, training, equipment, materials, or facilities are required" (pp. 332–333).

Although not generic, the term *physical and health impairment* refers to a very heterogeneous population displaying a wide range of conditions. Consequently, our discussion of specific disabilities or conditions will mean that generalizations to all physical impairments may not be valid. You should be aware that PHI can result from many different causes and can be classified in many different ways. For example, impairments may be *congenital* (the child has it from birth) or *acquired* (the child is normal at birth but something happens later). Whether the impairments are present at birth or appear later, the causes may include genetic factors, physical trauma, oxygen deprivation, chemical agents (poisoning), disease, or some combination of these or other factors. Furthermore, impairments may be classified according to the particular organ or organ system involved: for example, neurological impairments (involving the brain or spinal cord or peripheral nerves), cardiovascular conditions (involving the heart and blood vessels), hematological problems (involving the blood), orthopedic conditions (involving the bones and joints), and so on. Some types of disorders can be congenital or acquired, result from a variety of causes, and involve more than one organ system. So you can see that classification of physical and health impairments, while possible, is a topic that cannot be dealt with in much detail in a short space. However, the listing that follows attempts to classify various selected impairments, using one arbitrary system. If you want detailed information on what can go wrong with children's bodies and how to classify the various disorders, diseases, and traumas, consult a medical text.

Neurological	Cerebral palsy
	Multiple sclerosis
	Spina bifida
	Spinal cord injury
Musculoskeletal	Juvenile rheumatoid arthritis
	Limb deficiency
	Muscular dystrophy
	Scoliosis
Health Conditions	Allergies/asthma
	Cancer
	Cystic fibrosis
	Diabetes mellitus
	Epilepsy

	Heart problem
	Hemophilia
	Sickle cell anemia
Miscellaneous Physical	Accidents
Conditions	Burns
	Child abuse

SPECIFIC IMPAIRMENTS

Two specific conditions—cerebral palsy and epilepsy—have strong implications on the affected student's education (see Bigge, 1982; Bigge & Sirvis, 1986; Bleck & Nagel, 1982; Cruickshank, 1976; Hallahan & Kauffman, 1986 for a more extensive discussion from a special education perspective). These students may require various adaptations in their school environments and understanding from those around them.

Cerebral palsy

The largest group of physically impaired children needing special education services is the cerebral palsied population. Literally, cerebral palsy implies brain paralysis. According to Bleck (1975), *cerebral palsy* is "a nonprogressive disorder of movement or posture beginning in childhood due to a malfunction or damage of the brain (cerebral dysfunction)" (p. 37). Numerous causes, occurring before, during, or after birth, may be responsible for this condition. Some of the etiologies include anoxia, infection, intoxication, hemorrhaging, trauma, fever, and prematurity. The resulting physical impairment can range from barely inhibiting to profoundly debilitating. The prevalence of cerebral palsy has been estimated at 0.15% of the child population.

Cerebral palsied children can be classified in a number of ways: *(a)* limb involvement, also referred to as *anatomical* or *topographic* classification, and *(b)* nature of the motor disability. Limb involvement is not only applicable when describing cerebral palsied individuals, but is employed to classify various forms of paralysis as well. The specific topographic descriptions and the estimated percentage of cerebral palsied individuals with a given type of impairment can be outlined in the following manner (Denhoff, 1976):

Hemiplegia—upper and lower extremity
on the same side   35–40%

Diplegia—legs involved more than arms	10–20%
Quadriplegia—all four extremities	15–20%
Paraplegia—only legs	10–20%
Monoplegia—one extremity	rare
Triplegia—three extremities involved (usually one arm and both legs)	rare
Double hemiplegia—both halves of the body affected but in different ways	rare

The other method of classification refers to the type of motor disability displayed by the individual (regardless of the limbs involved) and is delineated as follows:

Spasticity—disharmony of muscle movements; the muscles involuntarily contract when movement or stretching is attempted.

Athetosis—involuntary, jerky, purposeless, writhing movements; purposeful coordinated movement cannot be achieved due to the uncontrollable contractions of the muscles.

Ataxia—uncoordination and awkwardness in the movements required for balance, position in space, and posture.

Tremor—rhythmic, involuntary shakiness of extremities

Rigidity—diffuse, continuous muscle tension

Mixed—several types of motor disability together, usually spasticity and athetosis.

These two classification systems, when used in combination with a laterality dimension, provide an accurate description of a child's impairment (e.g., cerebral palsy, left spastic hemiplegia) and for this reason they are used to facilitate communication.

The educational implications for this group of children are directly related to a number of factors. Although some cerebral palsied children have normal or above-average intelligence, the majority are below average in IQ. Many are mentally retarded. Second, many cerebral palsied children will have other impairments, possibly affecting hearing, vision, perception, language, and behavior. Third, because cerebral palsy involves motor impairment, it may be necessary to utilize special equipment and facilities for these children, especially if an appropriate education in the least restrictive environment is to be provided. Fourth,

CP individuals will usually require the cooperative efforts of a multidisciplinary team (MDT) of professionals. Finally, the teacher plays a very important role as reflected in the following sentiments:

> Careful analysis of the whole child taking into account the complexity of his disability and capitalizing on his strong points is the most demanding but important task for the teacher. (Bleck, 1975, p. 68)

Epilepsy

A seizure disorder is the result of "an abnormal discharge of electrical energy in the brain" (Hallahan & Kauffman, 1986, p. 340). *Epilepsy* is a disorder that involves recurrent episodes of seizure activity. The prevalence of epilepsy can range from 0.15–1% of the population depending on the definitional perspective employed.

Epilepsy can be caused by any event that results in brain damage, such as brain lesions, anoxia, trauma, poisoning, or tumors. If etiology can be determined, the term *symptomatic epilepsy* is used; however, if causation cannot be determined, which is the majority of the time, the appropriate term used is *idiopathic epilepsy.* Even if the original cause of the problem can be determined, the reason for the abnormal discharge of electrical energy under certain conditions (i.e., what triggers a seizure) may remain unknown.

One system for classifying the various forms of epilepsy is based on the localization of the seizure activity in the brain and can be briefly described in the following way:

> Generalized seizures—discharge is bilateral and symmetrical or is nonlocalized
>
> Partial seizures—localized discharge
>
> Miscellaneous—related to high fever (febrile seizure) or other cause

Included in the generalized seizure category are "grand mal," "petit mal," "myoclonic," and "akinetic seizures." The generalized seizure is characterized by a spontaneous loss of consciousness of varying length and expression.

The grand mal seizure (generalized tonic-clonic) is the type most people think of when they think of epilepsy. The person having a grand mal attack which is convulsive in nature usually lets out a cry, loses consciousness, falls, and goes through a short period of muscle contractions of the extremities, trunk, and head. This type of seizure may be preceded by an aura (an unusual sensory perception) which the individual can use as a warning for the onset of a seizure. The grand mal seizure also may include facial contortions, heavy breathing, perspiration, foaming at the mouth, loss of bladder and bowel control, and physical injury if the person strikes against objects while falling or convulsing. This behavior may last up to 5 minutes, after which the individual falls into a deep sleep, subsequently followed by natural sleep. Upon regaining consciousness, the individual may display the following characteristics: disorientation, depression, amnesia of the seizure, nausea, soreness, and exhaustion.

The petit mal (absence) seizure is less dramatic but can have a devastating effect on a student's educational progress. Berg (1982) describes the typical petit mal seizure as "the momentary suspension of all activity, a staring spell, or as some have called them, lapses or absence attacks" (p. 104). Often, this form of epilepsy is misperceived in a classroom setting as daydreaming, inattention, or misbehavior. The lapse of consciousness may last only a few seconds or may continue up to 30 seconds. Unlike the grand mal seizure, the onset of a petit mal seizure will not be accompanied by the aura phenomenon. Frequently, children will grow out of this type of seizure.

Partial (focal) seizures involve a focal discharge in a localized part of the brain, and as a result produce a specific motor or sensory effect. *Jacksonian seizure* is an example of a partial seizure and involves a pattern of rhythmic movements that start in one part of the body and progressively spread to other parts. Although not fully understood, *psychomotor seizure* (complex partial) is considered to be a type of focal seizure and is characterized by inappropriate behaviors such as being verbally incoherent, verbally abusive, or violent. Even though this type of seizure is brief, the behaviors nevertheless are socially unacceptable; and there is a good chance that they will be misinterpreted.

There have been many misconceptions about epilepsy throughout history. Unfortunately some of these misconceptions still exist. People with epilepsy have been stigmatized by the ideas that they are mentally ill and that seizures are somehow contagious. Seeing someone have a convulsion is upsetting and frightening to many people, especially to those uninformed or misinformed about the nature of seizures. Because people with epilepsy are no more disposed to mental illness than other individuals, they function quite normally between seizures. Mental retardation occurs in only 10% of this population; most people with epilepsy (approximately 70%) have average or above average intelligence. Most seizures (80%) can be totally or partially controlled with proper medication. Teachers can assist children who have seizures by ensuring their safety during seizures, by attempting to correct the misperceptions of others, and by being prepared to deal with learning problems that may arise.

BEHAVIORAL CHARACTERISTICS

The effect that physical impairments or health problems have on children and their families differs. As a result, it is often difficult to make generalizations about this group without acknowledging specific factors. The current age of the child, the age when the condition was acquired, the type and severity of the problem, how the problem was acquired, the visibility of the condition, and whether the impairment is progressive or nonprogressive must be taken into account (Hallahan & Kauffman, 1986; Heward & Orlansky, 1984). We will now examine two areas that relate to the behavior of physically or health impaired children.

Academic concerns

Having a physical or health impairment does not necessarily imply intellectual deficiency. While it is true that some PHI children are also mentally retarded or sensorily impaired, many are not. The learning capacity of most PHI is no different from their normal peers. These types of children have been excluded from school in the past because their needs could not be met; today they are guaranteed an appropriate education by law. However, some of these children are frequently absent from school due to medical factors. If this is the case, their achievement may suffer and remedial efforts may be indicated.

Psychological concerns

The successful adjustment of a physically impaired child depends greatly on the actions and attitudes of significant people such as parents, siblings, teachers, and peers in the child's immediate environment and of the public in the child's daily encounters.

The physically impaired child may experience feelings of insecurity, hopelessness, embarrassment, rejection, guilt, low self-esteem, and fear, which are contingent upon others' reaction to his or her impairment. These feelings may be manifested by withdrawing from interaction (avoidance), by attempting to hide the stigmatizing impairment, or by becoming overdependent. Such reactions can be avoided by sincere and thoughtful intervention whereby the child is accepted, integrated and included in the mainstream of life. In addition, it is also essential that realistic goals be set for the child. Inevitably, the physically impaired child will fantasize about being normal and participating in activities in which normal children usually engage.

We are often guilty of reacting to physically or health impaired individuals with fear, rejection, pity, discrimination, or low expectations, but most noticeably, awkwardness. We are probably just uncomfortable! We need to realize that these individuals, while limited in some way, can nonetheless be valuable contributors to society. When this understanding occurs, not only will the physically impaired have a better chance to minimize the handicapping nature of their problems, but we will have grown as well.

ADMINISTRATIVE AND EDUCATIONAL CONCERNS

In order to provide appropriate services to physically and health impaired children, alterations may need to be made in the usual educational system. The reorganization of schools and redesign of school buildings may be required; that is, they must be barrier-free. The successful coordination of many different ancillary services, necessitated by the nature of the impairment, must be addressed. Depending on the severity of the impairment, the delivery of educational services may include a hospital program, home-bound education, a special school setting, or a regular school setting. In addition, problems with mobility also become important considerations of special education administrators.

Integrating the physically impaired child into the regular schools requires more than making the building accessible. Mainstreaming physically impaired children involves preparing the school as a whole for this integration. As Bookbinder (1977) points out:

> Mainstreaming disabled children into the public school
> system will be successful only if all school personnel are

fully committed to trying to meet the special needs of these special children . . . We often overlook that understanding and commitment are required from the other children as well as from teachers and staff. (p. 31)

The ultimate importance of this endeavor for the adjustment of the special child has already been emphasized.

The educational goals and curricula for physically and health impaired students are usually similar to that of nondisabled peers. Reading, language arts, arithmetic, science, social studies, art, and music are certainly to be included in their education. However, when the impairments are severe, these children may be deprived of many educationally important experiences or may be unable to utilize the common materials found in the school settings. If this is the case, special education may be warranted to assure the acquisition of essential self-help, mobility, communication, vocational, and life-experience skills.

To maximize learning, an alternative teaching methodology might be needed. Task analysis and behavior modification techniques have proven to be quite successful in expediting the acquisition of basic skills in all children, including those with physical disabilities. *Individualization of instruction,* an often used term in education today, has precise meaning when applied to physically or health impaired learners. Adaptive measures that facilitate communication (e.g., use of computers and modified typewriters) and movement (e.g., use of myoelectric arms and wheelchairs controlled by sipping and puffing techniques) are available and have provided the physically impaired child with advantages that did not exist in the past.

Educational programming for the physically impaired can be conceptualized in the following hierarchical design:

Advanced educational, life, and occupational skills

↑

Basic academic skills

↑

Self-help/daily living/mobility/communication skills

All our efforts should be guided by the goal of independent functioning for this population. This goal usually implies the need for the higher level skills presented in this hierarchy; however, not every physically impaired child will be able to function independently in everyday life. As a result, a *modus operandi* that stresses sequential programming of skills from the most basic to the more advanced is essential.

PREVALENCE

It is very difficult to come up with a precise and valid figure for the number of people with physical or health impairments. Many individuals who may have this type of disability are classified as something else, occurring in combination with other conditions (Bigge & Sirvis, 1986).

Recent data collected by the federal government on the number of students (ages 3–21) who are identified as "orthopedically impaired" and "other health impaired" indicate that 110,019 students are being served (U.S. Department of Education, 1985). Caution must also be exercised in interpreting these figures.

Although an increase in physical impairments has been noticed in the past few years, this may be due to technological and medical advances that save the lives of many individuals who previously might not have survived. However, technology assumes a paradoxical role, because while advances that maintain lives and repair bodies are being made, other advances can increase problems (e.g., toxic waste, drug ingestion, faster automobiles).

TRENDS AND ISSUES

Technological advances

Monumental advances have been made in recent years in the areas of medicine, prosthetics/orthotics, adaptive technology, and cosmetology, all having had distinct positive effects for those with physical impairments. The medical field actually has had the most demonstrable impact on preventing and treating physical impairments (e.g., surgery, drug therapy) and health problems (e.g., fetal monitoring, immunization). In the area of prosthetics, the artificial replacement of missing body parts has enabled many individuals to regain some previously lacking functions. The use of prosthetic limbs and other adaptive technological advances, which include devices that allow the physically impaired to perform many everyday self-help tasks, are constantly being developed. Other examples of these engineering wonders are wheelchairs that are operated by miniature computers that can be told what to do; mouth-operated electronic devices that allow quadriplegic persons to perform certain actions from bed by varying their breathing patterns; puffing and sipping devices that can operate a telephone, radio, TV, lamp, typewriter, or door (Cohen, 1977). Cosmetological intervention is also helping some physically impaired individuals through plastic and reconstructive surgical procedures and through techniques that attempt to minimize the visibility of an impairment.

Costs

Costs for supporting research and providing services for this population are significant. However, these economic matters need to be considered from a long-term perspective. For instance, a computerized wheelchair, although expensive, may enable a person to work and function in society. In the long run, this fact becomes cost effective. More importantly is the benefit gained by the exceptional individual. What price can be put on that?

Accessibility

Historically, the concept of accessibility has been almost totally ignored until 1968 when the Architectural Barriers Act was passed. This legislation addressed the issue of federal funding in relation to the construction of public buildings. In 1973 the creation of the Architectural and Transportation Barriers and Compliance Board focused on the elimination of barriers. The problems associated with accessibility include obvious barriers such as steps, curbs, restrooms, doors, parking, and not so apparent barriers such as public telephones, thick carpeting, water fountains, and the use of elevators. The extent of this problem is clearly reflected in that:

> Every day, architectural barriers keep as many as 1 in
> 10 Americans from functioning as useful and con-

tributing citizens . . . approximately 52% of disabled persons are living below the poverty level . . . For them, the architectural barriers that daily keep them from obtaining a good education, from working, from realizing their potential, *must* come down. (DHEW, 1976, pp. 114–115)

CONCLUSIONS

The myriad problems that persons with physical or health impairments face are startling. These individuals can maximize their development and become contributing members of society if they are given the opportunities to do so. For this reason, it becomes imperative that we foster a society receptive to the needs of this special group. We must find ways for the more physically impaired to become more visible in our daily associations.

In introducing the reader to physical and health impairments, we are unable to provide you with a *real* understanding of what it is like to be physically or health impaired. So,we would like to conclude with this thought:

> Physical disability is a minority problem among the young and middle-aged, but among those who reach the life expectancy age of 70 it is a problem of the majority. A very small percentage of us will experience loss of mobility because of diseases like multiple sclerosis or muscular dystrophy; a somewhat larger, but still small percentage, will experience this loss because of accidents; most of us, however, will become old. (Cohen, 1977, p. 136)

SUGGESTIONS FOR WORKING WITH PERSONS WHO HAVE PHYSICAL AND/OR HEALTH IMPAIRMENTS

This section has been divided into four categories based on the specific suggestions relevant to each area.

General suggestions

1. Treat PHI persons in ways that are as normal as possible.
2. Do not underestimate their abilities because of their physical or health limitations.

3. Be aware of the individual's specific situation and the special needs and precautions that are warranted.

4. Be concerned about the psychosocial ramifications associated with the acquisition of a PHI.

For wheelchair-bound persons

1. Ask wheelchair users if they would like assistance before you help.

2. If conversation lasts more than a few minutes, consider sitting down or kneeling to get yourself on the same level as the wheelchair user.

3. Do not demean or patronize the wheelchair users by patting them on the head.

4. Give clear directions, including distance, weather conditions, and physical obstacles that may hinder travel.

5. When wheelchair users "transfer" out of the wheelchair to a chair, toilet, car, or bed, do not move the wheelchair out of reaching distance.

6. Do not assume that using a wheelchair is in itself a tragedy. It is a means of freedom that allows the user to move about independently.[5]

For individuals with severe forms of cerebral palsy

1. If the person has difficulties communicating clearly, do not be afraid to ask the person to repeat what was said.

2. Do ask persons with CP if they need assistance if they are experiencing difficulty in performing certain activities.

3. Be aware of the person's special needs (e.g., special chair for sitting).

4. Allow for additional time that will probably be needed for accomplishing various tasks (e.g., walking, writing).

For individuals who have convulsive types of seizures

1. Remain calm if a person has a seizure.

2. Try to prevent the person from injury by safeguarding the immediate environment.

---

[5]Adapted from Schoitz Medical Center. (n.d.). *What do I do when I meet a person in a wheelchair?* Waterloo, IA: Author.

3. Do not interfere with the person's seizure-related behaviors.

4. Do not force anything into the person's mouth (i.e., between the teeth).

5. If possible, place something soft beneath the person's head.

6. If possible, turn the person's face to one side to drain saliva.

7. Let the person rest upon regaining consciousness.

8. Seek medical assistance if the person seems to pass from one seizure to another without regaining consciousness.

9. Deal appropriately with the other people in the immediate environment.

PONDER THESE

Imagine that you are confined to a wheelchair for one day; then list all the "barriers" or "obstacles" that you would encounter in the course of your typical daily schedule.

If you catastrophically lost the use of your arms and legs, what functions would you first want to be able to reacquire or relearn?

Suppose you invited a wheelchair-bound friend over to your home for dinner. What adaptations would you have to make to accommodate your guest?

Consider how physically disabled individuals have been portrayed in various forms of the media (films, TV, cartoons, comics, advertisements, etc.). In general have these portrayals been positive or negative?

REFERENCES

Berg, B. O. (1982). Convulsive disorders. In E. E. Bleck & D. A. Nagel (Eds.), *Physically handicapped children: A medical atlas for teachers* (2nd ed., pp. 101–108). New York: Grune & Stratton.

Bigge, J. L. (1982). *Teaching individuals with physical and multiple disabilities* (2nd ed.). Columbus, OH: Merrill.

Bigge, J. L., & Sirvis, B. (1986). Physical and health impairments. In N. G. Haring & L. P. McCormick (Eds.), *Exceptional children and youth* (4th ed., pp. 313–354). Columbus, OH: Merrill.

Bleck, E. E. (1975). Cerebral palsy. In E. E. Bleck & D. A. Nagel (Eds.), *Physically handicapped children: A medical atlas for teachers* (pp. 37–89). New York: Grune & Stratton.

Bookbinder, S. (1977). What every child needs to know. *The Exceptional Parent, 7,* 31–34.

Cohen, S. (1977). *Special people.* Englewood Cliffs, NJ: Prentice-Hall.

Cruickshank, W. M. (Ed.). (1976). *Cerebral palsy: A developmental disability* (3rd rev. ed.). Syracuse, NY: Syracuse University Press.

Denhoff, E. (1976). Medical aspects. In W. M. Cruickshank (Ed.), *Cerebral palsy: A developmental disability* (3rd rev. ed.). Syracuse, NY: Syracuse University Press.

Department of Health, Education, & Welfare. (1976). Breaking down architectural barriers. *American Education, 17,* 114–115.

Haffner, T. (1976). The cap and gown feeling. *The Exceptional Parent, 6*(1), 13–17.

Hallahan, D. P., & Kauffman, J. M. (1986). *Exceptional children: Introduction to special education* (3rd ed.). Englewood Cliffs, NJ: Prentice-Hall.

Heward, W. L., & Orlansky, M. D. (1984). *Exceptional children: An introductory survey of special education* (2nd ed.). Columbus, OH: Merrill.

Sirvis, B. (1982). The physically disabled. In E. L. Meyen (Ed.), *Exceptional children and youth: An introduction* (pp. 382–405). Denver: Love Publishing.

Smith, R. M., & Neisworth, J. T. (1975). *The exceptional child: A functional approach.* New York: McGraw-Hill.

U.S. Department of Education. (1985). Unpublished document. Washington, DC: Author.

7

Visual Impairments

Blindness. What sort of image does this word evoke—dark glasses, a guide dog, a tin cup, the groping tap of a red-tipped white cane? The word *blindness* is commonly associated with thoughts of helplessness, pity, and a life of eternal blackness. But is this really blindness? What does blindness mean? To us it means, in part, working with people who are blind and forgetting that they can't see.

A young blind couple, with whom my wife and I were friends and professional associates, invited us to their home for an evening near the Christmas holidays. After a time of visiting, we went to the dining area where we enjoyed some refreshments. The colored holiday lights in the windows created a perfect effect for the late evening treats. The next morning, my wife received a very apologetic phone call from an embarrassed hostess. It was not until our host and hostess were retiring for the night that they discovered their light switch was in the off position. It was then that they realized they had fed us in a very dark room.

What I remember most from my philosophy class in my junior year of college is Joe, a blind student who sat behind me. He was a likable guy—good sense of humor and very bright. I think he was unable to see at all. He walked with cane and took all his class notes in Braille—I can still hear the peck, peck, peck of his stylus. One class session about midway through the semester, the professor was flamboyantly explaining a complex theory. He scribbled on the chalkboard to assist him in his instruction. As the professor paused for a moment, Joe raised his hand.

"Yes, Joe."

"I don't quite understand."

"What don't you understand, Joe?"

"The whole thing. It doesn't make any sense."

At this, the professor spun on his heel and frantically drew diagram after diagram, at the same time eloquently explaining the theory. After about 15 minutes, the professor turned around and gasped, "Now do you see?"

Joe stopped pecking with his stylus and calmly replied, "No, I still can't see, but I understand."

The professor cried, "Good!" wheeled around and started drawing again.

Sue, a young college student, desired a means of independent travel that would permit her greater range than by foot. Being legally blind, she obviously could not obtain a driver's license. However, she did have enough remaining vision to ride a bicycle. She purchased a bike and began making frequent trips about the college town and into the surrounding country, often riding several miles. On one occasion she made a visit to our home and decided to return to her dormitory by a new route that took her through the downtown area. As she rode the streets through the main business district, she began noticing numerous friendly people waving and smiling from the sidewalks. They seemed to be waving at her. As she continued, the number of people increased. Then there were crowds, looking, waving, and clapping—for her? Finally, she realized the reason for all the attention. She was riding in the middle of a major holiday parade!

Two adolescent friends attending a school for the blind went for a brief walk on the familiar sidewalks of the immediate neighborhood and left their travel canes behind. During their walk they encountered an unfamiliar patch of what felt to them like mud. They giggled and walked through it to "dry ground." Imagine the frustration on the face of the homeowner as he looked up from his troweling in time to see two young girls slogging through his freshly poured concrete driveway!

Little Teressa, a first-grader, was examining the various objects in a touch-and-tell box. She extracted a number of shapes from the box and described or named them: "square," "triangle," "circle." Finally she came to a cube that was different in shape and texture from those objects she had already handled. She paused, felt it intensely on all sides, and said, "A block—What's this? An H and R Block?"

As a graduate student in special education, I had never met Debbie in person. Debbie was a blind student in our department and was preparing to become a teacher of the visually impaired. Although I did not know Debbie personally, I had heard about her—about how independent she was and wanted to be. At this point in time, I still had much to learn about handicapped people in general and visually impaired people in particular.

It was an early winter morning and a fresh covering of snow blanketed the ground. I happened to be on my way to the campus center when I came upon Debbie. Debbie was on her way to breakfast; however, she seemed to be very disoriented and confused. Knowing that Debbie was a very independent person and fearing her wrath, I approached her somewhat timidly, not really sure whether I should ask her if she needed some assistance. Nevertheless, I introduced myself, highlighting our common bond or burden of being fellow graduate students. I then proceded to ask her if she needed any help.

Debbie told me that she certainly could use some help as the snow had covered the walkway that she normally used to go to the campus center where breakfast was served, thus negating the usefulness of her cane. I was delighted that she had allowed me to provide some assistance. Having had no prior experience as a sighted guide, I was anxious to learn the proper techniques. Debbie told me how to act and so off we went.

Everything went smoothly at first and I was so proud of how well I was doing. Then we came to a set of steps that descended to a lower level. Here I was trying to be so careful when I lost my footing on the icy steps and literally dropped out of the picture. I picked myself up off the ground, climbed back up the steps I had just rocketed over, and regained my position next to Debbie. I was worried that she would simply tell me not to get within 10 feet of her as I was a menace to her safety. However, Debbie was most understanding and after she realized the reason for my abrupt departure she got a good laugh out of it.

After I finally escorted her to her destination without any further mishaps, I realized that I might have needed Debbie's assistance in dealing with the hazards of mobility in the snow as much as she needed mine.

DEFINITION

Visual impairment is a malfunction of the eye or optic nerve that prevents a person from seeing normally. An individual has a visual impairment whenever anomalous development, disease, or injury reduce the ability of the eyes to function. When an individual cannot see normally in at least one eye, the person is considered visually impaired. People who are visually impaired may find that things look dim, blurred, or out of focus. They may have the sensation of seeing only a part of an object or seeing everything masked in a cloud. They may see occasional dark blotches that float or appear to remain in front of the object they are viewing. It may be that they can see things clearly but only straight ahead, as if looking through a drinking straw. Just as there are varying degrees of vision, the ability to use what vision there is also varies among people.

The terms *blindness, visual impairment, low vision,* or *visual handicap,* indicate significant visual problems; yet every definition includes varying degrees of vision. In fact, there are more children classified as blind who can see at least a little than there are those who cannot see at all (Jones, 1961).

Today regulations from PL 94–142 have produced the need for two definitions of visual impairment. One definition, the older legal definition, is based on visual acuity and field of vision while the second, more recent definition, is based on functional vision for educational purposes.

The first definition was needed to identify those persons who were eligible for benefits through federal programs, such as additional tax exemption, free mailing privileges, special materials from the Library of Congress, the privilege of operating vending stands in federal buildings, the opportunity of receiving special educational materials, and benefits from rehabilitation programs. This definition is still considered the legal definition for receiving benefits: "The legally blind are defined as those with a central visual acuity for distance of 20/200 or less in the better eye with correction or, if greater than 20/200, a field of vision no greater than 20 degrees in the widest diameter" (Hatfield, 1975, p. 4).

Barraga (1976) brought the second functional type of definition to the field by clearly describing the various terms used by professionals (i.e., blind, low vision, visually limited, and so on). This approach to defining visual handicaps has been most useful for educational placement and programming. Taylor (1973) divided severely visually impaired individuals into two categories, the blind and the partially seeing. Thus, blind individuals whose vision does not permit the use of print for reading can be educated by the use of Braille, tactile, and auditory devices. Partially seeing individuals are educated by the use of materials that complement their residual vision, such as large-print books or special illumination.

Although there may need to be a definition that is associated with the provision of services, it may be advantageous to describe the condition simply as severe visual impairment and devote more effort to describing the educational procedures and materials required to meet the needs of the visually impaired child.

PREVALENCE

The accuracy of estimates of prevalence in specific impairments is always subject to disagreement due to the ambiguity inherent in existing definitions and identification procedures. Visual impairment is a disability that affects only a small number of the school-aged population. Statistics indicate that only about 0.1% of the children are identified as having little or no vision. For the year 1983, the American Printing House for the Blind (1984) registered a total of 41,145 legally blind children between the ages of 3 and 21. Nearly 80% of this student population could use printed materials for educational purposes.

Visual impairment becomes a much more prevalent condition when we look at the elderly population. As a result, age becomes a significant factor that must be acknowledged when we speak of the prevalence of visual impairment.

ETIOLOGY

As reported by Livingston (1986), most visual problems can be attributed to malformations and malfunctions of the eye. Most visual impairments observed in school-age children are a result of events occurring prior to, during, or shortly after birth (Hatfield, 1963). The following categorizes selected types of visual impairments and provides brief explanations of each.

Refractive problems

Myopia—nearsightedness (eyeball too long)

Hyperopia—farsightedness

Astigmatism—uneveness in surface of cornea or lens

Lens abnormalities

Dislocation

Cataracts—clouding of the lens

Retinopathy of prematurity (retrolental fibroplasia)—scar tissue behind the lens (overconcentration of oxygen)

Retinal defects

Retinitis pigmentosa—progressive degeneration of retina

Diabetic retinopathy—interference of blood supply to retina

Macular degeneration—blood vessels of macula (part of retina) are damaged (loss of central vision)

Muscle control problems

Strabismus—cross-eyed

Nystagmus—involuntary, rapid, rhythmic, side-to-side eye movements

Amblyopia—"lazy eye"

Miscellaneous

    Glaucoma—pressure build-up of eye fluid

    Trauma—damage due to accidents, and so on

    Color vision—inability to detect certain colors

VISUAL IMPAIRMENT IN PERSPECTIVE

The anecdotes at the beginning of this chapter illustrate several points about visual impairment; these and other points will be further developed in this section.

    Most visually impaired (most blind) individuals can see. Only a small portion of those who are legally or educationally blind are totally blind or without vision.

    Most visually impaired individuals have all their other senses; that is, they are normal. Being visually impaired, even totally blind, does not impair or improve one's sense of hearing, smell, taste, or touch. A severely visually impaired individual is not endowed with a "sixth" sense as some believe. If such a person does do some things in different ways from most, it may be a very natural way of using the other senses in place of lost vision.

    Most totally blind persons, by making use of hearing, touch, smell, and kinesthetic perception can learn much about their environments. With good orientation and mobility skills and experience, those with little or no vision can use a cane as an aid for crossing intersections, taking walks, making shopping trips, and getting to just about any place within walking distance. Their hands help them to learn about a lot of things if they are just permitted to touch, handle, and move objects that are about them.

    Often, the biggest block to the blind person's living and learning naturally is other people who have normal vision. Family and friends, in their attempts to be helpful, too often forget the needs of a blind person: rather than permit a blind man to take an elbow, they may push him across the intersection; they may take the blind woman's order from her sighted friend across the table; or they may insist upon "look, but don't touch."

    As a group, people who are visually impaired comprise a normal range of personalities, interests, and abilities. Some visually impaired people are gifted, some are retarded, and most are intellectually normal. There are those who are emotionally disturbed and others with learning disabilities. We have visually impaired athletes as well as scholars. There are those who are socially adept, delinquent, prolific, dull, fascinating, obnoxious, or any other combination.

Severely visually impaired people have been successful in nearly every activity and vocation. However, society still judges these people not so much by their abilities as by their perceived differences. Because they are judged incapable *before* the fact, severely visually impaired adults often find locating jobs difficult and obtaining desirable employment nearly impossible.

Severe visual impairment can handicap people in their early experiences and in their ability to get from place to place. Important early experiences can be denied to visually impaired children if they are not permitted to be active and to use all of their senses to the maximum, thus often affecting concept and language development. Active early childhood and preschool experiences are important factors in assuring normal development for visually impaired children.

The difficulty in establishing one's position in the environment (orientation) and in moving from place to place (mobility) are two of the most direct handicaps caused by visual impairment. Some visually impaired individuals are only limited in their ability to operate a motor vehicle, while for others, visual impairment may cause a major mobility impediment.

Visual impairment can occur as one of the impairments in a multiply handicapped person. In about half the cases, severe visual impairment occurs as one of several difficulties in multiply handicapped persons.

The child with multiple impairments (e.g., deaf-blind) presents a unique educational problem. In many cases, particularly if the impairments are severe or profound, instruction must be highly individualized. Impairments come in all degrees of severity and in nearly every possible combination. Each additional impairment presents its own unique hurdle to normal growth and development, in addition to the problems that result from the particular combination of impairments.

To date, too little is still understood about multiply handicapped children. This misunderstanding has led in some cases to the misplacement and inappropriate treatment of these individuals. There are cases of deaf-blind persons with normal cognitive abilities being placed in special units of residential institutions designed for mentally retarded individuals. It is probably safe to say that, for some multiply handicapped people, too little has been done to assure their maximum potential for development.

EDUCATIONAL AND PRACTICAL CONCERNS

Education

The curriculum for students with visual impairment should be consistent with the regular education curriculum; however, additional instruction in certain areas of specific need may also be necessary. Mobility training is included to teach visually impaired individuals the most efficient means of interacting with their environment (Lowenfeld, 1971; Lyndon & McGraw, 1973). Depending on the extent of impairment, the curriculum may also include the use of Braille (the system of raised dots representing letters and symbols) for reading and writing, as well as the utilization of talking books, compressed speech, magnified print, embossed materials, and other technological advances. Most teaching methods found effective with normal seeing students are effective with visually impaired students. The obvious difference occurs with visual presentation that must be adapted or modified to utilize auditory or tactual sensory channels (Napier, 1973).

The issue of best placement of visually impaired students has provoked much debate over the years. With the implementation of PL 94–142, more students with milder problems have been provided services in the regular school settings, often in regular education classrooms. However, this has not always been the case. Furthermore, the question of best placement is more complicated for those students with more severe forms of impairment.

The question of residential versus day school for the visually impaired has engendered a quiet debate. Until the midpoint of this century, the majority of severely visually impaired children who received a quality education were educated at residential schools for the blind. Since that time, increased numbers of severely visually impaired children are being educated in local day school programs (Jones & Collins, 1966) or in regular public school settings (Heward & Orlansky, 1984), resulting in fewer numbers of students attending residential schools.

The major considerations of the debate are analyzed as follows:

Favoring day schools

1. It is important that children live at home with their families.
2. Dormitory living is detrimental to healthy development.
3. Segregation from normally seeing peers deprives visually impaired children of important experiences needed for normal development.
4. Larger local high schools can provide a wider range of curricular offerings than most small residential schools.

Favoring residential schools

1. Only the residential school is in a direct position to influence what learning takes place between the end of one school day and the beginning of the next.
2. The child can receive more individualized instruction than in the day schools where classes are often much larger.
3. Education will be better when the teachers can devote their entire interest and training to working with the visually impaired.
4. If the number of children or the number of handicapping conditions increases, the visually impaired will become a neglected minority, eventually losing out on educational services and materials as money is spent elsewhere.

To summarize, in order to ensure a nonrestrictive environment for visually impaired persons, it is necessary to *(a)* provide placement alternatives that are flexible and varied, and *(b)* consider the skill level of the person when selecting the most appropriate setting. The needs of visually impaired children must not be overlooked in the selection of educational placement.

Facets of everyday living

In addition to the educational needs of visually impaired people, other practical considerations must be addressed. Many everyday activities sighted persons routinely perform may have to be done in different ways by those with limited or no vision. For example, the selection and matching up of clothes will have to be determined in alternative ways. Some individuals use Braille tags; others simply buy clothes of certain colors that go together, then separate their closets accordingly. The acts of eating and drinking will be executed in modified ways. Telling time is accomplished by using specially designed watches with hands and raised dots (not Braille configurations) that can be touched.

Many typical household appliances will also need to be modified. The American Foundation for the Blind publishes a catalog entitled *Aids and Appliances for the Blind and Visually Impaired* that lists many such everyday items.

SUGGESTIONS FOR WORKING WITH PERSONS WHO HAVE VISUAL IMPAIRMENTS

The following suggestions have been divided into sections based on the nature of recommendation.

General suggestions

1. If a visually impaired person seems to be having problems (e.g., disoriented), ask whether you can be of any assistance. The worst that can happen is that she will say "No."

2. When acting as a sighted guide *(a)* let the visually impaired person take your arm rather than grabbing their arm and pushing; and *(b)* approach steps and other similar environmental realities at right angles.

3. Assist persons in getting a chair or into a car by placing their hand in the appropriate location (e.g., on the back of the chair or on the roof of the car).

4. Be sure to talk directly to the person and not to other companions. This is especially important for those working in restaurants who sometimes avoid talking to visually impaired persons.

5. When you enter or leave a room in which the only other person present is visually impaired/blind, let the person know you have come in or are leaving.

Educational suggestions

1. Seat visually impaired students in settings that maximize any residual vision and that avoid glare from the sun or lighting.

2. Try to minimize the reliance on visual materials when lecturing and, if they are needed, explain them fully.

3. Be careful not to talk at too quick a pace for students who use a slate and stylus for taking notes in Braille.

4. Avoid using materials that have low contrast features (such as purple ditto sheets) or glossy surfaces.

5. It may be necessary to allow some visually impaired students to take more breaks than usual. Their eyes may fatigue at quicker rates than other students'.

6. For visually impaired learners who can use printed materials, use large print materials and broad-tipped markers that contrast with the color of your materials.

7. Encourage students to tape record your presentations and to use readers if available.

8. Utilize the services of Recordings for the Blind as this organization has put much printed material on tape.

PONDER THESE

If a child with no travel vision entered your class, what specific things would you have to teach her in order for her to adapt successfully to the classroom? How might you and the children in your class have to change your habits or behaviors to facilitate the child's adaptation?

Imagine that you are a self-sufficient blind adult. How would you feel about receiving a special tax exemption simply because you are categorized as "legally blind?" Would you work for legislation providing special exemptions for persons categorized as handicapped (e.g., deaf) in other ways?

If you suddenly lost your vision, what special problems would you encounter in performing such everyday activities as eating, dressing and grooming, toileting, communicating, and getting around? What would you do for recreation?

Highlight the advantages and disadvantages of the following mobility techniques used by blind and visually limited people: sighted guide, guide dog, cane.

Find out how a congenitally blind person dreams.

REFERENCES

American Printing House for the Blind. (1984). *Annual report*. Louisville, KY: Author.

Barraga, N. C. (1976). *Visual handicaps and learning: A developmental approach*. Belmont, CA: Wadsworth.

Hatfield, E. M. (1963). Causes of blindness in school children. *The Sight-Saving Review, 33*, 218–33.

Hatfield, E. M. (1975). Why are they blind? *Sight-Saving Review, 45*, 3–22.

Heward, W. L., & Orlansky, M. D. (1984). *Exceptional children: An introductory survey of special education* (2nd ed.). Columbus, OH: Merrill

Jones, J. W. (1961). *Blind children, degree of vision, mode of reading*. Washington, DC: U. S. Government Printing Office.

Jones, J. W. & Collins, A. P. (1966). *Educational programs for visually handicapped children*. Washington, DC: U. S. Government Printing Office.

Livingston, R. (1986). Visual impairments. In N. G. Haring & L. P. McCormick (Eds.), *Exceptional children and youth* (4th ed., pp. 397–429). Columbus, OH: Merrill.

Lowenfeld, B. (1971). *Our blind children, growing and learning with them* (3rd ed.). Springfield, IL: Charles C Thomas.

Lyndon, W. T., & McGraw, M. L. (1973). *Concept development for visually handicapped children*. New York: American Foundation for the Blind.

Napier, G. D. (1973). Special subject adjustment and skills. In B. Lowenfeld (Ed.), *The visually handicapped child in school* (pp. 221–277). New York: John Day.

Taylor, J. L. (1973). Educational programs. In B. Lowenfeld (Ed.), *The visually handicapped child in school* (pp. 155–184). New York: John Day.

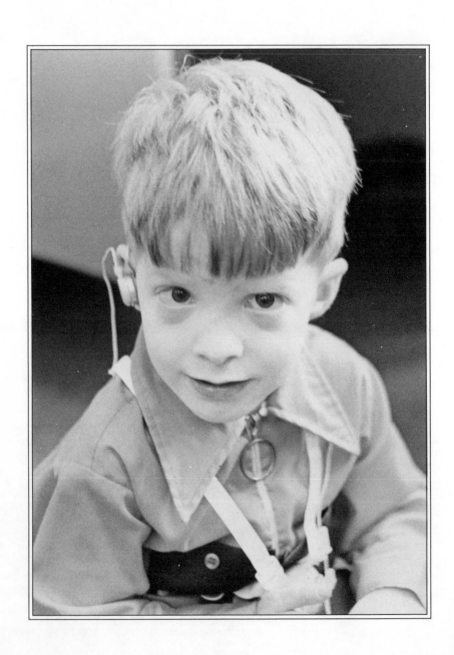

8

Hearing Impairment

At the age of 3, David began undergoing speech therapy. Each week his mother took him to the session, sat through as an observer, and then took him home. At the first visit, the therapist, who was aware of the fact that David had a little experience in speechreading, chose to test the skills by initiating a simple command, "Close door." David watched the therapist's face intently but made no move to carry out the command. The command was repeated and, again, no response. This continued for a while until it became obvious that both the therapist and David were confused. Not daring to initiate other commands or try other words under the circumstances, the therapist suggested to the mother that perhaps David was disturbed by the new situation. Calmly looking into the therapist's eyes, the mother patiently suggested, "Try 'shut door.'"

We were being trained to be teachers of the deaf. We had completed our course work and were preparing to do student teaching at a residential school. We had been trained strictly in teaching speech and speechreading (lip reading) without the use of signs or gestures. However, students and staff at the school made considerable use of manual signs and finger spell-

ing, none of which we understood. A few of us were given assignments at the secondary level which was particularly difficult since the use of signs at that level was considerable.

We were all having difficulty mastering sign language in addition to our student-teaching assignments. To improve our ability we practiced these skills by reading the Ann Landers column to our fellow student teachers in the evening. It was a laborious task and each day's column seemed to take forever.

During our learning period, one of my fellow student teachers returned to our dormitory at the end of an exhaustive day. She was embarrassed, concerned, and wondering aloud, "What do they think of me?" Only after considerable coaxing did the story come out. Her responsibility was to teach arithmetic. Because of her difficulty with manual signs and the inability of many students to speechread, she had devised a plan to use the overhead projector in writing out each problem for the students. Things went well until she indicated the operation of addition by writing the plus sign (+). This was greeted by a room full of blank faces. Try as she might, she was unable to make the children understand that they were to add. Exasperated, she finally decided to resort to finger spelling the word "add." Suddenly the room was astir with children's snickering and laughing. What had she done? There in the middle of a lesson, standing before all those young attentive faces, she suddenly realized that she had just signed the letters "a-s-s"!

I had just completed a university program in teaching the deaf, and the summer was mine to relax and prepare specifically for my first teaching experience in the fall. I was well armed with techniques and materials and very anxious to apply them to my class of early elementary children.

The first day of school finally arrived. Was I prepared! The room was ready and I was at school well before the hour. My course work and student-teaching experiences had taught me well that deaf children at the age of those I was soon to teach have difficulty in reading and require much work if they are ever to be able to speak. I also knew that a part of teaching deaf children involves surrounding them with a world of language. I thought that while my children might be unable to hear me and produce only the most gross approximations to words in their speaking, I would greet each child at the door with a "good morning." As they entered the room, I positioned myself so that my face was clearly visible and I carefully spoke and formed the words "good morning." I anxiously watched each small face for any sign of recognition or attempt at response. Response I got. To each greeting there was a well-spoken "Good morning, Mr. _____." I had just introduced myself to my "deaf" class, only to discover that they were not deaf but were an excited, talking, hearing group of "hearing impaired" children.

A few years ago, I was hired to interpret for one of the only deaf priests in the United States. He was to come to a Catholic Church up in Mililani, Hawaii. Through a friend, I was able to meet with him earlier than scheduled so I could become familiar with him, his style of signing, and what his needs were going to be.

Being the friendly lady that I am, I began to share with him who I was, what I did, and so on. He did the same. We sat in the church lounge. He began to tell me about his busy schedule, when I told him I was still shy/embarrassed, about interpreting in front of large audiences. The sentence began, "I am shy/embarrassed. . . ." The sign for shy/embarrassed is the back of your hand brushing against your right cheek, starting from your chin and moving upward. You need only do this one time. Being as nervous as I was I did not start at the chin and move upward; rather I started at the temple of the face and stroked downward.

It was at this point that the priest's eyes got extremely large with shock, he looked confused, and then he laughed. Now I was shocked, confused and needed an explanation. He told me to repeat what I had just signed. I did. He asked me what I was trying to say. I spelled it out and it was at this point that he told me what I'd done. What I had signed was not only incorrect but especially inappropriate for a priest. I had signed not that I was shy/embarrassed, instead that I was a whore. Now I was really embarrassed![1]

I was most impressed with Phyllis's emotional maturity and language facility. Her speechreading was excellent and proved a boon to her close friends. She often related conversations that were taking place well out of earshot, across the dining room

---

[1]Our thanks to Karen Ruff for sharing this story with us.

or lounge. Besides working at her studies, Phyllis was enjoy-
ing an active social life. During the course of college she began
dating one special fellow. After a period of time during which
she had been seeing her friend quite regularly, she returned
one night a little discouraged. She and John had broken up.
As she explained, going places together was enjoyable, and they
liked each other's company, but always having to say "good
night" or exchange "sweet nothings" while sitting under a light
was just too much for John to handle.[2]

DEFINITION

Whenever children are prevented from hearing environmental
sounds because of malfunction of the ear or of the associated
nerves, they experience some form of hearing impairment. Hearing impairments can be temporary or permanent, mild or profound. In discussing the problem of defining and classifying hearing impairment, Myklebust (1964) proposed that four variables
be considered: *(a)* degree of impairment, *(b)* age at onset, *(c)* cause,
and *(d)* physical origin. The variables of degree of impairment
and age at onset have the most direct relevance for education.
Both are accounted for in the definition provided by Streng, Fitch,
Hedgecock, Phillips, and Carrell (1958).

> The child who is born with little or no hearing, or who
> has suffered the loss early in infancy before speech and
> language patterns are acquired is said to be deaf. One
> who is born with normal hearing and reaches the age
> where he can produce and comprehend speech but sub-
> sequently loses his hearing is described as deafened. The
> hard of hearing are those with reduced hearing acuity
> either since birth or acquired at any time during life. (p.
> 9)

More recent definitions continue to stress the development
of spoken language as it is related to hearing impairment.
Hearing impairment is a generic term indicating a hearing

---

[2]Special gratitude is extended to Lois Schoeny and Lynn Mann, experienced
teachers of hearing impaired children, who kindly provided some of the anecdotal material used in this chapter.

disability that may range in severity from mild to profound. It consists of two groups, the deaf and the hard of hearing:

A *deaf* person is one whose hearing disability precludes successful processing of linguistic information through audition, with or without a hearing aid.

A *hard-of-hearing* person is one who, generally with the use of a hearing aid, has residual hearing sufficient to enable successful processing of linguistic information through audition.

PREVALENCE

It is estimated that 5% of the school-aged population possess some degree of hearing impairment (Silverman & Lane, 1970). Of this 5%, approximately 1–1.5% are in need of special education services. Unfortunately only 0.18% of the school population was receiving services as reported by the Department of Education to Congress in the 1984 annual report. There are a great number of children who have hearing impairments that *need attention* but who do *not require special education placement* because their impairments are minor or correctable.

ETIOLOGY

In a study of school-aged, hearing impaired children enrolled in special education programs, more than half had impaired hearing at birth. The etiology was undetermined for approximately 38% (Myklebust, 1964). Reviews of the literature indicate 25–50% of all childhood deafness is due to heredity (Hoemann & Briga, 1981). This figure is explained to a certain degree by the high incidence of marriage among people who are hearing impaired.

Impairments of hearing in the outer or middle ear (conductive), even when that portion of the auditory system is totally nonfunctional, leave some potential for using residual hearing (Myklebust, 1964), whereas impaired hearing resulting from loss of inner-ear or nerve functions (sensorineural) can be a more serious, irreversible type of hearing loss.

Hearing impairments can result from a variety of causes. Excess ear wax and placement of small objects in the ear by children are frequent causes of conductive hearing impairments, as is otitis media, inflammation of the middle ear (Davis, 1970).

Pregnant women contracting rubella during the first trimester frequently give birth to children with sensorineural hearing loss (Northern and Downs, 1974). Some childhood diseases which involve viral infections of the upper respiratory tract can also cause hearing loss. Other causes include the use of certain antibiotics (McGee, 1968), excessive exposure to loud noises, viral infections of the pregnant mother prior to the child's birth, and Rh incompatibility (Davis, 1970).

ASSESSMENT

Although parents, teacher, and other key individuals in a child's life may suspect that a hearing problem may exist, it is usually an audiologist who conducts the more accurate and elaborate assessment procedures. As Hallahan and Kauffman (1986) have pointed out, there are three general types of hearing tests: pure-tone audiometry, speech audiometry, and specialized tests designed for use with very young children.

Pure-tone audiometry assesses an individual's hearing sensitivity (loudness) at various frequencies. Intensity of sound is measured in decibel (dB) units and frequency is measured in Hertz (Hz) units. The intensity of sounds that we come into contact with every day range from 0 dB (the zero hearing threshold) to well over 100 dB (very loud sounds like auto horns). The frequencies of most speech sounds which are important to humans fall between 125 to 8000 Hz. Pure-tone tests can be administered either by earphones (air conduction) or by placing a vibrating device on the person's forehead (bone conduction). By administering these two types of tests, an audiologist can determine if the hearing loss is conductive or sensorineural.

Speech audiometry is simply a test of whether a person can understand speech. At the heart of this procedure is an attempt to determine at which dB level the examinee is able to understand speech (known as the *speech reception threshold*).

Inherent in these assessment techniques is the examinee's ability to respond to the stimulus situation. For very young children this voluntary response may not be possible. Three techniques that have been developed for utilization with this age group include play audiometry, reflex audiometry, and evoked-response audiometry (Hallahan & Kauffman, 1986).

IMPRESSIONS

Many times people have certain incorrect impressions about hearing impaired children, such as *(a)* "deaf" children cannot hear, *(b)* children who cannot hear cannot talk, and *(c)* "deaf" children are retarded. These three notions have direct educational and social implications; therefore, they will receive focal attention in this chapter.

Deaf children cannot hear. Children classified as profoundly hearing impaired may still have some ability to hear. They may be able to hear loud noises such as automobile horns or slamming doors. The ability to hear even this much may provide vital information to alert or warn the child of danger. Of all hearing impaired children, relatively few can properly be labeled profoundly deaf. Many have enough usable hearing to develop language. The typical breakdown of degrees of hearing impairment is as follows:

Classification	Degree of dB Loss
Mild	26–54
Moderate	55–69
Severe	70–89
Profound	90+

There are two ways in which hearing impaired children can be helped with respect to the information they receive. First, they can be helped to understand and use what sounds they can hear. Then, of course, if the hearing impairment is such that the variety of sounds can be increased through amplification, they can be given access to more information through use of the hearing aid. However, it is worth noting that hearing aids amplify all sounds in the environment. As a result, while these devices provide a useful function to many hearing impaired people, they have limitations as well. For these reasons, it is important that hearing impaired children be identified as soon as possible, and that they be exposed to experiences in listening and interpreting sounds (auditory training).

Deaf children cannot talk. In language acquisition, receptive language precedes expressive language. Profoundly deaf children, because they cannot receive language aurally, are handicapped in their expression of the language. However, children with all degrees of hearing impairment are able and do learn to communicate.

With amplification and auditory training, hard-of-hearing children can usually use their hearing to develop spoken language. They can and do talk. Some deaf children, with the benefit of little or no residual hearing, are able to develop successful speechreading (lip reading) and some speaking skills. While ability in speechreading is difficult and skill level may vary, the acquisition of clear, intelligible speech by the child born profoundly deaf is usually a laborious task. Both receptive and expressive language are available to profoundly deaf persons through the use of sign language. American Sign Language (ASL) is a system that includes thousands of conceptual signs; it is not a word-by-word representation of the English language having syntactic and semantic differences. Although this system is popular with adult hearing impaired persons, it may not be suitable for children who are beginning to learn the English language. The importance of this task for later learning (e.g., reading) should be obvious. Other sign languages such as morphemic-based Signing Exact English (SEE II) also exist. Another recognizable system is the manual alphabet (also known as fingerspelling). This includes individual finger signs for each letter of the alphabet and numbers from 1–10 as in the illustration that follows.[3]

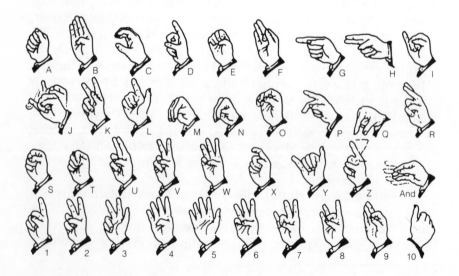

---

[3]Source: The Pennsylvania Society for the Advancement of the Deaf.

For a long time there has been great controversy over whether educators should rely strictly upon oral language (oralism) or should use manual sign language (manualism) when teaching deaf children. Unfortunately, the issue has not, as yet, been resolved. There is some trend toward a combined use of oral and manual methods in a procedure identified as "total communication."

Deaf children are retarded. The measurement of intelligence has traditionally relied heavily upon language, and language is precisely the area of greatest handicap for the seriously hearing impaired child. Both professionals and laypersons have wrongly inferred that because hearing impaired persons evidence a language deficit there may also be an intellectual or cognitive deficit. More recent, broader conceptualizations of intelligence include considerations of nonverbal or performance aspects (Myklebust, 1964). With language factors accounted for, the intelligence of hearing impaired children approximates the norm for hearing children (McConnell, 1973; Wiley, 1971).

Observations of behavior of the profoundly deaf may also give the impression of retardation. A child who fails to respond to another's voice, fails to respond to very loud noises, demonstrates problems in balance, or produces strange vocalizations may mistakenly be judged as mentally retarded. These behaviors alone or in combination actually may indicate serious hearing problems. The alert observer should have the child checked for hearing loss.

COGNITION AND COMMUNICATION

The mistaken impressions of the preceding discussion highlight areas of educational need for hearing impaired children. Programs benefitting such children should include some or all of the following elements: *(a)* early identification, *(b)* parent counseling and participation, *(c)* concept development, *(d)* preschool education, *(e)* auditory training, *(f)*speech training, and *(g)* speech reading and /or sign language.

Early identification of the child with a hearing impairment is essential in order to initiate auditory and speech training before lack of exposure to language results in a more serious deprivation. Gentile (1972) found that high-school-aged deaf students averaged fourth-grade level on a test of comprehension and averaged sixth-grade level on a test of computation. Early and intensive intervention in the area of language development is imperative for the hearing impaired child to approach normal achievement in academic areas. Assistance in providing concrete hearing and language experiences can serve to enrich the child's total fund of information, enhancing intellectual and social growth. Parents should participate directly in providing these experiences.

The development of basic social skills is not so much a matter of the hearing impairment itself but that of how individuals in the environment respond (Hoemann & Briga, 1981). Matters are further complicated because hearing impaired children cannot easily communicate their feelings of isolation, rejection and frustration (Meadow, 1975). Emphasis upon exposure can help foster healthy social and interpersonal relationships. It can also minimize the limitation hearing impairment places upon the amount of information that the child obtains from the environment.

Hearing impaired children need activities that contribute to conceptual development. Skills should include comparisons of sizes, shapes, and colors of objects (Evelsizer, 1972). Understanding of these concepts will increase the opportunities for meaningful experiences in which there is variety, novelty, and occasion for selection. Such experiences can contribute to development of divergent thinking and evaluation. It is in these two areas, divergent thinking and evaluation, that hearing impairment most directly and generally affects intelligence (Myklebust, 1964).

Furth (1973) suggests that development of cognition and intelligence should precede emphasis upon language under the theoretical framework that thought precedes language. Placing primary emphasis upon early identification and diagnosis, conceptual development, auditory training, and building a base of general experiences should be consistent with such a conceptualization.

It has been the experience of educators of the hearing impaired that early work on language is important to language development in the child (McConnell, 1973). The longer the deprivation, the greater the handicap. Approaches to language may include speechreading and speech training in which the child is exposed in a systematic way to oral language. One advantage of acquiring ability in speech and speechreading rather than just manual communication skills is that it enables the child to communicate with normally hearing persons.

The use of sign language in the form of manual signs or finger spelling permits the deaf child to communicate with other deaf individuals. Signs and gestures may be used when total lack of hearing, visual impairment, or reduced mental functioning render an individual unable to acquire speech and speechreading skills with reasonable facility. While some educators tend to feel that use of manual signs may retard or interfere with development of speaking and speechreading skills if introduced early (McConnell, 1973), there is some evidence that use of manualism may not interfere and perhaps may even facilitate overall language development (Alterman, 1970; Meadow, 1968; Stuckless & Birch, 1966; Vernon & Koh, 1970).

POSTSCRIPT

It would be a mistake to argue that hearing impaired children are just like all other children. They are not. By virtue of their exceptionalities they are different. Boothroyd (1982) points out, what begins as a sensory problem has consequences that can create:

1. A perceptual problem
2. A speech problem
3. A communication problem
4. A cognitive problem
5. A social problem
6. An emotional problem
7. An educational problem
8. An intellectual problem
9. A vocational problem

These problems are often compounded by:

10. Parental problems
11. Societal problems

The personal and social success of hearing impaired children depends upon the degree to which we as individuals and as a society will accept their differences and upon the quality of methods, techniques, and devices developed to ameliorate their handicapping condition.

SUGGESTIONS FOR WORKING WITH PERSONS WHO HAVE HEARING IMPAIRMENT

General

1. Write messages or key phrases down if necessary.
2. Talk directly to the hearing impaired person when there is an interpreter.
3. Use gestures and facial expressions as much as possible.
4. Consider trimming facial hair if you work with hearing impaired people on a regular basis.
5. Get the person's attention by waving your hand or tapping on the shoulder.
6. Familiarize yourself with the basic operation of a person's hearing aid as well as the capabilities of the person using it.
7. Speak naturally and clearly; do not over dramatize or over enunciate.

Educational

1. Seat hearing impaired persons appropriately. This usually means near the speaker or interpreter.
2. Do not stand in front of a window or light source as this makes speechreading difficult.
3. Avoid talking while writing on a blackboard (i.e., face the hearing impaired person while talking).
4. Discuss new concepts and provide new vocabulary in advance.
5. Use visual aids whenever possible.
6. Occasionally ask hearing impaired students to repeat what you have said to determine whether they understood.

PONDER THESE

Think of some methods you could use to determine the possibility of a hearing loss in young children.

Discuss the pros and cons of teaching communication skills to deaf people using the following methods:

Oral communication

Manual communication (e.g., signing and finger spelling)

Simultaneous oral and manual communication

Investigate the impact of technology on the lives of hearing impaired individuals. Consider areas like:

Using telephones

Computer technolgy

Medical advances (e.g., cochlear implants)

List the major concerns that arise for a profoundly hearing impaired person in the following situations:

Driving

Staying at a hotel or motel

Responding to someone knocking at the door

Crossing the street

Playing softball

REFERENCES

Alterman, A. I. (1970). Language and the education of children with early profound deafness. *American Annals of the Deaf, 115,* 514–521.

Boothroyd, A. (1982). *Hearing Impairments in young children.* Englewood Cliffs, NJ: Prentice-Hall.

Davis, H. (1970). Abnormal hearing and deafness. In H. Davis and S. R. Silverman (Eds.), *Hearing and deafness* (3rd ed., pp. 87–146.). New York: Holt, Rinehart & Winston.

Evelsizer, R. L. (1972). Hearing impairment in the young child. In A. H. Adams (Ed.), *Threshold learning abilities: Diagnostic and instructional procedures for specific early learning disabilities.* New York: Macmillan.

Furth, H. G. (1973). *Deafness and learning: A psychosocial approach.* Belmont, CA: Wadsworth.

Gentile, A. (1972). Academic achievement test results or a national testing program for hearing impaired students: 1971. *Annual Survey of Hearing Impaired Children and Youth.* Gallaudet College Office Demographic Studies, Ser. D, No. 9.

Hallahan, D. P., & Kauffman, J. M. (1986). *Exceptional children: Introduction to special education* (3rd ed.). Englewood Cliffs, NJ: Prentice-Hall.

Hoemann, J. W., & Briga, J. S. (1981). Hearing impairments. In J. M. Kauffman & D. P. Hallahan (Eds.), *Handbook of special education* (pp. 222–247). Englewood Cliffs, NJ: Prentice-Hall.

McConnell, F. (1973). Children with hearing disabilities. In L. M. Dunn (Ed.), *Exceptional children in the schools: Special education in transition* (2nd ed., pp. 351–410). New York: Holt, Rinehart & Winston.

McGee, T. M. (1968).Ototoxic antibiotics. *Volta Review, 70,* 667–671.

Meadow, K. P. (1968). Early manual communication in relation to the deaf child's intellectual, social, and communicative functioning. *American Annals of the Deaf, 113,* 29–41.

Meadow, K. P. (1975). Development of deaf children. In E. M. Hetherington (Ed.), *Review of child development research* (Vol. 5, pp. 441–508) Chicago: University of Chicago.

Myklebust, H. R. (1964). *The psychology of deafness: Sensory deprivation, learning and adjustment* (2nd ed.). New York: Grune & Stratton.

Northern, J. L., & Downs, M. P. (1974). *Hearing in children.* Baltimore: Williams and Wilkins.

Silverman, S. R., & Lane, H. S. (1970). Deaf children. In H. Davis and S. R. Silverman (Eds.), *Hearing and deafness* (3rd ed., pp. 433–482). New York: Holt, Rinehart & Winston.

Streng, A., Fitch, W. J., Hedgecock, L. D., Phillips, J. W., & Carrell, J. A. (1958). *Hearing therapy for children* (2nd ed.). New York: Grune & Stratton.

Stuckless, E. R., & Birch, J. W. (1966). The influence of early manual communication on the linguistic development of deaf children. *American Annals of the Deaf, 111,* 499–504.

U.S. Department of Education. (1984). *Sixth annual report to Congress on the implementation of P.L. 94–142: The Education for All Handicapped Children Act.* Washington, DC: U.S. Government Printing Office.

Vernon, M., & Koh, S. D. (1970). Early manual communication and deaf children's achievement. *American Annals of the Deaf, 115,* 527–536.

Wiley, J. A. (1971). A psychology of auditory impairment. In W. M. Cruickshank (Ed.), *Psychology of exceptional children and youth* (3rd ed., pp. 414–439). Englewood Cliffs, NJ: Prentice-Hall.

9

Communication Disorders

Our anecdotes to this point have depicted what it is like to work with handicapped people. We have not attempted to convey directly what it is like to be handicapped. Almost everyone has at some time or other experienced some embarrassment, guilt, frustration, anxiety, or pride stemming from verbal interaction with others. Few of us, however, have felt the overwhelming emotions that accompany severe difficulties in oral communication. Listening and talking are such ubiquitous social experiences that we tend to underestimate the handicap that can result from even minor speech deviations. We find it relatively easy to form an empathic relationship with an individual who has an obvious physical, emotional, or mental disorder, but we tend to feel that the individual with a speech disorder suffers no lasting penalty and could easily overcome the difficulty with a little determination. Consequently, we have chosen the following anecdotes to call your attention to the feelings and problems of children with speech and language disorders.

I must be pretty tough because I'm not in the bug house. The constant experience of starting to say something and never having it come out when I want it to should have driven me crazy long ago. I can't even say my own name. Once in a while I get a little streak of easy speech and then wham, I'm plugged, tripped up, helpless, making silent mouth openings like a gold-fish. It's like trying to play the piano with half the keys sticking. I can't even get used to it because sometimes I can fear a word and out it pops; then again when I am expecting smooth speech and everything's going all right, boom I'm stuck. It sure's exasperating. (p. 72)

Even when I was a little girl I remember being ashamed of my speech. And every time I opened my mouth I shamed my mother. I can't tell you how awful it felt. If I talked, I did wrong. It was that simple. I kept thinking I must be awful bad to have to talk like that. I remember praying to God and asking him to forgive me for whatever it was I must have done. I remember trying hard to remember what it was, and not being able to find it.(p. 61)

The most wonderful thing about being able to pronounce my sounds now is that people aren't always saying "What? What's that?" I bet I've heard that fifty thousand times. Often they'd shout at me as though I were deaf and that usually made me talk worse. Or they'd answer "Yes" when that just didn't make sense. I still occasionally find myself getting set for these reactions and steeling myself against them and being surprised when other people just listen. (p. 72)

After I came to high school from the country, everybody laughed at me whenever I tried to recite. After that I pretended to be dumb and always said "I don't know" when the teacher called on me. That's why I quit school. (p. 42)

Yesterday, when we made that tape recording of my new voice and I heard it, I felt all mixed up inside. I told you it sounded much better, and it does. Compared to my old voice, it's a great improvement. But it isn't ME! It just isn't. I sound like a phony or like an actor playing a part. I know it's better but I don't want to talk so strangely. I just couldn't keep my appointment with you today because I'm so upset about it. I'm even thinking of quitting. I know you said I'd get used to it, but right now I don't think I ever could. (p. 181)

THERAPIST

When you were stuck that time, what were your feelings?

SUBJECT

I don't know. All, All mmmmmmmmmmmmmixed up, I gggggguess.

THERAPIST

You probably felt helpless . . . sort of as though your mouth had frozen shut . . .

SUBJECT

And, and I cccccouldn't open it. Yeah.

THERAPIST

You couldn't open it. It was almost as though you had lost the ability to move a part of yourself when you wanted to . . . Sure must be frustrating . . .

SUBJECT

Sssure is. BBBBBurns me up. I, I, I, jjjust hate mmmmm . . . Oh skip it . . . I don't know.

THERAPIST

(Acceptingly) It almost makes you hate yourself when you get stuck like that.

SUBJECT

Yeah, dih-dih-sigusted with mmmmmmyself and everything else . . .

THERAPIST

Some stutterers even find themselves hating the person they are talking to.

SUBJECT

Yyyyeah, I,I,I,I, I wwwwwas huh-huh-huh-hating yyyyyyyyou just then.

THERAPIST

Uh huh. I know.

SUBJECT

(Blurting it out) How, how come you know all these th-things? (pp. 384–85)[1]

When I was 15, I participated with a group of five other boys in a stuttering therapy program. All of us in the group had a common problem—Mrs. Shinn, the lady who worked in our favorite ice cream parlor. We'd go into the store to order a straw-

[1]Charles Van Riper, *Speech Correction: Principles and Methods*, 4th ed. (Englewood Cliffs, N.J.: Prentice-Hall, Inc., 1963), pp. 41–42, 61–63, 72, 181, 384–385. Copyright © 1963. Reprinted by permission of Prentice-Hall, Inc.

berry cone and say, "I want a st-st-st-st-st-. . .," and before we could finish the word she'd hand us a strawberry cone. Sometimes she'd even say, "Yeah, I know, strawberry." Well, that's pretty irritating to have someone think she can always predict what you're going to say. It's even worse when someone finishes a sentence for you. Much as we liked the ice cream she dished out, we all started to hate old Mrs. Shinn. So we thought of a way to teach her a lesson. One day we went into the ice cream parlor one after another. Each of us said the same thing, "I want a st-st-st-st-st-. . ." and just as Mrs. Shinn was about to hand us the strawberry cone we finished, ". . .st-st-st-chocolate cone." From that day on, she always let us finish our orders before she started to dip.[2]

When I was a boy, my parents made sacrifices to give me stuttering lessons. I got pretty good at stuttering after a while. I could stutter in iambic pentameter, a feat that turned the most patronizing grown-up pale, and I could speak my name to the rhythm of the first 32 bars of "Tiger Rag." That is top stuttering. I suppose today stuttering lessons, like everything else, are much more expensive, but at that time, when Calvin Coolidge was on the march and the 1930s just a threat, lessons were offered at about $5 an hour and were "guaranteed" to stop stuttering instantly, or at least somewhere on the lively side of the statistical expectancy. The people who administered these courses were, and probably still are, great practical jokers. Each stuttering school "arranged" that their method proceed under a form of group therapy. Any stutterer knows that no group of stutterers can be persuaded to stop talking to each other, if only in the hope of picking up a new style such as a stammer or a bilateral emission lisp, the way interested new side men do at a solid jam session. The result of such conversation exchange was a gregarious sort of nervous shock which in no time halted the power of speech altogether.

At last my parents found the Neurological Institute. The experts there shrugged casually. It was a lead pipe cinch. It seems that I stuttered because of my hands. Essentially, they explained,

---

[2]We are grateful to C. Lee Woods, Ph.D., for contributing this anecdote.

I was an addled chirognostic. I was right-handed when I should have been left-handed, and whoever had insisted that I use my right hand for eating and writing while I had been growing had scrambled my speech centers. And they were right. It was on- ly a crutch, someone told me patiently, but it worked. Today I can talk fast and long and I hardly stutter at all.[3]

Speech and language disorders are particularly complex problems. For this reason speech-language therapists typically receive rigorous training and are required to meet high profes- sional standards. Correction of speech and language disorders is carried out in many different, often multidisciplinary settings. Therefore, in many universities, training programs for speech- language pathologists are located in departments other than special education, such as departments of speech pathology and audiology. Basic knowledge of speech and language disorders and their correction is important for all professionals working with disabled students because many children with other primary handicaps, such as mental retardation and emotional disturb- ance, also experience difficulties in speech and language.

DEFINITION

Often the concepts of communication, language, and speech are confused. It is imperative for professionals and lay people to employ the proper use of these terms. Hallahan & Kauffman (1986) aptly differentiate these concepts:

> Speech and language are tools used for purposes of com-
> munication. Communication requires . . . sending . . .
> and receiving . . . meaningful messages . . . Language is
> the communication of ideas through an arbitrary system
> of symbols that are used according to semantic and
> grammatical rules . . . Speech is the behavior of forming
> and sequencing the sounds of oral language. (p. 194)

We can consider speech as a part of oral language, in a subcate- gory of the more generic use of the term language. In this chap-

---

[3]From R. Condon, "A Show of Hands," *Holiday Magazine* 36, no. 3 (1964): 12. Reprinted by permission of the Curtis Publishing Co., Indianapolis, Indiana.

ter, we will be most concerned with oral language—a system of communication incorporating spoken sounds.

Unfortunately, the identification of a speech or language impairment can be a matter of subjective judgment. Just how much a language or speech pattern must differ from normal before it becomes a disorder often depends upon characteristics of both the listener and the speaker. For instance, a mother having grown accustomed to her 9-year-old's unusual articulation may overlook the fact that the child's speech is unintelligible to his peers. Moreover, whether a speech difference is considered a disorder depends upon the age of the speaker. That is, in a 3-year-old, faulty articulation is normal and certainly would not be thought of as a disorder, as it might be for an older child. VanRiper (1978) notes that abnormal speech is so different from normal speech that it *(a)* draws the listener's attention to itself rather than to what is being said, and *(b)* interferes with communication, or *(c)* produces distress in the speaker or the listener. Defective speech is conspicuous, unintelligible, or unpleasant.

In spite of difficulties involved in precisely defining speech and language disorders, usable definitions have been developed by speech-language pathologists. McLean (1978) notes that the identification and classification of communication disorders, while not an easy task, is usually based on two comparisons:

> Judgments of which children should be considered to have a communication disorder requiring special education or clinical programming are made from two basic comparisons. The first is a comparison of the child's language with the standard language form of the culture. The second is a comparison of the child's language with the language of other children at the same age level. (p. 271)

ETIOLOGY

The cause of speech and language disorders may be either biological, or functional. *Biological* etiologies involve known neurological deficits or structural malformations such as cleft palate, cleft lip, enlarged adenoids, hearing impairment, cerebral palsy, damage to various muscles that are used in articulation (dysarthria) or phonation, deformities of the vocal organs, and ear infections, to name a few.

Most disorders of speech and language, however, have no known biological cause and are, therefore, termed *functional* disorders. This implies that there is a definite functional loss of a certain ability, but it cannot be attributed to any organic cause. Functional disorders may include articulation and voice problems, stuttering, and specific language disabilities. Many theories, attempting to explain the etiology of various problems, have been offered, but no single explanation is generally accepted at this time.

LANGUAGE DISORDERS

To fully understand how language is disordered, we must know what constitutes normal language. The development of language begins with the early cry of an infant and progresses through stages of differentiated crying, babbling, vocal play, single words, holophrastic speech (a single word representing a whole phrase or sentence), syntactical utterances, multi-word expressions, and sentences. Recently, there has been some discussion whether language comprehension precedes language production. The prevailing attitude seems to favor an interactive mechanism. That is, children progress through these stages in a predictable manner; however, this process is very complex and problems can occur. Because language acquisition is greatly complex, there are conflicting theories of language development. Individuals such as Chomsky, Skinner, Bloom, Nelson, and Bruner all have theories to explain the hows and whys of language development (see Schiefelbusch & McCormick, 1981). Research does not yet conclusively support any single orientation; we must therefore await the further investigation of this complex phenomenon.

Language problems occur in all the following areas: oral, written, and even gestural. However, our concern with the various aspects of oral language disabilities relates to Hull and Hull's (1973) description: "Disability in oral language occurs when an individual is unable to comprehend meaningful ideas which have been spoken or when he is unable to use spoken words to effectively express meaningful ideas" (p. 303). In other words, this individual is not effectively able to use the elemental symbols of oral language.

Naremore (1980) notes that in thinking about different types of language disorders one should keep in mind these three things: *(a)* the language and nonlanguage behaviors a child imitates, because a lot of language learning involves learning to imitate; *(b)* the language the child comprehends, because receptive language (understanding what is heard) is so important in early learning; and *(c)* the language the child uses spontaneously, because effective communication in natural situations is the ultimate goal of language remediation. Besides these three points, Naremore suggests four classes of disordered language.

First, some children do not develop receptive and/or expressive language by the age of 3 years as most children (Bangs, 1982). The *absence of language* may be due to deafness, brain damage, mental retardation, or childhood psychosis. Regardless of the cause, the important thing is that the child shows no signs of understanding or being able to use language. These children need direct instruction in how to make speech sounds and say words. They also need to be given many opportunities to hear and use language. And these opportunities must be structured to teach the child how language is used for communication—to influence the environment for a desired result (for example, to get something the child wants).

A second class of language disorder is *qualitatively different language.* That is, the child may make speech sounds and even have an extensive vocabulary but not know how to use language to communicate effectively. Speech may be echolalic (parrotlike repetition of what is heard) or just not make sense or not accurately convey meaning. Such difficulties may have any number of causes, and often the causes are not really known in a specific case. Whatever the cause, a child with qualitatively different language needs remedial instruction in the *functions* of language—how it is used in social contexts (i.e., pragmatic language) and how it is related to thinking and behaving.

Delayed language, a third type of disorder, means that the child appears to be acquiring language by the normal processes and in the normal sequence, but at a significantly later age than most children. Finally, *interrupted language development*—the child has acquired language normally but loses it due, for example, to hearing impairment or brain damage—is another class of disorder. Again, the cause of the language disorder may or may not be known. Certainly, language instruction may be different for a hearing child than for one who is deaf. But, in any case, a remedial language training program must take into account what the child knows about, how the child talks about those things, and how the child communicates his or her wishes, intentions, demands, feelings and so on (see Schiefelbusch & McCormick, 1981).

SPEECH IMPAIRMENT

"Speech is defective when it is ungrammatical, unintelligible, culturally or personally unsatisfactory, or abusive of the speech mechanism" (Perkins, 1971, p. 4). Remember that "unintelligible" and "unsatisfactory," terms used in the preceding statement, are subjective descriptors. Just as beauty is in the eye of the beholder, defective speech can be in the ear of the listener. Speech can vary along numerous dimensions. Several that are the basis of classification of speech disorders include phonological disorders, voice disorders, and fluency problems. And these classifications are not mutually exclusive because an individual may exhibit more than one type of speech problem.

Phonological disorders

Phonology has to do with the way speech sounds are made (articulation). Phonological disorders consist of omissions (e.g., "tha" for "that"), substitutions (e.g. "thnake" for "snake"), and distortions (e.g., "s" produced by lateralized emission of air). Children with phonological difficulties are sometimes described as using "baby talk," being "tongue-tied," or not "talking plain." The causes of phonological difficulties include slow development, missing teeth, cleft palate or lip, neurological impairment, emotional problems, and faulty learning. In the vast majority of cases with which a speech-language pathologist works, the phonological problem is functional; that is, the etiology is unknown. It must be remembered that some children may not master all of the speech sounds until approximately 8 years of age. It is not uncommon or pathological for children between the ages of 5 and 8 to misarticulate some sounds and for children younger than 3 years of age to be unintelligible except to their parents. When evaluating a child's phonology, one must always keep in mind the child's overall developmental level.

Voice disorders

Phonation or voice is the tonal or musical quality produced by vibration of the vocal folds. Voice disorders can affect pitch, loudness, tonal quality, and cause the voice to have the sound of nasality and hoarseness (Perkins, 1980). More specifically, deviations along these dimensions may involve abuse of the larynx, interference with communication, or unpleasantness to the ear. The individual's voice may consistently be too high- or low-pitched, too loud or too soft, too monotone, or too breathy, harsh, or hoarse. These disorders of voice may be caused by malformation, injury or disease of the vocal folds, psychological factors, hearing loss, and so forth. Damage to the vocal folds can result from the person's persistent misuse of the voice, for example, through excessive screaming. It is also possible for voice disorders to arise from faulty learning.

Disorders of speech flow

The dimensions of speech-flow include sequence, duration, rate, rhythm, and fluency (Perkins, 1980). Normal speech is perceived as relatively fluent or smooth-flowing with various natural interruptions. All of us have experienced difficulties in speech fluency, usually when we try to speak too quickly or forget what we were saying in mid-sentence.

The most common problem associated with speech fluency is stuttering. Dysfluencies or disruptions in the flow of speech are one aspect of stuttering. Normal speech contains disruptions of rhythm or dysfluencies, but when these occur so frequently and severely that the listener's attention is drawn to them and they interfere with communication, the speaker may be considered to have a speech problem. The speech disruptions that characterize stuttering include repetitions or prolongations of sound, word, syllable, or speech posture and/or avoidance and struggle behaviors. Stuttering has been classified into two types: (a) "primary" involving the normal, disfluent repetitions characteristic of a young child and (b) "secondary" referring to the more severe speech impairments that are compounded by the disfluent nonspeech behaviors just noted.

Usually caused by a complex interaction of factors, stuttering involves social, emotional, and physiological reactions in both speaker and listener. Among the few facts about stuttering that we do know are:

1. Stuttering is a natural phenomenon of childhood. In learning speech and language, all children become dysfluent to some degree. Many children develop patterns of

dysfluency that are transitory but do, nevertheless, cause their parents grave concern. In almost all cases, stuttering begins before adolescence, and, by late adolescence, approximately three-fourths of these stuttering children stop spontaneously. This phenomenon occurs independently of the assistance of speech-language pathologists or other professionals.

2. Most individuals who stutter have particular trouble with certain words or specific situations. For instance, speaking to strangers or talking on the phone may pose great difficulties while reading aloud or singing are not affected.

3. Stuttering is more prevalent among boys than girls. Various studies have reported boy:girl ratios ranging from 3 : 1 to 8 : 1.

4. Stuttering runs in families. This may or may not be due to hereditary factors. One should remember that religious beliefs also run in families, but religion is not transmitted genetically.

5. There are numerous theories of stuttering, with none sufficient to explain all cases. Hereditary, psychoanalytical, organic, and learning theories have been proposed. It is also believed by some researchers that children become stutterers primarily because parents show exaggerated concern for the young child's normal dysfluencies ("diagnosogenic" theory).

6. Although a large number of treatment methods have been applied, none has been universally successful. Therapeutic efforts have included systematic desensitization, negative practice, ego building, psychotherapy, operant conditioning, voluntary control, modification of stuttering patterns, chemotherapy, surgery, hypnosis, and rhythmic speech. While no universal "cure" has been found, it appears that some of the most successful treatments known to date are those based on learning principles.

MULTIPLE DISORDERS

Often speech and language disorders will be found together in an individual. Both problems often occur simultaneously under certain handicapping conditions.

Disorders associated with hearing impairment

If a child has a significant hearing impairment, speech may be characterized by voice disorders and many errors of articulation. This child is most likely to misarticulate unvoiced high frequency sounds such as "s", "f," "p," "t," and "sh." For this individual, the task of learning the sounds of language is severely impeded by the hearing difficulty. If the impairment is too severe, it may be necessary to use another language system such as signing.

Disorders associated with cerebral palsy

The type of brain damage which results in cerebral palsy may make it difficult or impossible for the child to control the muscles necessary for proper phonation and articulation. The speech of such individuals may be characterized by fluctuating patterns of pitch, timing, intensity, and phonology. In addition, both cognitive and perceptual motor difficulties may inhibit the acquisition of language and speech. However, because of the considerable variance of this population, some individuals will display severe impairment while others with milder forms of CP will demonstrate normal speech and language abilities.

Disorders associated with cleft palate or cleft lip

Cleft palate is a structural defect in the palate or roof of the mouth that may make it difficult or impossible for the individual to close off the nasal air passage, which is necessary for proper phonology. Speech associated with an unrepaired or inadequately repaired cleft palate is hypernasal; that is, too much air escapes through the nose as the person talks. Cleft lip (often inappropriately referred to as "harelip") is a structural defect in the upper lip that, if unrepaired, may also result in defective articulation. Both cleft palate and cleft lip result from failure of the bone and/or soft tissue of the palate or lip to fuse during approximately the first trimester of pregnancy. Language facility in the young child may be hindered by the communication problems stemming from these physical disorders.

Disorders associated with mental retardation, emotional disturbance, and learning disabilities

Mentally retarded children may exhibit speech problems and delays in language development. Mentally retarded children will more likely develop greater speech problems than normal children of the same developmental age. It is also a fact that as the severity of the retardation increases so does the probability that the individual will have significant speech and/or language problems. Severely emotionally disturbed children may display peculiar language patterns such as meaningless statements, parrotlike speech (echolalia), or frequent, inappropriate use of personal pronouns. Although the distinction between language disabilities and learning disabilities is not clearly demarcated, there is a strong relationship. Some professionals (Bryan & Bryan, 1978) believe that language disorders may be the focal issue in regard to learning disabilities.

PREVALENCE

It was reported by the U.S. Department of Education for 1983–84 that 2.37% of the school population was determined eligible for speech services. However, most authorities estimate that 5% of school-age students have some type of speech handicap. The estimated breakdown (of school age population) of specific speech problems is:

phonological disorders	1–3%
voice disorders	1–2%
stuttering	less than 1%

The prevalence of language disorders is difficult to estimate because there are no satisfactory figures for this impairment at present. The issue of determining a prevalence figure for language disorders becomes compounded by the significant overlap of language problems and learning disabilities.

SPEECH AND LANGUAGE PROGRAMS

Speech therapists perform their services in a wide variety of settings, including elementary and secondary schools, speech and hearing clinics, residential facilities, and rehabilitation hospitals. As one might expect, schools serve the largest number of individuals needing intervention.

School speech and language programs are the most feasible means of providing services to children. Working together, teachers and speech-language specialists can identify and provide assistance to large numbers of children who otherwise might never be taken to a speech center. Unfortunately, because most school systems continue to hire too few speech-language therapists, only those children with the most severe speech or language handicaps are typically served by them on a regular basis. Some speech and language impaired children may receive assistance from a learning disabilities specialist or resource teacher if the particular school is able to provide this type of service.

Teachers, then, play a vital role in assisting those children not seen regularly by the speech-language therapist. After a careful assessment of the child's speech, the specialist can recommend activities that the child can work on in the classroom. Only through the cooperative efforts of teacher and specialist can assistance be provided for all children with speech and language handicaps.

POSTSCRIPT

We have outlined only major disorders of speech and language and the major etiological factors contributing to these conditions. There are other less common or more specific disorders and etiological factors that are beyond the scope of this chapter. Moreover, within each of the broad categories we have outlined, there is a wide variation in degree or severity of the handicap. Additionally, an individual's speech may be disordered by more than one of the conditions already discussed. For more detailed treatment of speech and language impairments see Devany, Rincover, and Lovaas (1981), Hixon, Shriberg, and Saxman (1980), Schiefelbusch and McCormick (1981), Tarver and Ellsworth (1981), or Van Riper (1978).

Speech is one of an individual's most personal attributes. Certainly, as the anecdotes at the beginning of this chapter demonstrate, having a speech problem can be extremely embarrassing and painful. When people continually respond more to the sound than to the content of speech, a person's desire to communicate thoughts and feelings can be inhibited. Although children with speech disorders may choose a world of silence rather than face the disturbing reactions on a listener's face, they can, with help, overcome or learn to cope with their difficulties. At times, they can make light of their situation. Having a speech or language handicap, like having any other handicap, does not exclude a child from the world of fun and humor.

SUGGESTIONS FOR WORKING WITH PERSONS WHO HAVE SPEECH/LANGUAGE DISORDERS

General

1. Teachers, parents, and friends should be informed of what skills and/or behaviors the therapist is targeting so they can appropriately respond and reinforce them in educational settings, at home, or in the community.
2. Listen attentively and patiently when the person is talking. Give the person time.
3. If you do not understand what the individual said, explain what you did understand and ask for clarification of the rest.
4. Remember that the speech/language impaired person has trouble talking, not hearing; do not shout or yell.
5. Laugh with, but not at, the speech/language impaired individual.

Working with those who stutter

1. Accept them as they are.
2. Look at and not away from them when they talk. Obvious uneasiness can make them uncomfortable.
3. Encourage but do not force them to talk.
4. Do not say things for them. That is, do not complete their words or statements when they get hung up.
5. Build their self-confidence by emphasizing their assets.
6. Encourage them to participate in group activities.
7. Create an environment in which these individuals can feel comfortable. Let them know that you are aware of but accept their problem.

PONDER THESE

We judge one another's speech to a large degree on the basis of what we are accustomed to hearing. Which, if any, of the following individuals would you judge to have defective speech? What specific characteristics of their speech distract you from the content of what they have to say?

Jimmy Carter	Norm Crosby
Mel Tillis	Jimmy Stewart
Kim Karnes	Charo
Barbara Walters	Pee Wee Herman

Imagine that a parent comes to you with one of the following descriptions of a child's speech or language. What specific questions would you ask the parent to help you determine whether the child may in fact need the services of a speech-language specialist?

"Now my little boy—he just don't talk plain so you can understand him."

"Melinda stutters."

"Fred sounds like he's talking through his nose."

"I don't know what's the matter. She just hardly ever talks. I mean almost *never!* She doesn't say more than a couple of words in a day, and sometimes you can't even understand those."

To get some idea of what it is like to have a speech impairment, try one of the following activities. In public or in the company of strangers or on the telephone, speak with a severe phonological or voice deviation or with marked dysfluency (stutter). Describe your listener's reactions and the feelings they engendered in you.

REFERENCES

Bangs, T. E. (1982). *Language and learning disorders of the pre-academic child with curriculum guide* (2nd ed.). Englewood Cliffs, NJ: Prentice-Hall.

Bryan, T. H., & Bryan, J. H. (1978). *Understanding learning disabilities* (2nd ed.). Sherman Oaks, CA: Alfred Publishing.

Devany, J. M., Rincover, A., & Lovaas, O. I. (1981). Teaching speech to nonverbal children. In J. M. Kauffman & D. P. Hallahan (Eds.), *Handbook of special education* (pp. 512–529). Englewood Cliffs, NJ: Prentice-Hall.

Hallahan, D. P., & Kauffman, J. M. (1986). *Exceptional children: Introduction to special education* (3rd ed.). Englewood Cliffs, NJ: Prentice-Hall.

Hixon, T. J., Shriberg, L. D., & Saxman, J. H. (Eds.). (1980). *Introduction to communication disorders.* Englewood Cliffs, NJ: Prentice-Hall.

Hull, F. M., & Hull, M. E. (1973). Children with oral communication disabilities. In L. M. Dunn (Ed.), *Exceptional children in the schools* (2nd ed., pp. 299–348). New York: Holt, Rinehart, & Winston.

McLean, J. E. (1978). Language structure and communication disorders. In M. G. Haring (Ed.), *Behavior of exceptional children* (2nd ed., pp. 253–288). Columbus, OH: Merrill.

Naremore, R. C. (1980). Language disorders. In T. J. Hixon, L. D. Shriberg, & J. H. Saxman (Eds.), *Introduction to communication disorders.* Englewood Cliffs, NJ: Prentice-Hall.

Perkins, W. H. (1971). *Speech pathology: An applied behavioral science.* St. Louis: Mosby.

Perkins, W. H. (1980). Disorders of speech flow. In T. J. Hixon, L. D. Shriberg, & J. H. Saxman (Eds.), *Introduction to communication disorders.* Englewood Cliffs, NJ: Prentice-Hall.

Schiefelbusch, R. L., & McCormick, L. P. (1981). Language and speech disorders. In J. M. Kauffman & D. P. Hallahan (Eds.), *Handbook of special education* (pp. 108–140). Englewood Cliffs, NJ: Prentice-Hall.

Tarver, S. G., & Ellsworth, P. S. (1981). Written and oral language for verbal children. In J. M. Kauffman & D. P. Hallahan (Eds.), *Handbook of special education* (pp. 491–511). Englewood Clifs, NJ: Prentice-Hall.

U.S. Department of Education. (1984). *Sixth annual report to Congress on the implementation of P.L.94–142: The Education for All Handicapped Children Act.* Washington, DC: U.S. Government Printing Office.

Van Riper, C. (1978). *Speech correction: Principles and methods* (6th ed.). Englewood Cliffs, NJ: Prentice-Hall.

THREE

Other Exceptional Areas

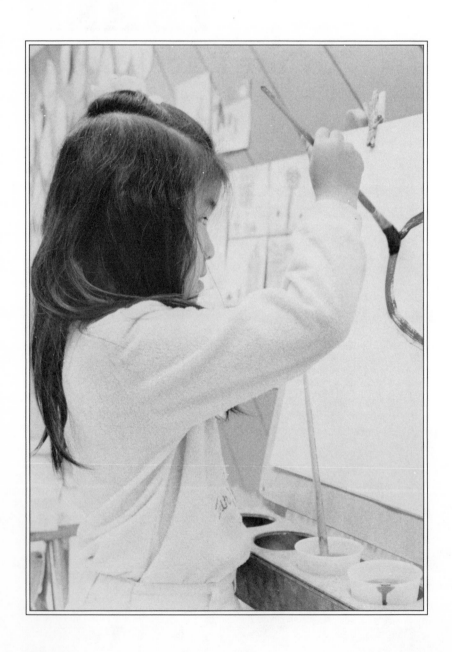

10

Giftedness

I was standing at the front of the room explaining how the earth revolves and how, because of its huge size, it is difficult for us to realize that it is actually round. All of a sudden Spencer blurted out. "The earth isn't round."

I curtly replied, "Ha, do you think it's flat?"

He matter-of-factly said, "No, it's a truncated sphere."

I quickly changed the subject. While the children were at recess I had a chance to grab a soft drink in the teacher's lounge. While sipping my drink, I looked up the word "truncated" in the dictionary. I'm still not sure if he was right, but it sounded good; so good that I wasn't going to make an issue of it. Spencer said the darndest things.

At 4 Ellie was reading on a third grade level. AT 5 she could complete long arithmetic problems in her head. At 6 she played sonatinas on the piano. At 7 she said, "At Sunday school they told us that God created all the things in the world. I already knew that, so I didn't learn anything new. What I'm anxious to know is how did he make everything. Do you know what I mean? When are they going to teach me how he created all these things?"

Not long ago, I was invited to go on a "reef walk" with a class of gifted third and fourth graders. It was a very educational experience.

While we were wading in shallow water, we came upon a familiar marine organism commonly called a feather duster. Forgetting that these students had vocabularies well advanced of their nongifted age peers, I was ready to say something like, "Look how that thing hangs on the rock."

Before I could get my highly descriptive statement out, Eddie, who always amazes us with his comments, offered the following. "Notice how securely anchored the organism is to the stationary coral."

All I could reply was: "Yes, I did."

It was explained quite clearly to his father that Albert would never make a success of anything, and when Albert was expelled from the "gymnasium" he was emphatically told, "Your presence in the class is disruptive and affects the other students." According to Clark (1971, p. 12) Albert's last name was Einstein.

Barlow (1952), quoting from the mid-nineteenth-century Chamber's Journal, *reported the arithmetical examination given to Truman Stafford, a child prodigy. The examination was given by the Rev. H. W. Adams when Truman was 10 years old.*

> *I had only to read the sum to him once. . .Let this fact be remembered in connection with some of the long and blind sums I shall hereafter name, and see if it does not show his amazing power of conception and comprehension. The questions given him became continually harder. What number is that which, being divided by the product of its digits, the quotient is 3; and if 18 be added, the digits will be inverted? He flew out of his chair, whirled around, rolled up his eyes and said in about a minute, 24. Multiply in your head 365, 365, 365, 365, 365, 365 by 365, 365, 365, 365, 365, 365. He flew around the room like a top, pulled his pantaloons over the tops of his boots, bit his hands, rolled his eyes in their sockets, sometimes smiling and talking, and*

*then seeming to be in an agony, until, in not more than
one minute said he, 133,491,850,208,566,925,016,658,
299,951,583,225! (p. 43)*

---

*Mr. Palcuzzi, principal of the Jefferson Elementary School, once
got tired of hearing objections to special provisions for gifted
children, so he decided to spice an otherwise mild PTA meeting with his proposal for the gifted. The elements of the Palcuzzi
program were as follows:*

1. *Children should be grouped by ability.*
2. *Part of the school day should be given over to special
   instructon.*
3. *Talented students should be allowed time to share their
   talents with children of other schools in the area or even
   of other schools throughout the state. (We will pay the
   transportation costs.)*
4. *A child should be advanced according to his talents,
   rather than according to his age.*
5. *These children should have special teachers, specially
   trained and highly salaried.*

*As might be expected, the "Palcuzzi program" was sub-
jected to a barrage of criticism:*

*"What about the youngster who isn't able to fit into the
special group; won't his ego be damaged?"*

*"How about the special cost; how could you justify trans-
portation costs that would have to be paid by moving a special
group of students from one school to another?"*

*"Mightn't we be endangering the child by having him inter-
act with children who are much more mature than he is?"*

*"Wouldn't the other teachers complain if we gave more
money to the instructors of this group?"*

*After listening for 10 or 15 minutes, Mr. Palcuzzi dropped
his bomb! He said that he wasn't describing a new program for
the intellectually gifted, but a program the school system had
been enthusiastically supporting for a number of years—the
program for gifted basketball players! Gallagher (1975) refers
to this as the "Palcuzzi Ploy" (p. 83).*

The Palcuzzi Ploy illustrates the very real problem of selling the general public on differential education for the gifted. There has been a tendency to view *equal* education for all as being the *same* educational practices for all, even though the major objective of public school education is to provide educational programs that will allow all individuals to develop their maximum potential. When children reach a certain intellectual criterion we tend to say, "Enough is enough! You only need to learn so much and we don't need a bunch of intellectual elitists around here anyway."

The gifted are generally perceived as being capable of shifting for themselves. In fact, many people feel that they will learn even under the most adverse learning conditions. The fact of the matter is that the gifted possess a unique array of learning characteristics that are best utilized through nontraditional teaching techniques for children of their age. In other words, the learning and thinking of gifted pupils are best facilitated through a *special* education. Lindsley (1971), when talking about exceptional children, emphasized that while retarded students drop out of the bottom of the normal class gifted students pop out of the top. "Gifted and learning disabled students are retarded by the curriculum assigned them in the average classroom. The gifted child is not stimulated to perform to his ultimate; the retarded child can't perform to the average" (p. 115).

While handicapped children can arouse sympathy and empathy, the gifted are left to fend for themselves in the regular classroom with their chronological peers. They may be capable of learning at such a high level of cognition that traditional instruction for children of their age is often boring, tedious, and redundant. It is no wonder that many case histories of very bright individuals reveal that at some time in their lives they experienced difficulties in school. Kirk (1972) reported that Norbert Wiener, one of the great men in cybernetics, read *Alice in Wonderland* and *The Arabian Nights* by age 4 but was refused admission to school because he was not old enough. At age 7 he was placed in the third grade. At age 18 he received his Ph.D. in mathematics.

It is common knowledge that Albert Einstein was bored in school and maintained a below-average to mediocre school record. Thomas Edison, at the age of 7, was at the bottom of his class. His mother got so upset with the school that she pulled him out of class and taught him at home. He was never again admitted to a public school. Stories like these tend to confirm the popular belief that the gifted can and will learn on their own.

But what about the gifted children who do not make it? The talented children who drop out of school because they are bored and unchallenged? What about Dorothy J., a middle-aged Cahuilla Indian woman? In spite of Dorothy's fear of teachers and lack of knowledge of English, she completed high school. As reported by Martinson (1973), "She is co-author, with university professors, of several books in linguistics, ethnobotany, and music and has served as a university lecturer in both the United States and abroad. Meanwhile, because she lacks formal higher education, she earns a living on an assembly line in a factory near her reservation" (p. 205).

Our relative unconcern for exceptional children who are gifted is reflected by the fact that federal spending for special education of the gifted and talented through the 1980s has been only about 0.5% of the federal allocations for education of the handicapped. In 1972 and again in 1983 the U.S. Commissioner of Education, in a report to Congress, noted that the group of youngsters identified as gifted are the most neglected in American education.

DEFINITION

It would seem that there are as many definitions of the gifted as there are authorities in the field. In fact, there is little agreement about whether high IQ alone should define giftedness or whether other characteristics like high creativity, achievement, motivation, or special talents (for example, in music, dance, or athletics) should be considered. The most recent federal definition, included in the Gifted and Talented Children's Act of 1978 (*Congressional Record,* 1978) reads:

> . . ."gifted and talented children" means children. . .who are identified. . .as possessing demonstrated or potential abilities that give evidence of high performance capabilities in areas such as intellectual, creative, specific academic, or leadership ability, or in the performing and visual arts, and who by reason thereof, require services or activities not ordinarily provided by the school.

Gallagher (1979) and Renzulli (1978) have noted that the federal definition may be misleading in some respects. No one has devised a reliable means of measuring "leadership ability" or "potential abilities." And while the federal definition gives the impression that there are many *independent* features of giftedness, in reality many of the characteristics listed (e.g., intellectual, creative, and specific academic abilities) are highly correlated.

Definitions of giftedness have changed over the years. Early definitions relied almost exclusively on IQ. Contemporary definitions typically refer to creativity, motivation, and/or exceptional performance in some culturally valued activity as well. All definitions state that gifted children are clearly superior in some ability area to most children of the same age. How far superior they should be, who should be the comparison group for judging superiority, and in what specific ways they should be superior—these are the major issues in defining giftedness.

Renzulli, Reis, and Smith (1981) have suggested that giftedness should be conceptualized in a multifaceted way. They suggested that gifted individuals have demonstrated or show potential in the following areas:

1. High ability (includes intelligence)
2. High creativity (implies the development and application of innovative ideas)
3. High task commitment (related to high degree of motivation and diligence)

Tests of intelligence as well as of other abilities are essential to identification. Making realistic judgments about children's potential is difficult for educators and parents alike (Webb, Meckstroth, & Tolan, 1982). Most teachers are unable to identify over half the children determined as gifted by individual intelligence tests (Fox, 1981).

While it might be said that identifying gifted students has been often overlooked in education, this definitely is the case with certain groups of children (Wolf & Stephens, 1986). Four different groups of students are typically underrepresented in gifted education; these include children who are culturally different, female, handicapped, or underachieving. There are gifted learners in all these groups and efforts must be undertaken to identify them.

PREVALENCE

As definitions change, so do the prevalence figures. That is predictable. Based on the normal curve, approximately 15 to 16% of the population earns IQs of 115 or above, while only 2 to 3% earn IQs of 130 or above. Because of the difficulty of assessing giftedness among children from disadvantaged cultures, Martinson (1973) has posed an interesting idea, designating the upper 3% of each cultural group as gifted. Thus, different IQ cut-off limits may be selected for each cultural group. Federal government sources do not really indicate clearly what percentage of the population is thought to be gifted, although figures of 3–5% are sometimes mentioned (Sisk, 1981). Obviously, both the definition and the prevalence of giftedness are arbitrary.

CHARACTERISTICS

In describing gifted persons, however they are defined, mention must be made of Terman's monumental contribution, *Generic Studies of Genius* (Burks, Jensen, & Terman, 1930; Cox, 1926; Terman, 1925, Terman & Oden, 1947; Terman & Oden, 1959). Terman actually devoted his life to the study of 1,528 gifted (high IQ) children, following them for 35 years from 1920 to his death in 1956. This five-volume study is expected to continue to the year 2010. The study is not only noted for its large sample size and longitudinal contribution, but for its consistent accuracy. The findings of Terman's investigation have been confirmed and reconfirmed to the point of "bordering on redundancy" (Getzels & Dillon, 1973, p. 694).

Basically, Terman's study counteracts the stereotypic concept that gifted individuals are physically weak, are small in stature, wear glases, read all the time, are not interesting to be around, and are "book-wormish." Terman's findings indicate not only that the gifted are superior in intellect, but that they also are physically, socially, emotionally, and morally advanced. Terman's gifted subjects were reported to be taller, stronger, and heavier than nongifted children. They walked earlier and had a lower incidence of sensory defects, malnutrition, and poor posture. They came from above-average to high-income homes, and their parents were well educated. When compared with the general population, they had a low incidence of delinquency, mental illness, and alcoholism. The gifted seemed to be more happily married, to have fewer divorces, and to have fewer offspring. Of over 1,500 offspring, there is a reported mean IQ of 132, with only 2 percent falling below 100 and 33⅓ percent scoring over 140. After studying Terman's classic work you cannot help but wonder what causes giftedness.

We enter a word of caution here: Gifted children are not necessarily superchildren. Some do, in fact, fit a negative stereotype. Individuals may vary from the generally superior description one gets for Terman's studies. Some gifted children are physically or emotionally handicapped (see Maker, 1977). Those with *extremely* high intelligence (IQ over 180) may be particularly prone to difficulties in social adjustment simply because their advanced abilities are so *exceedingly* rare among persons their age (see Hollingworth, 1942).

ETIOLOGY

Galton's (1869) classic contribution to the quantitative psychological study of giftedness touched off the nature-nurture controversy. His examination of adult geniuses lent support to the argument for a hereditary cause. In the years after his study, environmental aspects were accentuated by the majority of authorities in the field of giftedness. However, it was observed that gifted individuals walked, talked, and read much earlier than "normals," and such early acceleration in behavioral development was difficult to attribute primarily to environmental events. Yet it was also observed that the environments in which the majority of the gifted developed were unquestionably wholesome and stimulating. Because the nature-nurture controversy became so complex and conjured up emotional overtones, a pragmatic resolution evolved: "We are unable to genetically manipulate variables by selective breeding, but we are able to manipulate environmental events that may facilitate intellectual growth." This practical approach is best summed up by Gallagher (1964):

> Environment can have either an inhibiting or encouraging effect on the development of intellectual talent. Such an assumption places a heavy responsibility on the culture and its educational system, but it is also an exciting one for the educator and social scientist. The concept of *intelligence* as a genetically determined trait has

been replaced by the concept of a pliable and plastic intellect which is responsive to the environment in which it is placed. The place of genetics and intelligence has not been denied; rather, the first place of environment in its interaction with genetics has been reaffirmed. (p. 20)

While the logic of this approach seems irrefutable, Jensen (1966, 1969) insisted that genes and prenatal develoment account for 80% of the variance in intelligence while only 20% of the variance can be accounted for by the environment. Citing research studies, growth figures, and models of intelligence, Jensen presented a convincing case. Torrance (1971) summarizes Jensen's position as follows:

He especially questioned the idea that IQ differences are almost entirely a result of environmental differences and the cultural bias of intelligence tests. As in his earlier papers, he argued that environmental factors are less important in determining IQ than genetic factors. After examining the recent research concerning compensatory educational programs for young children, Jensen concluded that extreme environmental deprivation can keep a child from performing up to his genetic potential, but an enriched educational program cannot push the child above the potential. Jensen argues, however, that there are other mental abilities not included in intelligence tests that might be capitalized upon in educational programs. He believes that current educational attempts to boost IQ have been misdirected, and he advocates the development of educational methods that are based on other mental abilities besides IQ. (p. 550)

Early childhood studies have established that environmental factors can have a significant influence on intelligence and school success (Schweinhart & Weikart, 1985). Just how much environmental versus genetic factors play in determining functional intelligence has yet to be established. While researchers and educators debate the question of how much the environment affects intelligence, a growing number of parents currently are doing their best to create "superbabies." Glenn Doman (1984) in *How to Multiply Your Baby's Intelligence* tells parents that high and low intelligence are products of the environment and to produce superior intellectual abilities in their children, parents should present stimulating learning activities from birth onward. David Elkind (1981) in reaction to the drive for early development of abilities warns parents that too much early pressure to learn can create depression in young children. Certainly both educators and parents eagerly await some clarification on how much early stimulation and skill training are appropriate in developing children's full capacity for superior functioning and emotional well-being.

CREATIVITY

Another classic work on the gifted is Getzels and Jackson's (1962) study of the relationship between IQ and creativity. Two groups were identified: *(a)* high on IQ and low on creativity (mean IQ 150) and *(b)* low on IQ and high on creativity (mean IQ 127). High IQ–low creativity was defined as the top 20% on IQ but low on creative thinking; low IQ–high creativity was defined as the top 20% on creativity but lower on IQ. Despite a 23-point difference in IQ, both groups performed equally well on standardized achievement tests. The major finding was that while creativity may be a facet of intelligence, it is not being measured by the typical standardized intelligence tests. Apparently, creativity is not being tapped by conventional methods of measurement and evaluation.

Since there exists a low tolerance for noncomformity in our society, creativity is often discouraged, Torrance (1965) attempted to accelerate creativeness in children by offering them $2 prizes for stories that were interesting, exciting, and unusual. He found that children would produce such stories when reinforced for doing so. By using reinforcement techniques, other researchers too have found that creativity in story-writing, easel-painting, block-building, and selection of word combinations can be increased (Baer, Rowbury, & Goetz, 1976; Brigham, Graubard & Stans, 1972; Glover & Gary, 1976; Goetz & Salmonson, 1972). Torrance and others have demonstrated that creative thinking abilities need to be energized and guided, and that the earlier this is done the better.

DIFFERENTIAL EDUCATION

As listed by Ward (1962), the logic of special education services for the gifted is based on the following assumptions and observed facts:

1. Gifted children as a group differ from others in learning ability; they learn faster and remember more, and they tend to think more deeply with and about what they learn.

2. As adults, gifted persons tend to remain similarly advanced beyond the average and tend to assume distinctive social roles as leaders in the reconstruction and advancement of whatever lines of activity they pursue.

3. The regular school curriculum only barely approximates the demands of either the greater learning capacity or the anticipated social roles of gifted persons.

4. An educational program *can* be devised which *does* more adequately meet these basic demands, and which on the whole being uniquely suited to the gifted is both unnecessary for and impossible of accomplishment by students of lesser ability.

5. Differential educational provisions for the gifted promise to discover more gifted persons, to improve their education, and to launch them earlier into their chosen careers so that society, as well as the persons themselves, may enjoy longer the fruits of their productive and creative labors. (p. 22)

Ward's points, though written two decades ago, are hard to argue against; nearly all current educational programs for the gifted are built around most or all of his assumptions. Getzels and Dillon (1973) list nearly 30 specific programs and practices, but we will discuss only 3: ability grouping, enrichment, and acceleration (see Callahan, 1981, and Sisk, 1981, for further discussion).

Ability grouping

In this method the gifted are separated into more homogeneous groupings through special classes, ability tracks, and so forth. Although the results of research on ability grouping are somewhat contradictory, sufficient evidence suggests that the gifted benefit from such programs to provoke further investigation. Getzels and Dillon (1973) quote Gold as saying, "Grouping apparently is a helpful but not automatically effective instructional adjustment; achievement seems to improve only when grouping is accompanied by a differentiation in teacher quality, curriculum, guidance and method" (p. 716).

As the "Palcuzzi Ploy" illustrates (see page 165),

American schools support ability grouping in athletics, but they are not very positive toward ability grouping in academics. Legal action in the 1960s and 1970s tended to eliminate special "tracking" or ability grouping on the grounds that it is a discriminatory practice. The feeling of many Americans seems to be that equality should be the overriding concern in public education. But, as Gallagher and Weiss (1979, p. 2) noted, "society's notion of 'equality' tends to be destructive of giftedness in elementary and secondary school." It seems likely that public schools will maintain an emphasis on integration and heterogeneous grouping— for the retarded *and* the gifted. The practice of ability grouping will be found most often in private schools where the government policy of equality is not an issue.

Enrichment

Referring to some adaptation of the regular educational program, enrichment usually implies that the gifted are not to be separated from their normal peers. Enrichment is of two kinds: horizontal and vertical. *Horizontal enrichment* refers to providing *more* educational experiences at the same level of difficulty, while *vertical enrichment* refers to providing higher-level activities of increasing complexity. Although the majority of gifted students receiving special services are involved in enrichment-type programs, there is little evidence to support their efficacy.

Renzulli (1977) observes that a lot of activity that passes as enrichment (especially the horizontal kind) is actually a waste of gifted children's time. He has proposed a three-stage model for enrichment activities. Two levels of enrichment—general exploratory activities and group exercises to increase creativity, affective awareness, and problem solving skills—are appropriate for *all* children, including the gifted. But a third type—individual and small group investigations of real-life problems—is particularly suited for the gifted. In this kind of enrichment, the child actually carries out an experiment or project as a chemist, politician, writer, meteorologist or what have you. The child *becomes* a professional or artisan, working like an adult counterpart and producing valuable information or creating a valuable product.

Perhaps children are gifted sometimes (not necessarily always) or in some specific areas (not in others). This idea has led Renzulli, Reis, and Smith (1981) to propose a "revolving door" plan for enrichment. This plan means children will be phased in and out of the special third level of enrichment—the real-life investigations or projects—as they demonstrate their ability and interest by producing something valuable. If and when a "gifted" child hasn't the motivation, creativity, or intelligence to pursue a particular project at this level, then he or she returns to regular class activities and another child who does have the necessary characteristics for the project is included in the special enrichment.

Acceleration

By this means the student is moved through the traditional program at a faster rate or begins schooling earlier. Gifted children may enter school early, skip grades, go to summer school, earn college credit in high school, and the like. Research seems clearly to support acceleration, but programs of this type meet with criticism and disfavor.

> Apparently the cultural values favoring a standard period of dependency and formal education are stronger than the social or individual need for achievement and independence. This is an instance of the more general case one remarks throughout education: when research findings clash with cultural values, the values are more likely to prevail. (Getzels & Dillon, 1973, p. 717)

Both at the preschool level (Robinson, Roedell, & Jackson, 1979) and the high school level (Keating, 1979; Stanley, 1979), researchers have found that *gifted children's learning is quantitatively, not qualitatively different* from that of normal children. In other words, they learn just like children who are older; they work faster and at a more advanced level. It is not surprising, then, that acceleration typically proves to be an effective plan. What is surprising is that our schools hold such a strong bias against this economical, effective way of dealing with intellectual difference.

Although administrative arrangements for handling any student—handicapped, normal, or gifted—assist or interfere with instruction, the major educational concerns focus on what goes on in the classroom. No administrative manipulation of environmental variables can *assure* learning. This is not to minimize the importance of administrative approaches, but it is commonly recognized that although appropriate facilities, materials, and wholesome environmental conditions are necessary, these important facets are no substitute for a conscientious, sensitive, skillful, and competent teacher.

CONCLUSIONS

Gifted students are very bright, yet they too need attention and selected stimulation, and their learning and thinking can most certainly be inhibited or suppressed. If we are to do what we say *should* be done, that is, develop each individual to his or her optimum or maximum potential, then we must take another look at our educational services for the gifted.

Not only is differential instruction important to gifted individuals themselves, it may very well be important to society. We are living in a world that grows more complex every day. War, crime, drugs, alcoholism, overpopulation, and pollution are problems that threaten our very survival. How may these problems be resolved now and in the future? It just may be that we will have to turn to today's gifted students and hope they will come up with some answers.

In the 1950s, during the era of Sputnik, the nation turned to the gifted for solutions to problems in the physical sciences (i.e., space exploration). The public at that time supported differential educational programs for the gifted, especially those programs relating to science. Unfortunately, the programs were short-lived, as the United States quickly caught up in the space race. At present, it is the social sciences that need a booster shot. We should now begin to train and entice our gifted individuals into the area of social science exploration.

Maslow's (1971) analogy of how tall our species can grow and how fast we can run brings the value and importance of the gifted into meaningful perspective.

> If we want to answer the question how tall can the human species grow, then obviously it is well to pick out the ones who are already tallest and study them. If we want to know how fast a human being can run, then it is no use to average out the speed of a "good sample" of the population, it is far better to collect Olympic gold-medal winners and see how well they can do. If we want to know the possiblities for spiritual growth, value

growth, or moral development in human beings, then I maintain that we can learn most by studying our most moral, ethical, or saintly people.

On the whole I think it is fair to say that human history is a record of the ways in which human nature has been sold short. The highest possibilities of human nature have practically always been underrated. Even when "good specimens," the saints and sages and great leaders of history, have been available for study, the temptation too often has been to consider them not human but supernaturally endowed.[1]

As we begin to think about the gifted as a human resource to solve society's problems, we must be aware that we have no right to harness their intellectual talents at the cost of their basic freedoms. Getzels (1957) reminds us that there comes a time when we must look at the gifted as people and not be compelled to figure out how we can get the most out of them. Hopefully, if they are properly treated in our educational settings, gifted persons will find gratification as well as intriguing challenges in all learning.

SUGGESTIONS FOR WORKING WITH PERSONS WHO ARE GIFTED

1. In helping an underachieving child become motivated, present ideas and tasks in terms of the needs and interests of the child.

2. Help children set realistic goals.

3. Give children choices of learning goals and activities. Choices give the child an opportunity to develop self-esteem and a sense of competency.

4. Do not expect perfection. Gifted children need to know that mistakes are a natural part of growing and learning.

5. Provide extra activities and experiences for the gifted, but be thoughtful about scheduling. Be sure the gifted child does not become overscheduled.

---

[1]From Maslow, A., *The Farther Reaches of Human Nature*, Copyright © 1971 by Bertha G. Maslow, p. 7. Reprinted by permission of The Viking Press, Inc., New York.

6. Be sure the gifted child and the other children in his class or neighborhood understand that he is more like them than different. Like everyone else, the gifted child sometimes has feelings of fear and inadequacy, a huge need for love and acceptance, and desire to play and have fun.

7. Be sure that educational experiences challenge the child and awaken his interest in learning. Watch for signs of boredom. Gifted children need schools to be exciting, not places where they must sit through long hours of learning activities below their level.

8. Provide opportunities for creative problem solving.

9. Avoid comparisons of the gifted child with other children, particularly siblings.

10. Help the gifted child develop a respectful attitude toward the feelings, skills, and abilities of his nongifted peers.

11. Help the gifted child develop leadership skills.

12. Appreciate the gifted child simply for being a fine human being. Communicate that you like the child, not just because of his or her superior ability, but because he or she is just a good person and a delight to spend time with.

PONDER THESE

By what criteria could the following individuals be judged to be gifted?

Thomas Jefferson	Itzhak Perlman
Jesse Jackson	Beverly Sills
Will Rogers	Madonna
Ralph Sampson	Ann Landers
Ronald Reagan	Adolf Hitler

Is it possible to become nationally known—a household word—without being gifted?

Read some accounts, factual or fictional, of giftedness (for example, *The Child Buyer* by Lewis Hersey or *Mental Prodigies* by Fred Barlow). How would you handle the child described in a regular public school class?

Plan a hypothetical educational program to *make* children gifted. Would the opposite of your program *make* children retarded?

REFERENCES

Baer, D. M., Rowbury, T. G., & Goetz, E. M. (1976). Behavorial traps in the preschool: A proposal for research. In A. D. Pick (Ed.), *Minnesota Symposia on Child Psychology* (Vol. 10, pp. 3–27), Minneapolis: University of Minnesota.

Barlow, F. (1952). *Mental prodigies.* New York: Greenwood.

Bringham, T. A., Graubard, P. S., & Stans, A. (1972). Analysis of effects of sequential reinforcement contigencies on aspects of composition. *Journal of Applied Behavior Analysis, 5,* 421–427.

Burks, B., Jensen, D., & Terman, L. M. (1930). The promise of youth. *Genetic studies of genius* (Vol. 3). Palo Alto, CA: Stanford University.

Callahan, C. M. Superior abilities (1981). In J. M. Kauffman & D. P. Hallahan (Eds.), *Handbook of special education* (pp. 49–86). Englewood Cliffs, NJ: Prentice-Hall.

Clark, R. W (1971). *Einstein: The life and times.* New York: World.

Congressional Record. (1978, October 10), H–12179.

Cox, C. M. (1926). The early mental traits of 300 geniuses. *Genetic studies of genius* (Vol. 2). Palo Alto, CA: Stanford University.

Doman, G. (1984). *How to multiply your baby's intelligence.* New York: Doubleday.

Elkind, D. (1981). *The hurried child.* Reading, MA: Addison-Wesley.

Fox, L. H. (1981). Identification of the academically gifted. *American Psychologist, 36,* 1101–1111.

Gallagher, J. J. (1975). *Teaching the gifted child* (2nd ed.). Boston: Allyn & Bacon.

Gallagher, J. J. (1979). Issues in education for the gifted. In A. H. Passow (Ed.), *The 78th yearbook of the National Society for the Study of Education, Part I: The gifted and talented: Their education and development* (pp. 28–44). Chicago: University of Chicago.

Gallagher, J. J., & Weiss, P. (1979). *The education of gifted and talented students. A history and prospectus.* Washington, DC: Council for Basic Education.

Galton, F. (1969). *Hereditary genius: An inquiry into its laws and consequences.* London: Macmillan.

Getzels, J. W. (1957). Social values and individual motives: The dilemma of the gifted. *School Review, 65,* 60–63.

Getzels, J. W., & Dillon, J. T. (1973). The nature of giftedness and the education of the gifted. In R. M. W. Travers (Ed.), *Second handbook of research on teaching.* Chicago: Rand McNally.

Getzels, J. W., & Jackson, P. W. (1962). *Creativity and intelligence: Explorations with gifted students.* New York: Wiley.

Glover, J., & Gary, A. L. (1976). Procedures to increase some aspects of creativity. *Journal of Applied Behavior Analysis, 9,* 79–84.

Goetz, E. M., & Salmonson, M. M. (1972). The effect of general and descriptive reinforcement on "creativity" in easel painting. In G. Semb (Ed.), *Behavioral analysis in education—1972.* Lawrence: University of Kansas Department of Human Development.

Hollingworth, L.S. (1942). *Children above 180 IQ, Stanford-Binet: Origin and development.* Yonkers-on-Hudson, NY: World Book.

Jensen, A.R. (1966). Verbal mediation and educational potential. *Psychology in the Schools, 3,* 99–109.

Jensen, A.R. (1969). How much can we boost IQ and scholastic achievement? *Harvard Educational Review, 39,* 1–119.

Keating, D.P. (1979). Secondary school programs. In A.H. Passow (Ed.), *The 78th yearbook of the National Society for the Study of Education, Part I: The gifted and talented* (pp. 186–198). Chicago: University of Chicago.

Kirk, S.A. (1972). *Educating exceptional children* (Rev. ed.). Boston: Houghton Mifflin.

Lindsley, O.R. (1971). Precision teaching in perspective: An interview with Ogden R. Lindsley. *Teaching Exceptional Children, 31,* 114–119.

Marker, C.J. (1977). *Providing programs for the gifted handicapped.* Reston, VA: Council for Exceptional Children.

Martinson, R.A. (1973). Children with superior cognitive abilities. In L.M. Dunn (Ed.), *Exceptional children in the schools* (2nd ed., pp. 191–241). New York: Holt, Rinehart & Winston.

Maslow, A.H. (1971). *The farther reaches of human nature.* New York: Viking.

Renzulli, J.S. (1977) *The enrichment triad model: A guide for developing defensible programs for the gifted and talented.* Wethersfield, CN: Creative Learning.

Renzulli, J.S. (1978). What makes giftedness? Re-examining a definition. *Phi Delta Kappan, 60,* 180–184, 261.

Renzulli, J.S., Reis, S.M., & Smith, L.H. (1981). *The revolving door identification model.* Mansfield Center, CN: Creative Learning.

Robinson, H.B., Roedell, W.C., & Hackson, N.E. (1979). Early identification and intervention. In A.H. Passow (Ed.), *The 78th yearbook of the National Society for the Study of Education, Part I: The gifted and talented* (pp. 138–154). Chicago: University of Chicago.

Schweinhart, L.J., & Weikart, D.P. (1985). Evidence that good early childhood programs work. *Phi Delta Kappan, 66,* 545–551.

Sisk, D.A. (1981). Educational planning for the gifted and talented. In J.M. Kauffman & D.P. Hallahan (Eds.), *Handbook of special education* (pp. 441–458). Englewood Cliffs, NJ: Prentice-Hall.

Stanley, J.C. (1979). The study and facilitation of talent for mathematics. In A.H. Passow (Ed.), *The 78th yearbook of the National Society for the Study of Education, Part I: The gifted and talented* (pp. 169–185). Chicago: University of Chicago.

Terman, L.M. (1925). Mental and physical traits of a thousand gifted children. *Genetic studies of genius* (Vol. 1). Palo Alto, CA: Stanford University.

Terman, L.M., & Oden, M.H. (1947). The gifted child grows up. *Genetic studies of genius* (Vol. 4). Palo Alto, CA: Stanford University.

Terman, L.M., & Oden, M.H. (1959). The gifted group at mid-life. *Genetic studies of genius* (Vol. 5). Palo Alto, CA: Stanford University.

Torrance, E.P. (1965). *Rewarding creative behavior: Experiments in classroom creativity.* Englewood Cliffs, NJ: Prentice-Hall.

Torrance, E.P. (1971). Psychology of gifted children and youth. In W.M. Cruickshank (Ed.), *Psychology of exceptional children and youth* (3rd ed., pp. 528–564). Englewood Cliffs, NJ: Prentice-Hall.

U.S. Senate Report of the Gifted and Talented Subcommittee on Labor and Public Welfare. (1972, March). Washington, DC: U.S. Government Printing Office.

Ward, V.S. (Ed.). (1962). *The gifted student: A manual for program improvement.* Charlottesville, VA: Southern Regional Educational Board.

Webb, J.T., Meckstroth, E.A., & Tolan, S.S. (1982). *Guiding the gifted child.* Columbus, OH: Ohio Psychology Publishing.

Wolf, J.S., & Stephens, T.M. (1986). Gifted and talented. In N.G. Haring & L.P. McCormick (Eds.), *Exceptional children and youth* (4th ed., pp. 431–473). Columbus, OH: Merrill.

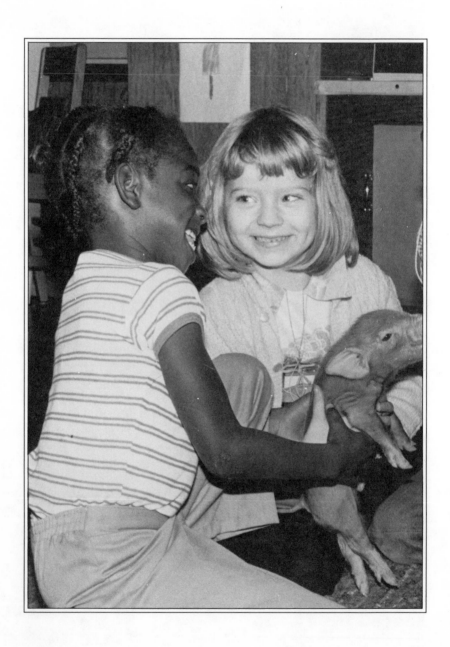

11
Cultural Diversity

What may be functional behavior in one context may be disfunctional in another as the following example illustrates: *A kindergarten teacher shared a recent experience about a child who, she said, refused to talk to her for months except during the times when she asked her direct questions, or singled her out for a response. The child, at these times, would answer briefly and to the point. Further inquiry revealed that the child did not have a language problem and was observed to be friendly and normally sociable with her peers. One day, toward the end of the school year, this child suddenly began to initiate verbal contacts with the teacher and spoke in class like the rest of her highly verbal peers. The teacher was relieved and concluded that the child had a "head on her shoulders." An implication seems to be that one who does not speak is incapable of thought. To this teacher, thinking was synonymous with speaking. What to say, when to speak, who [sic] to talk to are culture-related behaviors. In this teacher's culture, it is obvious that talk is valued.*[1]

---

[1]*Note.* From "Beyond the language needs of children from minority cultures" by V. Chattergy, 1983, *Educational Perspectives*, 22(2), pp. 26–28.

It is not by design that culturally different children are discriminated against in our schools. But observe how our well-intentioned educational system subliminally chips aways at that which is not the Ango-American norm. Take, for example, something as innocuous as a lesson in nutrition taught by a competent, experienced first-grade teacher. Through many years of teaching, she has perfected this lesson—one of her favorites. Moreover, she is armed with the most modern visual aids on the market. And so she begins: "Children, today we are going to study diet. Our diet is made up of those things that we eat to build strong, healthy bodies." And with a rubber-tipped pointer she taps the flip chart and says, "For example, a good breakfast consists of orange juice for vitamin C." Then she flips to the next chart and points to a large bowl of whole grain cereals and a loaf of bread and says, "Whole grain cereal for vitamin B. Toast, preferably whole wheat, children." She flips that chart and concludes with, "Sausage, bacon, or eggs for additional protein." No problem. That's not a bad breakfast. But [one] first grader is sitting in that [class] and he's had papas fritas con chile verde, una tasa de cafe con leche, y una tortilla. You know what he says to himself? He says, "I understand. Those are the kind of things I should eat. Those are the right things to eat. What I've been eating must not be too good." And the next time he comes to school with a sack lunch filled with things he normally eats, he goes beneath the bleachers or behind the building to eat them in private so that his friends or the teacher won't perceive him as someone who does not eat the right things.[2]

For a significant number of exceptional children, school becomes the vehicle that differentiates them from "normal" students. Many students who are identified as mentally retarded, learning disabled, or emotionally disturbed are not so identified until they enter school. For these students, *school* seems to become the culprit. The academic and behavioral demands they encounter are major impediments to success.

For another segment of the school-age population, school also

[2]Taken, with minor adaptations, from "Cultural Conflict and Cultural Diversity in Education," by J. Aragon. In *Cultural Diversity and the Exceptional Child* (p. 27) L. A. Bransford, L. Baca, and K. Lane (Eds.), 1974, Reston VA: The Council for Exceptional Children.

is a major obstacle. However, these students may not lack the requisite academic and behavioral skills for appropriate achievement. Rather, they happen to have been raised in families whose cultural heritage differs from that of the majority of their peers. This fact can have a dramatic impact on a student's schooling.

Interestingly, some students can be included in both of the groups mentioned above. They can have academic or behavioral difficulties along with being culturally different. In effect, these students possess a dual handicap: their recognized disability and their cultural divergence from their peers (Chinn & Kamp, 1982; Fair & Sullivan, 1980). Moreover, because the families from which many of these students come are poor, it has also been suggested that these students actually might be in triple jeopardy due to their handicap, their ethnicity, and their low socioeconomic status (Baca & Chinn, 1982).

INTRODUCTION

The purpose of this chapter is twofold: *(a)* to discuss the nature of cultural diversity and *(b)* to examine the complexities of exceptionality in relation to cultural differences. Although this area of public and professional interest has been receiving much attention within the last few years, there is an appreciable lack of programming and research. For this reason, the "state of the art" on providing appropriate services for culturally different handicapped students is only beginning to be formulated. Unquestionably, many issues must be addressed before substantial progress can be made.

There are three guiding principles from which efforts to educate cuturally different exceptional students have emerged. These principles are desegregation, equal educational opportunity, and appropriate education. The first of these, desegregation, initially surfaced in the 1954 Supreme Court decision in *Brown v. Topeka Board of Education.* Segregated education for certain students was declared unconstitutional. The second principle, equal educational opportunity (related in many ways to desegregation), was firmly established n 1974 in a landmark case involving Chinese-speaking students in California (*Lau v. Nichols*). The Supreme Court unanimously decided that these students whose primary language was not English were being denied a meaningful education in a system where instruction was presented solely in the language of the majority. The third factor, an appropriate education, was mandated upon the enactment of the Education for All Handicapped Children Act of 1975 (PL 94–142). This federal legislation guaranteed that all handicapped students are entitled to an education tailored to their particular needs and abilities. Furthermore, this law safeguards the rights of both students and parents.

These forces notwithstanding, the nature of cultural diversity in relation to exceptionality is not as clear or straightforward as we would like. As a matter of fact, there are a number of problems. Consequently, it is well worth looking more closely at these problems surrounding this issue. For, if we can understand the problems, perhaps we can do something about them.

THE NATURE OF CULTURAL DIVERSITY

The United States is a nation that prides itself upon the fact that the many people who first came to this country were from a variety of ethnic backgrounds, were able to live in relative harmony, and collectively were able to build a strong, democratic society. Over the years, the ethnicity of these people was subsumed to a great extent; everyone was an American. Nevertheless, while we do not today think of people of Italian heritage as an ethnic minority, we do think of other groups, such as American Indians, Asian Americans, Blacks, and Hispanics, in this way. Very recently, we have also witnessed the immigration of other people such as Southeast Asians, Haitians, and Cubans.

What makes these people different? Basically it stems from culture. Hilliard (1980) provided a succinct yet acceptable conceptualization of culture. "*Culture* means the distinctive creativity of a particular group of people. *Creativity* includes world view, values, style, and above all language" (p. 585). Therefore, it follows that the variables of culture cited by Hilliard will differ, and at times significantly, across ethnic groups. Unfortunately, customs and social values can set individuals apart from the majority in negatively-perceived ways.

Cultural diversity, at one level of analysis, is a desirable feature of life in that it exposes us to different people and customs. However, when cultural differences are great and they are set in the context of formal schooling, significant problems often arise. Aragon (1974) referred to this situation as "cultural conflict." The major discrepancy is between the culture of various minority groups and the Anglo culture upon which the public school system is based and implemented throughout the country. Although discussing IQ testing, Gonzalez (1974) used a term that is quite apropos for referring to the fact that our schools are oriented in a non-ethnic direction—in other words, *anglocentric.*

An example of how cultural values can differ across various groups is presented below. Selected items related to how "an individual" is viewed from three cultural perspectives are presented (Project HO'OKOHO, n.d.)

Polynesian *Native American*	*Asian*	*Western*
1. individual valued as part of family	1. individual valued as part of family	1. individual held as supreme value
2. self-control, humility	2. self-control, humility	2. self-expression, pride
3. submit to family system	3. submit to family rule	3. negotiates within family
4. spiritual harmony	4. spiritual harmony	4. spiritual duality
5. reverence/respect for life	5. partnership with nature	5. master nature
6. cooperation, mutual help	6. cooperation, mutual help	6. competition, self-reliance
7. loyalty, obedience, shared responsibility	7. obedience, duty, honor	7. self-pride, honor, duty
8. do what is necessary, play more	8. hard work, little play	8. work hard, then play

The fundamental cause of cultural conflict comes from trying to achieve a "cultural fit." As the first vignette demonstrated, we often attempt to fit culturally diverse students into a system that is frequently at odds with the way they are, the way they think, and the way they behave. If we truly adhere to the ideal that students' individuality must be taken into consideration when programming for their educational needs, then it is hypocritical to ignore their cultural heritage.

At this point, it is important to clarify the fact that just being culturally different does not automatically make one eligible for special education. As mentioned before, it is certainly possible for minority students to have disabilities as well. The perplexing dilemma is distinguishing culturally diverse students with linguistic differences (i.e., non-English proficient [NEP]; limited-English proficient [LEP]) from students who have true language disabilities.

MAJOR ISSUES

Many issues are involved in educating exceptional students from culturally diverse backgrounds. Only a selected number of them will be addressed in this chapter, however. The major concerns to be discussed include *(a)* the disproportionate number of minority students who are in special classes, *(b)* the problems related to assessment of these students, and *(c)* the elements of appropriate education for these students.

Disproportionate numbers

There is strong documentation (Killalea Associates, 1980; Mercer, 1973) that minority students are overrepresented in special education classes. For example, Chinn and Kamp (1982), in reporting on data accumulated by the Office of Civil Rights, stated that "Blacks constituted 38 percent of the EMR (educable mentally retarded) students, which is over twice the percentage found in the general population (16 percent)" (p. 372). In Hawaii, it is interesting to note that, while 20.4% of the public school population is Hawaiian or part Hawaiian, this group comprises 31.8% of the special education population (Native Hawaiian Assessment Project, 1983).

Dunn (1968) suggested that special education classes contained disproportionate numbers of ethnically different children. However, it was during the early 1970s that concern regarding this disrepresentation reached the point whereby a number of lawsuits were filed.

Quite notable among the court cases were *Larry P. v. Riles* and *Diana v. the State of California. Larry P.* was a class action suite filed in federal district court in California on behalf of black students who were allegedly placed inappropriately into classes for mentally retarded students. The case was decided in favor of the plaintiffs and upheld twice upon appeal. A major factor in this case was the use of discriminatory testing practices that were used to place these black students. *Diana,* a case also filed in federal district court in California, involved virtually the same issues; however, this time the plaintiffs were Hispanic. This case, although settled out of court, resulted in acknowledgment that Hispanic students had been misplaced and in the setting of guidelines for the future assessment and placement of other minority students (MacMillan, 1982).

As can be detected, a primary culprit in the misplacement of minority students seems to be the methods by which we determine eligibility for special education. Furthermore, as illustrated by the arguments in *Lau v. Nichols,* a very limited range of appropriate and cost-effective options seems to be available to school systems for educating minority students. Even though special education is conceptually based on the principle that teaching methodology and materials are geared to the individual needs of students who differ from their school-age counterparts, it is not the best setting for students who are not disabled but rather culturally different. Special education *may be* appropriate for those culturally different students who also have disabilities; we will discuss this issue further in the conclusion of this chapter.

Assessment

Criticism has long been levied at the nature and practices of assessing culturally different students. Attention has primarily focused on the issue of bias. More specifically, bias has been attached to various standardized tests themselves as well as to the process in which these tests are used. Among the many problems found with most of the tests used for making educational decisions are:

> Test information and questioning techniques that are related to the majority culture (Nazarro, 1979)

> Tests that demand linguistic styles that are similar to the majority culture (Bailey and Harbin, 1980)

> Norms that are obtained from standardization samples which are mostly white and middle class (Bailey and Harbin, 1980)

Other problems, more specifically related to student performance variables, have also been cited:

> Reluctance to participate in such a way as to maximize performance (Nazarro, 1979)

> Cognitive styles of minority students that differ from the majority culture (Chinn and Kamp, 1982)

Cummins (1984) has highlighted some other problems associated with the assessment process. First, psychologists and teachers do not seem to be sensitive to the limitations of formal tests typically used with minority language children. Second, there is a distinction between *surface language* involved with basic communication and *language proficiency* needed to deal successfully with various cognitive/academic tasks. This distinction is particularly important when examining the skill levels of students whose primary language (L_1) is not English (L_2):

> The fact that immigrant students require, on the average, 5–7 years to approach grade norms in L_2 academic skills, yet show peer-appropriate L_2 conversational skills within about two years of arrival, suggests that conversational and academic aspects of language proficiency need to be distinguished. (Cummins, 1984, p. 149)

The implication of this second point is that formal measures (e.g., Verbal scale of the Weschler Intelligence Scale for Children–Revised) given to NEP/LEP students may be inappropriate. Langdon (1983) has suggested that it may be unwise to subject students who have been in this country less than a year to the typical test batteries, unless there are indications the student has definite language problems.

It may be well worth taking a closer look at examples of test items that are very much culturally determined. Gouveia (n.d.) has developed an instrument entitled *The Hana-Butta Test.* He based this device on the Hawaiian plantation culture. A few examples from the Hana-Butta test illustrate the nature of a culturally specific, or biased, test:

A "puka" is a _____ .
   a. fish
   b. star
   c. curve
   d. hole
   e. vine

A woman who is "hapai" is _____ .
   a. available
   b. married
   c. pregnant
   d. sexy
   e. a mother

"Hana-butta" is known statewide as _____ .
   a. high-fat butter made in Hana
   b. margarine from the Hana Dairy
   c. a famous peanut butter shake from Tutu's Snack Bar, Hana
   d. mucus running from the nose of a person with a bad cold
   e. a peanut butter sandwich

If you answered the above questions by choosing letters *d, c,* and *d* respectively, you are correct. However, chances are that unless you have lived in Hawaii or you have visited Hawaii and spent considerable time outside of Waikiki, you did not know the answers. It is obvious that cultural background can be very important for successfully answering culturally specific questions. For many culturally different students, taking tests that have been based on white, middle-class experiences and values may prove just as difficult. Furthermore, poor performance may lead to placement into special education programs, even though culture and not disability is the determining factor.

Suggestions have been offered to minimize the negative effects of bias inherent in traditional assessment practices. Chinn (1980) presented five ways in which the assessment of culturally different students can be improved:

1. Use of culture-free tests
2. Development of tests that are specific to one culture and thereby deemed as fair
3. Use of culture-fair tests (usually designed to minimize linguistic requirements)
4. Modification of existing tests in order to create new norms and change the test sample
5. Differential weighing of verbal and nonverbal portions of the present intelligence and achievement tests. (p. 54)

Additional recommendations include:

1. Obtaining pertinent school record information and information from parents/guardians (Langdon, 1983);
2. Collecting data over longer periods of time—"longitudinal monitoring" (Cummins, 1984);

3. Delaying assessment practices until students have had a chance to become language proficient.

One instrument that has been developed with cultural differences in mind is the *System of Multicultural Pluralistic Assessment* (SOMPA) (see Chinn and Kamp, 1982; or Mercer and Lewis, 1977). Cummins (1984) has stated that instruments such as the *Kaufman Assessment Battery for Children* (Kaufman & Kaufman, 1983) and the *Learning Potential Assessment Device* (Feuerstein, 1979) may be more appropriate for use with culturally different students than the Weschler devices if in the hands of knowledgeable examiners.

The problems of bias in assessment are not only specific to the tests used and student characteristics. There is more to assessment than testing. Bailey and Harbin (1980) have suggested that bias can be found in other stages of the diagnostic and placement process:

> Decision making is a step-by-step process. For example, the steps in the diagnostic and placement process typically include *(a)* referral, *(b)* testing, *(c)* interpretation of results, *(d)* determination of eligibility, *(e)* recommendation for placement, and *(f)* actual placement. While much criticism has been aimed at the testing component of this process, each step has the potential for bias against certain individuals or groups of children. (p. 594)

Assuming that we can adequately identify and effectively place culturally diverse disabled students, we are now faced with the task of providing them with an appropriate education. As will be seen, this is not an easy objective to accomplish.

Appropriate education

"It should be clear that cultural diversity requires no unusual special education" (Hilliard, 1980, p. 587). This statement is both true and false depending on the level of analysis. On a very general level, it can be argued that special education for minority students involves the same type of individualized programming to which all disabled students are entitled. On a more specific level, however, it becomes evident that in order to address the needs of some minority students it may be necessary to undertake some major changes.

One type of programming alternative beginning to be initiated in some school districts is *bilingual special education.* Baca and Chinn (1982) have defined this approach as the "use of the home language and the home culture along with English in the individually designed program of special education for the student" (p. 42). Two types of bilingual programs include transitional and maintenance programs (ERIC, n.d.) and characterize variant philosophies. *Transitional programs* are designed with the primary goal of making linguistically different students competent in the use of English. *Maintenance programs* strive to develop competence in both languages (L_1 and L_2) and in both cultural environments. Although the maintenance type of program is attractive to many bilingual educators, the transitional is the most commonly found program. Relatively few maintenance-type bilingual classes exist because few people who are professionally qualified as special education teachers are also bilingual. Moreover, some professionals who support a philosophy of cultural assimilation oppose bilingual education.

A program often confused with bilingual education is English as a Second Language (ESL) (Baca & Cervantes, 1984). The principal focus of ESL programs is to develop English proficiency, only one of the goals of bilingual education. As was pointed out earlier, bilingual education also attempts to develop students' native language and culture.

If the ultimate question is appropriate education and if it is to be provided to culturally different students (whether disabled or not), the following areas must be further examined and addressed. *Teaching techniques* should be identified and implemented that take into account a student's linguistic background, cognitive and learning styles, and other learning-related characteristics. *Curriculum modifications* are necessary in order to acknowledge what Aragon (1974) called "the life style and heritage of all our students" (p. 28). Most of the curricular materials used in our schools still reflect a rather Anglocentric perspective. Along this line of thought, Almanza and Mosley (1980) have referred to traditional curriculum as having "a monolithic orientation relative to race, ethnicity, and culture" (p. 608). It seems warranted that instructional materials should be sensitive to cultural differences and encompass a wide range of cultural values and heritages. Moreover, classroom practices and methodology should be "compatible with the culture of the client population in ways that contribute to effective education"

(Jordan, 1981, p. 16). The majority culture has traditionally found its values and heritage reflected in teaching materials; why should it not be so for minority cultures as well? For without cultural relevancy in school subjects:

> . . .the culturally different student who comes through our school system is bewildered and frustrated. By the time he finishes, he doesn't know what has "truth, beauty, or value"—whether it's those things he's learned in school or those things he's learned and practiced at home. (Aragon, 1974, p. 29)

As educators, our goal must be to prepare competent citizens who demonstrate purpose and possess self-worth.

Teacher competencies

A corollary to this topic of appropriate education is the need for appropriately prepared teachers. Jones (1976) has reported that teacher attitudes and expectations toward minority students are negative in many instances. If this is indeed a trend, then it may be prudent to provide preservice and inservice teachers with accurate information on and techniques for working with various cultural groups. Suitable models for incorporating multicultural concepts into teacher training programs in special education have been developed (see Rodriguez, 1982).

CONCLUSIONS

Earlier in this chapter, a statement was made that indicated that special education *may be* appropriate for students who are culturally different *and* disabled. The uncertainty of the "may be" stems from a number of *ifs:*

> *If* we can effectively identify culturally diverse students who are disabled
>
> *If* we can develop appropriate placements, suitable techniques, relevant materials, and individualized programs for teaching these students
>
> *If* we can adequately prepare competent professionals
>
> *Then* and only then we will be able to provide an education that is *appropriate* and *special.*

Although progress is being made, it still remains "easier to identify the problems of educating culturally diverse exceptional children than it is to solve the problems" (Baca & Chinn, 1982, p. 41).

SUGGESTIONS FOR WORKING WITH PERSONS WHO ARE CULTURALLY DIFFERENT

The following suggestions were originally developed by Bessant-Byrd (1981, pp. 94–103) with teachers in mind. They are relevant for others as well.

1. Knowledge of the role of a value system and ability to evaluate its influence on behavior
2. Knowledge of the philosophy of various cultures and an interest in expanding that knowledge
3. Use of relevant information and materials characteristic of both traditional and contemporary lifestyles of various cultures
4. Understanding of different patterns of human growth and development within and between cultures
5. Recognition of potential cultural and linguistic biases in the composition, administration, and interpretation of existing assessment instruments
6. The ability to provide a flexible learning environment which meets individual needs of learners from various culture groups

PONDER THESE

The *Peabody Individual Achievement Test* (PIAT) assesses general achievement; one subtest in this instrument is entitled "General Information." One of the test items asks, "What do we call the last car on a freight train?" Children from which of the following groups would be unable to answer this question—a failure more related to their cultural upbringing than to a lack of achievement?

Southeast Asians
Haitians

Hawaiians

Native Americans

List some of the problems and possible solutions for identifying gifted students who come from culturally different
groups.

How are students from culturally diverse groups affected
when the educational curriculum differs from their
knowledge of their own cultural heritage? For example,
how might a Hawaiian or a Native American child react
when told that *Christopher Columbus* discovered their
country?

REFERENCES

Almanza, H. P., & Mosley, W. J. (1980). Curriculum adaptations and modifications for culturally diverse handicapped children. *Exceptional Children, 46,* 608–613.

Aragon, J. Cultural conflict and cultural diversity in education. In L. A. Bransford, L. Baca, & K. Lane (Eds.), *Cultural diversity and the exceptional child,* (pp. 24–31). Reston, VA: The Council for Exceptional Children, 1974.

Baca, L. M., & Cervantes, H. T. (1984). *The bilingual special education interface.* St. Louis: Times Mirror/Mosby.

Baca, L., & Chinn, P. C. (1982). Coming to grips with cultural diversity. *Exceptional Education Quarterly, 2*(4), 33–45.

Bailey, D. B., & Harbin, G. L. (1980). Nondiscriminatory evaluation. *Exceptional Children, 46,* 590–596.

Bessant-Byrd, H. (1981). Competencies for educating culturally different exceptional children. In J. N. Nazzaro (Ed.), *Culturally diverse exceptional children in school.* Reston, VA.: ERIC Clearinghouse on Handicapped and Gifted Children.

Chinn, K. A. (1980). Assessment of culturally diverse children. *Viewpoints in Teaching and Learning, 56*(1), 50–63.

Chinn, P. C. & Kamp, S.H. (1982). Cultural diversity and exceptionality. In N. G. Haring (Ed.), *Exceptional children and youth* (3rd ed., pp. 371–390). Columbus, OH: Merrill.

Cummins, J. (1984). *Bilingualism and special education: Issues in assessment and pedagogy.* San Diego: College-Hill Press.

Dunn, L. M. (1968). Special education for the mildly retarded: Is much of it justifiable? *Exceptional Children, 35,* 5–22.

ERIC. (n.d.). *Bilingual education for exceptional children: Fact sheet.* Reston, VA: ERIC Clearinghouse on Handicapped and Gifted Children.

Fair, G. W., & Sullivan, A. R. (1980). Career opportunities for culturally diverse handicapped youth. *Exceptional Children, 46,* 626–631.

Feuerstein, R. (1979). *The dynamic assessment of retarded performance.* Baltimore: University Park.

Gonzalez, G. (1974). Language, culture, and exceptional children. In L. A. Bransford, L. Baca, & K. Lane (Eds.), *Cultural diversity and the exceptional child* (pp. 2–11). Reston, VA.: The Council for Exceptional Children.

Gouveia, W. (n.d.). *The Hana-Butta Test.* Maui, HI: Author.

Hillard, A. G. (1980). Cultural diversity and special education. *Exceptional Children, 46,* 584–588.

Jones, R. L., & Wilderson, F. B. (1976). Mainstreaming and the minority child: An overview of issues and a perspective. In R. L. Jones (Ed.), *Mainstreaming and the minority child* (pp. 1–13). Reston, VA.: Council for Exceptional Children.

Jordan, C. (1981). The selection of culturally-compatible classroom practices. *Educational Perspectives, 20*(1), 16–19.

Kaufman, A., & Kaufman, N. (1983). *Kaufman Assessment Battery for Children.* Circle Pines, MN: American Guidance Service.

Killalea Associates. (1980). *State, regional, and national summaries of data from the 1978 civil rights survey of elementary and secondary schools. Prepared for the U.S. Office of Civil Rights.* Alexandria, VA.: Killalea Associates.

Langdon, H. W. (1983). Assessment and intervention strategies for the bilingual language-disordered student. *Exceptional Children, 50,* 37–46.

MacMillan, D. L. (1982). *Mental retardation in school and society* (2nd ed.). Boston: Little, Brown.

Mercer J. R. (1973). *Labeling the mentally retarded.* Berkeley: University of California.

Mercer, J. R., & Lewis, J. F. (1977). *System of Multicultural Pluralistic Assessment: Technical manual.* New York: Psychological Corporation.

Native Hawaiian Assessment Project. (1983). *Final report.* Honolulu: Author.

Nazarro, J. (1979). *Assessment of minority students* (Fact Sheet). Reston, VA.: ERIC Clearinghouse on Handicapped and Gifted Children.

Project HO'OKOHO. (n.d.). *Bilingual special education* (Module No. 62a). Honolulu: Department of Special Education, University of Hawaii.

Rodriguez, F. (1982). Mainstreaming a multicultural concept into special education: Guidelines for teacher trainers. *Exceptional Children, 49,* 220–227.

FOUR
Exceptional Perspectives

12

Early Childhood

Darrell was the kind of preschooler every teacher dreads having in the class—a 4-year-old public nuisance. Unable (or unwilling) to follow the simplest directions, he could usually be found poking an innocent classmate or doing his best in any number of ways to disrupt my Head Start class. But Darrell was not incapable of showing affection. I cannot easily forget the day he interrupted his finger painting to "lovingly" hug me and run his paint-covered fingers through my hair. I thought I caught a devilish gleam in his eye when he released his grip, but I quickly dismissed it. Darrell had long been tagged mentally retarded, and his misbehavior, we all knew, was due to his mental disability. Thus, Darrell was forgiven for this and other equally trying acts in the classroom.

It was George Washington's birthday, and I stood the class in a circle and put on a favorite record, "Chopping Down the Cherry Tree." The record was ideal for gross-motor development. I instructed the children to swing their arms rhythmically to the "chop chop" of the music as if they were all little Georges chopping away at the proverbial cherry tree. The children loved it. Everyone swung his imaginary ax with the greatest enthusiasm—everyone of course except "dumb" Darrell who just stood there with his arms straight out in front of him, hands clasped together making a huge fist. Patiently, I attempted to teach Darrell the act of chopping. But even after much demonstrating and coaxing, he stubbornly refused to change his original position and continued to stand motionless with his "ax" extended. Close to the end of my patience, I cried, "Darrell, why won't you chop with your ax like the rest of us?"

The reply shocked me into reassessing Darrell's mentally retarded label: "I don't need to chop. Can't you see I have a power saw!"[1]

Richard was a blond, blue-eyed 6-year-old who had been living in a residential school for emotionally disturbed children for 3 years. On weekends he went home with his family. He was diagnosed as autistic and displayed many of the typical behaviors of children so labeled. Although he was quick to complain with high-pitched squeals, he never spoke and showed no emotion when people talked to him. He avoided eye contact with teachers, staff, or other children, preferring to isolate himself in a corner whenever he could. He liked to hold a toy truck upside down so that he could push its wheels and intently watch them spin. In the hope that some day Richard could learn to make letters and write his name, the staff had spent every school day reinforcing Richard for going to the table and making an approximation of a circle or a triangle, prerequisite skills for writing words. After so many days, weeks, and months of no improvement, the staff became discouraged and feared that Richard would never learn to make shapes, not to mention write his name. It was on one of these days that Richard left his corner, stepped up to the chalkboard, on which he had never written, and in perfect letters wrote, "PANTRY PRIDE." Never having written a letter before, he produced the name of the grocery store where his mother shopped. We were shocked and overjoyed, but our hearts sank when Richard returned to his corner and refused to produce another word. Yet Richard had stepped out of his usual behavior to show us his capacity for learning if only for a few minutes. We were then in a much better position to plan appropriate learning experiences.

---

[1]We are grateful to Ms. Roxana G. Davison for contributing this anecdote.

Placed in a strange environment, the one thing that pre-schoolers are not is predictable. Thus, I prepared myself for the worst when I took my Head Start class of 30 inner-city 4-year-olds to the famous Bronx Zoo. How could I expect them to be orderly and restrained? Flashing through my mind were fright-ful fantasies of Freddy taking a bath with the walruses or Lin-da slipping through the bars to pet the leopards. To my great surprise, the children were very well-behaved despite their ob-vious excitement at viewing the many wild animals that had previously only been magazine pictures. My major problem in controlling the children occurred quite unexpectedly as we rounded a corner and faced a large square of lush green grass bearing several "Keep off the grass" signs. After having sur-vived elephant pens and monkey cages, I was hardly concerned about a grassy plot of ground. I was, in fact, stunned when almost every child bolted from our orderly little procession and tumbled onto the grass screaming with delight. It took me several seconds to realize that these inner-city children were growing up playing on concrete sidewalks and black asphalt streets covered with broken glass. That simple plot of green grass gave them their greatest thrill of our entire zoo trip.

Craig was the precocious one of the group. I was continually in awe of his insight and his eagerness to solve the mysteries of his world. Of course, there were a few times when even Craig put two and two together and came up with five.

    Craig's mother, a divorcee, was dating an obstetrician. Like so many preschoolers, Craig kept his teachers and classmates well informed about his mother's personal life by frequently making announcements such as, "My mother dates a doctor named Phil, and he delivers real babies."

    One day as we were out for a drive, Craig shouted, "Oh, look! There's Dr. Phil's house!" Pointing to a van parked in front of the house, he said, "There's his truck too!"

    Since I was acquainted with Dr. Phil and knew that he owned no truck, I said gently, "No, Craig, that truck doesn't belong to Dr. Phil."

    Looking me squarely in the eyes, he impatiently retorted, "Well, I bet it is too his truck. He must have a truck because Mommy says he delivers babies!"

RATIONALE FOR EARLY CHILDHOOD EDUCATION

Early scholars such as Montessori, Froebel, and Hall first directed attention toward early childhood as important foundation years for learning. A widespread interest in early childhood education, however, did not develop until the 1960s when psychological research began to reveal that the early years are indeed most critical for a child's future development.

Research findings suggested that the rate of learning roughly parallels a child's physical growth. It appears that learning occurs quite rapidly in the first 2 years, slightly less rapidly for the next 4, and then begins to level off to a lower and gradually decreasing rate. In fact, Benjamin (1964) asserts that 50% of a child's total intellectual capacity has been developed by age 4, and 80% by age 8. Skeels's (1966) classic study of orphanage children dramatically demonstrated that modifying the environment during the early formative years can greatly improve a child's capacity for intellectual and social development at a later age.

More recently Schweinhart and Weikart (1985) reviewed seven longitudinal studies of the effects of early education on children living in poverty and found that every comparison of scholastic placement was favorable to the group that had received early childhood education. Moreover, avoiding later placement in special education programs emerged as one of the major financial benefits of preschool education.

Today a sound foundation during the early childhood years is considered essential for subsequent success in school. In fact, Burton White's (1975) research at Harvard University's Pre-School Project led him to conclude that the period that begins at 8 months and ends at 3 years is a period of primary importance to the development of human intelligence and social skill. White insists that "to begin to look at a child's educational development when he is 2 years of age is already much too late" (p. 4). The need for thoughtful and rich early stimulation is critical for all children, particularly for those children with physical, emotional, mental, or social handicaps (Hayden, 1979). McDaniels (1977) argues that we cannot wait until age 6, or even 3, to begin our interventions with young children. Programs for some young exceptional children should begin not long after birth.

Nagera (1975) warns that poorly conceived school-based centers for infants and toddlers may do more harm than good. During the 1970s educators learned that parents play a critical role in facilitating development. Today's educators recognize that well-conceived programs involve parents in the teaching of their young children (Anastasiow, 1981). In particular, home and center-based parent training can greatly change the young exceptional child's chances for developing to his full potential (Sandler, Coren, & Thurman, 1983; Shearer & Shearer, 1972; Sontag, 1977).

Recent legislative action, specifically Public Law 94–142, has mandated programs for all handicapped children between the ages of 3 and 21. As a result of this significant law, the area of early childhood education has moved into the spotlight of attention. The guarantees of this law assure parental participation, protection of rights, written notification of any placement changes, teacher training efforts, and incentive funding to the states. Efforts to locate and identify preschool-age handicapped children (commonly referred to as *child find*) must also be initiated. A U.S. Department of Education (1984) report to Congress argues that early intervention with handicapped children results in significant decreases in services required later. In those cases where early intervention eliminates or reduces the services otherwise needed when the child enters school, it results in notable cost savings.

A legal basis now exists for early childhood services to handicapped youngsters. Unfortunately, the present law does not go far enough in assuring services to all young exceptional children. In 1980, states were mandated under PL 94–142 to provide services to all handicapped students ages 3 to 21 but less than half of the states actually mandated services for the full 3-to-5 year range. Moreover, 21 of the states report no specific standards governing teachers of young handicapped children (O'Connell, 1983). Those at their most critical stage of development, from birth to 3 years, have yet to receive the assurance of a free appropriate public education (O'Connell, 1983). One thing is certain: special educators and parents will continue their civil rights struggle for the handicapped until appropriate educational support is available to all exceptional children and their parents from birth onward.

DEFINITION OF EARLY CHILDHOOD EDUCATION

Early childhood education was traditionally conceived of as the group learning experiences provided for children from the ages of 3 to 8. Thus, programs for early childhood education encompassed nursery schools, kindergartens, and primary grades. The growing realization, however, that infancy and toddlerhood are critical years for later social and intellectual development has largely accounted for the current notion that early childhood education embraces programs for all children under 9 years of age. Quite logically, a significant proportion of educational and psychological research is now focused on the infant and toddler years and on parental involvement.

Early childhood education relies on the continued execution of various important dimensions: *(a)* early identification, *(b)* continuous assessment, *(c)* appropriate curricula, *(d)* effective teaching procedures, *(e)* parental involvement, and *(f)* multidisciplinary interaction. The omission of any of these dimensions in any early childhood program is detrimental to the education of handicapped children. The curriculum for a young handicapped child's educational program is generally determined by the child's strengths and delays in seven areas of development: self-help skills, gross motor development, fine motor development, communication skills, perceptual development, conceptual development, and social-emotional development.

PREVALENCE OF YOUNG HANDICAPPED CHILDREN

Although exact incidence figures are unavailable, in 1976, the National Advisory Committee on the Handicapped reported that in the U.S. approximately 1,187,000 preschool children displayed physical, emotional, and mental handicaps. These figures include children from infancy to 5 years, yet only a few states provide services to those under 3 years old (Hayden, 1979).

Of those children identifiable as needing special services, many are multiply handicapped, having secondary deficits accompanying their major disability. Most of the young exceptional children do not fit neatly into the traditional special education categories. Many of the milder disabilities (e.g., mild retardation, learning disabilities) may not be evident until a child is of school age. Many of these children may be considered "at risk" for potential future school failure. They should be provided with services in various early intervention programs that do not specifically identify them as "handicapped."

Some states have designated special categorical distinctions for preschool age handicapped children. Terms such as *learning impaired* may be used with this population until these children reach school age. Then a reevaluation would be conducted and the children would be either declassified or reclassified. Unfortunately, some disabled infants and preschoolers are not receiving the educational experiences necessary to insure continued progress and later successful school adjustment.

ETIOLOGY

The causes of disabilities in young children can be divided into five major categories: *(a)* genetic, *(b)* prenatal, *(c)* perinatal, *(d)* postnatal, and *(e)* cultural. Although a child's difficulty often results from a complex interaction of two or more factors, most educators focus attention on remediation rather than search for causes. However, remediation can sometimes be facilitated when etiological, or causative, factors are understood.

Genetic difficulties include biochemical disorders, such as galactosemia and phenylketonuria (PKU), and such chromosomal abnormalities as Down syndrome. Today both PKU and galactosemia can be detected by urine tests, and, if found early enough, the harmful effects can be controlled by putting the infant on special diets. Some *prenatal* conditions frequently associated with childhood disabilities are *(a)* anoxia (i.e., premature separation of the placenta), severe anemia, or a heart condition of the mother; *(b)* Rh factor incompatibility; and *(c)* rubella contracted by the mother during the first trimester of pregnancy. Birth injuries, asphyxia, and prematurity are among the *perinatal* conditions that may affect the child during or immediately preceding birth. During infancy and early childhood, handicapping conditions can result from malnutrition, accidental physical trauma (especially to the brain), child abuse/neglect, and from diseases and infections such as encephalitis, meningitis, and chronic otitis media. Finally, it appears that a great proportion of the children suffering from school learning difficulties have simply not received the necessary experiential and cultural prerequisites such as social and educational stimulation.

Obviously, the early medical, nutritional, social, and educational needs of children must be satisfied in order to maximize their opportunities for healthy development. And it is equally true that the sooner an etiological factor is arrested or ameliorated, the less profound will be its debilitating effects. Unfortunately, early delivery of services, which may be of great importance to some young children and their families, is frequently difficult. Not only are funds and services limited, but also the identification of children with less severe but potential handicapping conditions is no easy task.

LANGUAGE DEVELOPMENT

That language and intellectual competence are closely intertwined is becoming increasingly obvious. Often accompanying immature language are such immature thought processes as delayed discrimination and reasoning skills. Indeed, severe language delay or inadequacy is the most significant single behavioral sign indicating a young child's need for special help in order to succeed in school.

Socialization depends upon experiences with language and communication. The ability to abstract the essence of experiences and the urge and power to express complex thoughts and feelings is uniquely human. Although animals may respond to symbols for specific things, such as a dog knowing he is going for a walk when he sees his leash, only people can generalize from their experiences and share an analysis and synthesis of their ideas with others. From infancy on, human learning is dependent upon the acquisition of the communication code of that culture.

The very young child faces the task of learning to understand the world's confusing happenings. Understanding is restricted to the immediate and concrete during early childhood. Concomitant with the development of language skills, the child gradually begins to deal with abstractions, and begins to use symbolization in more complex ways.

Unfortunately, as all educators know, the path leading from simple and concrete communication to the complex and abstract variety of understanding is a treacherous one that can be followed only if the child is afforded appropriate environmental experiences. A rich and stimulating language environment during the early childhood years is required to develop the verbal and intellectual skills essential for later school success (Horton, 1974; Vygotsky, 1978; White, 1975). Moreover, to develop intellect and expressive skills, a child must be provided with stimulating sensory and social experiences that involve the child emotionally and help create a need for communication. Clearly, insufficient and unsatisfying experiences with the social and physical worlds can hamper the drive to talk and question. They may eventually reduce the child's motivation and create language and thought patterns that cause school failure.

The language patterns of many children from lower socioeconomic levels are a source of considerable concern to linguists, psychologists, and educators. The language of lower-class children often differs significantly from the standard English spoken by middle-class children and expected by teachers within the public schools. Bereiter and Engelmann (1966) go so far as to equate cultural deprivation with language deprivation, insisting that for lower-class children to succeed in school, they must learn the middle-class language of the school system. Similarly, Bloom, Davis, & Hess (1965) treat the speech of lower-class children in terms of "language deficit." They maintain that the language and future learning of lower-class children are inhibited because their parents are less likely to provide the quantity and quality of verbal "corrective feedback" found in typical middle-class environments. Unfortunately, viewing a child from a language-deficit perspective suggests that the child is deprived of a structurally systematic and functionally adequate language. Further, it suggests that the lower-class child is generally deprived of culturalization when, in fact, the deprivation may relate only to middle-class culture. Hence, perceiving the lower-class child as having "language differences" rather than "language deficiencies" is preferable (Baratz, 1969).

Whether viewed as different or deficient, the language used by lower-class children in their homes varies considerably from that used in school. Hess and Shipman (1967) conducted class-related research that found language learning and intellectual growth to be by-products of the verbal interaction between mother and child. Their research revealed that middle-class mothers most often employed a democratic type of control, used expanded sentences, and provided labels for objects. Most lower-class mothers, on the other hand, used an imperative type of control, spoke in a restricted form of language, and failed to provide their children with labels for objects. Although language style does vary within lower socioeconomic groups, lower-class children typically develop a mode of communication, perhaps adequate at home, which nonetheless may not be sufficient enough for progress in school.

Language difficulties, however, are not unique to lower-class youngsters. Many middle- and upper-class parents fail to provide their children with a language environment conducive to later school success. Moreover, language disabilities result not only from faulty learning, but often from emotional disturbance, hearing impairment, central nervous system dysfunction, and mental retardation, none of which know social-class distinctions.

EARLY INTERVENTION PROJECTS

Head Start

Because large numbers of children within the lower class have experienced school difficulties, the nation's first comprehensive effort to provide prerequisite educational opportunities focused on economically disadvantaged children. Within this population were found the highest incidence of language differences as well as all other types of handicaps. The first nationwide program specifically designed for children likely to experience later educational difficulties was Project Head Start. Head Start programs began with the hope of providing not only rich language environments, but also a wide range of health, nutritional, and educational experiences for economically disadvantaged preschoolers.

The commencement of Project Head Start in the spring of 1965 engendered hope in some circles of one day significantly reducing personal failure and poverty in society. Born under the auspices of the Office of Economic Opportunity, Project Head Start authorized the organization and establishment of 6-week summer programs for children whose family income fell below the poverty level set by Congress. Geared to the early childhood years, the program attempted to provide whatever environmental supplements were needed to prevent failure in the elementary grades. Following the first summer's operation, Head Start programs for the full academic year were initiated. Although the personnel of early Head Start centers were left free to determine specific objectives and their means of achievement, greater levels of program specificity were gradually introduced. And because of abundant differences in beliefs among centers as to the needs of children, substantial variation in programs developed. The creators of some programs emphasized development of social skills while others concentrated on the development of good health and dietary habits. Many programs resembled a traditional nursery school, but others emphasized intensive directive instruction in language, reading-readiness skills, science, and math. Thus, Head Start was in effect many different programs with centers varying widely in terms of what and how they taught.

One of the most innovative and exciting aspects of Project Head Start was its concept of parent involvement. Active parents can add continuity to the child's home and school experiences while also encouraging at-home practice of the cognitive skills disadvantaged children may lack. In addition, a parent's active contribution to the child's education often engenders new feelings of adequacy and self-worth in the parent that, in turn, may enhance affectional relationships in the home (Evans, 1971). However, while federal Head Start officials encouraged parent participation, they failed to adequately specify how parents were to be involved and there was substantial variation from center to center.

The nationwide interest in early childhood education and the exciting possibilities presented by Project Head Start appear in retrospect to have generated some unfortunate side effects. Amid the excitement, child development experts failed to caution the nation that a 6-week summer session or even a full-year program prior to school entrance would provide only a beginning in meeting the educational needs of young children. And specialists did not adequately inform the public that the scientific study of child development, in its infancy, could provide only a few clues about the necessary social and educational experiences required for optimal development of young children. Moreover, at the time, educators had not fully recognized the critical influence of the years from birth to age 3 and had not included infants and toddlers in the project. Thus expectations of success for Head Start ran unrealistically high.

Although significant increases on cognitive measures were found, especially from those children from the southeastern geographical region and from large urban areas (Caldwell, 1972; Payne, Mercer, Payne, & Davidson, 1973), the effects of the Head Start experience appeared to wash out as children entered school.

Some time after the initiation of Head Start, the nation's attitude toward early intervention became perceptibly more skeptical and disillusionment displaced the former climate of optimism. Although Head Start had doubtlessly helped many young children overcome classroom difficulties, it failed to realize its promise of healing the nation's educational ills. Unfortunately Head Start as initially conceived did not include many important aspects of educational planning more clearly understood by today's educators.

Educators now know that unless the content of a program is carefully defined a preschool is just another place for a child to be (Schweinhart, Berrueta-Clement, Barnett, Epstein & Weikart, 1985). Current Head Start programs have improved their content and are proving to have significant short and long term positive effects on low income children (Schweinhart & Weikart, 1985). Today the federal government invests about a billion and a half dollars annually in such early childhood programs.

After the need for early educational experiences for handicapped children received wide recognition in the late 1960s, Head Start legislation was amended to require that at least 10% of the enrollment opportunities in each state be made available to handicapped children. Although the available spaces do not begin to equal the number of young handicapped children, today many exceptional preschoolers are participating in this program.

Follow through

In many primary schools throughout the nation, Project Follow Through has been implemented as a means of sustaining early gains produced by Head Start experiences. Authorized in 1968 under the Office of Economic Opportunity, the programs provide continued educational enrichment for primary-grade children formerly enrolled in Head Start classes. Clearly, all special services for young children have the greatest chance for lasting success when continued assistance is provided in the elementary grades.

Originally conceived as an extension of Head Start, Follow Through changed its focus as time progressed. The Office of Education altered it to one that was described as a *planned variation experiment*. The major portion of a report conducted on this project was produced by Abt Associates, Inc. Their data analysis compared various features of thirteen of the early intervention models.

Although many conclusions could be drawn from the final report, there seemed to be two major findings: *(a)* the existence of substantial intersite variation across programs and *(b)* the superiority of the "basic skills" type of model. House, Glass, McLean, and Walker (1978) reviewed the evaluation giving support to the first finding, but seriously questioning the second. In their article, they present a number of arguments that challenge the second conclusion. House and his colleagues stress the very intricate dynamics of Project Follow Through and the lack of definitive answers:

> The truth about Follow Through is complex. No simple answer to the problem of educating disadvantaged students has been found. . . . Unique features of the local settings had more effect on test scores than did the models. This does not mean that federal programs are useless or inappropriate for pursuing national objectives; however, many of the most significant factors affecting educational achievement lie outside the control of federal officials. (p. 156)

RECENT FEDERAL INITIATIVES SUPPORTING PRESCHOOL PROGRAMS

Four federal initiatives—Education for All Handicapped Children Act-B (EHA-B), the Preschool Incentive Grant Program, the State Implementation Grant Program and the Handicapped Children's Early Education Program (HCEEP)—have played a critical role in encouraging preschool programs. The U.S. Department of Education (1984) reports that the number of states choosing to participate in these preschool programs has more than doubled since fiscal year 1978. They report that the accomplishments of the HCEEP, better known as the First Chance Network, are greater and more varied than those of any other documented education program.

MAJOR ISSUES IN EARLY CHILDHOOD EDUCATION

Educational strategies

Today, there are a variety of intervention strategies as evidenced by the variety of models in the Follow Through Project. The

Follow Through Project classifies their various orientations into three main categories (Stebbins, St. Pierre, Proper, Anderson, & Cerva, 1977, pp. 131–132):

Basic Skills	These models focus first on the elementary skills of vocabulary, arithmetic computation, spelling, and language.
Cognitive-Conceptual	These models emphasize the more complex "learning-to-learn" and problem-solving skills.
Affective-Cognitive	These models focus primarily on self-concept and attitudes toward learning, and secondarily on "learning-to-learn" skills.

Underlying each of these orientations is a theoretical foundation derived from years of psychological research. Although a full discussion of these orientations currently in use is beyond the scope of this book, we can presently state that more research is needed before establishing the superiority of any specific orientation.

Parent involvement

In past years the advice given to parents of exceptional children by physicians, teachers, and psychologists was often ill-founded: "Just wait and see what happens. He'll probably grow out of it." Instead, difficulties were compounded and the children fell further and further behind their nonhandicapped peers.

Cleary, the efforts to educate parents and to involve them in the total educational program of their handicapped child are warranted. The impact of parental (or primary caregiver) behavior is so profound that it not only greatly influences intelligence (Garber & Heber, 1973; White, 1975), but it even affects the rate of neuromotor attainments such as sitting, crawling, and walking (Anastasiow, 1981; Kearsley, 1979). Furthermore, not only does the parent affect the child, but the presence of a handicapped child can have a powerful influence on parents. As Hayden (1978) points out: "Having a handicapped child can be a traumatic experience for parents, not only when they first learn of the child's disability but throughout the child's growing years" (p. 42).

Although some parents are quick to recognize when something is wrong with their child, some parents have difficulty accepting the reality of their child's handicap. Such reality-avoidance often prevents the handicapped child from receiving professional attention in the early years when remediation could be advantageous. And this unfortunate fact underscores the importance of the teacher's role in identifying handicaps.

Public Law 94–142 assures a minimum amount of parental involvement, but the need to educate and involve parents as soon as possible in primary intervention programs far exceeds what is required by law. Although some handicapping conditions are immediately obvious, others are more subtle and difficult to detect. Developmental lags or deviations in children are frequently overlooked because parents lack basic knowledge concerning child development and have little opportunity to compare their child's development with that of others (Allen, Rieke, Dmitriev, & Hayden, 1972). Moreover, even those few parents who can quickly detect minor disabilities in other children can be oblivious to their own child's slight limp, speech delay, or vision impairment. Understandably, many parents find it difficult to admit that their child is handicapped.

Identification

Teachers should proceed with considerable caution, however, in their efforts to avail disabled children of needed services. Their job should be simply to observe the children carefully and alert parents that additional help *may* be needed. Teachers must remember that they are not in a position to render a definitive medical diagnosis of a disorder.

Before causing parents needless alarm, teachers should recognize that whether or not a particular developmental skill is appropriate may depend on the community in which the child lives. Personal judgments of disability may be subject to cultural or educational bias. Branding a child as handicapped can have devastating effects on his or her self-esteem, and the label may well become a self-fulfilling prophecy. Stated differently, low expectations can encourage low performance.

Clearly, it is within the teacher's proper role to observe children carefully and to obtain professional assistance in interpreting behavioral signs. Appropriate parental warnings and referrals for further diagnosis should be made only after the teacher systematically records observations of the child's behavior. All early childhood teachers should familiarize themselves with developmental, age-appropriate behaviors and with potentially troublesome behaviors in young children. Teachers should keep in mind that even among "normal" children vast differences abound in the physical, social, and intellectual growth rates of individuals. Only those children who after careful observation appear well behind their peers in some basic facet of development will need to be referred for further diagnosis and special services. (For lists of specific behaviors indicative of potential problems, see Allen, Rieke, Dmitriev, & Hayden, 1972; and Wallace & Kauffman, 1986.)

In addition to the teacher's identification of students who need special services, there is now a trend toward the early identification of handicapped infants. With our present knowledge, approximately 6.8% of handicapped children can be identified at birth or very shortly thereafter. Pediatricians, then, are in the best position to identify handicapped infants and toddlers and, if appropriately trained, can communicate helpful suggestions to parents. Major efforts are currently being made to educate physicians in normal and exceptional child development (Guralnick, Richardson, & Heiser, 1982). Techniques for postnatal evaluation are presently available. To be useful, or perhaps justified, this early identification must be followed up with the appropriate commensurate services. Presently, only a few of these services are available to handicapped neonates. However, along with increasing research in this area emphasizing the importance of the child's first 3 years of life, appropriate services are being developed as well.

Prevention

Early identification and intervention sometimes become a vehicle for preventing or inhibiting the further development of handicapping conditions. If services for the child and the parents can be provided at a very early point in the infant's development, many major problems can be avoided at a later time. However, the prevention of severe problems also depends on the continued improvement of medical and health services and on the ability to improve environmental factors (e.g., proper nutrition, adequate medical care, healthy living conditions).

CONCLUSION

Early childhood programs are here to stay. Research has clearly documented their importance. We have no substantial evidence, however, to indicate that any one teaching approach is superior in every situation and with every child. We do know that some exceptional children require positive reinforcement and direct instruction before they begin to manipulate and meaningfully interact with the physical environment. On the other hand, many young children clearly respond to directive teaching with greater enthusiasm and more correct responses if first given the opportunity to manipulate concrete objects. The likelihood is that the young handicapped child's optimum development is best fostered in an environment that provides ample opportunity for self-directed exploration supplemented by directive instruction in areas of the child's greatest need. Parent involvement can maximize training efforts.

The study of human behavior is still in its infancy. Seventy years ago, Freud and Watson were only beginning their studies on the nature of behavior and learning. The real impetus for early childhood education began as late as the 1960s, and the importance of the first 3 years is just beginning to be widely recognized.

We have learned much in a very short time. Yet, we are still falling far short in meeting the needs of our young handicapped children. However, with continued progress in our commitment to educational programming and research, the future for young exceptional children is full of promise.

SUGGESTIONS FOR WORKING WITH EARLY CHILDHOOD HANDICAPPED CHILDREN

1. Be familiar with milestones for normal development and focus instructional activities around the handicapped child's delays. Help him or her enjoy and appreciate his or her strengths.
2. Don't waste time teaching unnecessary skills. Focus on those skills that the child must have to succeed in school and in his social world.
3. Break down learning tasks so that the child proceeds one step at a time.

4. High expectations that the child can take the next developmental step are critical to her willingness to try.

5. Spend some time helping parents learn teaching principles such as goal setting, breaking down tasks, and so on. Parents can then support your educational program at home.

6. Ask parents about the most time-consuming and frustrating parts of their time with the child. Help parents set up at-home programs for the areas where they would like to see their child's behavior change. Frequent problem areas are bath taking, dressing, eating, discipline, bedtime routine, and success with neighborhood children.

7. Preschool handicapped children need a good, sound educational program where time is not wasted on nonessential learning tasks. They also need a warm, loving connection with the teacher and an abundance of affirmation.

8. Low teacher-child ratios can enhance the progress toward learning goals.

PONDER THESE

Suppose you suspect that a child in your preschool group has a language deficiency. What would be the advantages and disadvantages of alerting the child's parents to this possible difficulty?

A 6-year-old child with whom you work exhibits the following:

Antisocial behavior (kicking, hitting, scratching, spitting on others)

Severe language and speech disorders (poor articulation, poverty of expression)

Lack of independent play skills (cannot play alone with toys)

Lack of appropriate self-help skills (cannot feed himself without spilling or dress himself without help)

Which of the child's problem behaviors would you work on first? Why? How would you go about changing these behaviors?

Consider what a "learning disability" is in a preschool youngster. How can it be manifested and identified?

Identify some specific concerns associated with the following areas that might put a preschool age child at risk for future school failure:

- Medical factors
- Environmental factors
- Cultural factors

REFERENCES

Allen, K. E., Rieke, J., Dmitriev, V., & Hayden, A. H. (1972). Early warning: Observation as a tool for recognizing potential handicaps in young children. *Educational Horizons, 50,* 43–55.

Anastasiow, N. J. (1981). Early childhood education for the handicapped in the 1980's: Recommendations: *Exceptional Children, 47,* 276–282.

Baratz, J. (1969). Linguistic and cultural factors in teaching reading to ghetto children. *Elementary English, 46,* 199–203.

Bereiter, C., & Englemann, S. (1966). *Teaching disadvantaged children in the preschool.* Englewood Cliffs, NJ: Prentice-Hall.

Bloom, B. S. (1964). *Stability and change in human characteristics.* New York: Wiley.

Bloom, B., Davis, A., & Hess, R. (1965). *Compensatory education for cultural deprivation.* New York: Holt, Rinehart & Winston.

Caldwell, B. M. (1972). Consolidating our gains in early childhood. *Educational Horizons, 50,* 56–62.

Evans, E. D. (1971). *Contemporary influences in early childhood education.* New York: Holt, Rinehart & Winston.

Garber, H., & Heber, R. (1973). *The Milwaukee Project: Early intervention as a technique to prevent mental retardation.* Stoors: The University of Connecticut Technical Paper.

Guralnick, M. J., Richardson, H. B., Jr., & Heiser, K. E. (1982). A curriculum in handicapping conditions for pediatric residents. *Exceptional Children, 48,* 338–346.

Hayden, A. H. (1978). Special education for young children. In N. G. Haring (Ed.), *Behavior of exceptional children* (2nd. ed., pp. 29–43). Columbus, OH: Merrill.

Hayden, A. H. (1979). Handicapped children, birth to age 3. *Exceptional Children, 45,* 510–516.

Hess, R. D., & Shipman, V. (1967). Cognitive elements in maternal behavior. *The craft of teaching and the schooling of teachers.* Denver: U.S. Office of Education, Tri-University Project, 57–85.

Horton, K. B. (1974). Infant intervention and language learning. In R. L. Schidfelbusch & L. L. Lloyd (Eds.), *Language perspectives—Acquisition, retardation and intervention* (pp. 469–491). Baltimore, MD: University Park.

House, E. R., Glass, G. V., McLean, L. D., & Walker, D. F. (1978). No simple answer: Critique of the Follow Through evaluation. *Harvard Educational Review, 48,* 128–160.

Kearsley, R. B. (1979). Latrogenic retardation: A syndrome of learned incompetence. In R. B. Kearsley & I. E. Sigel (Eds.), *Infants at risk:*

Assessment of cognitive functioning. Hillsdale, NJ: Lawrence Erlbaum Associates.

McDaniels, G. (1977). Successful programs for young handicapped children. *Educational Horizons, 56,* 26–33.

Nagera, H. (1975). Day-care centers: Red light, green light or amber light. *The International Review of Psycho-Analysis, 2* (1), 121–137.

National Advisory Committee on the Handicapped. (1976). *Annual report.* Washington, DC: U.S. Office of Education.

O'Connell, J. C. (1983). Education of handicapped preschoolers: A national survey of services and personnel requirements. *Exceptional Children, 49,* 528–540.

Payne, J. S., Mercer, C. D., Payne, R. A., & Davison, R. G. (1973). *Head Start: A tragicomedy with epilogue.* New York: Behavioral Publications.

Sandler, A., Coren, A. & Thurman, S. K. (1983). A training program for parents of handicapped preschool children: Effects upon mother, father and child. *Exceptional Children, 49,* 355–358.

Schweinhart, L. J., Berrueta-Clement, J. R. Barnett, W. S., Epstein, A. S., & Weikart, D. P. (1985). The promise of early childhood education. *Phi Delta Kappan, 66,* 548–553.

Schweinhart, L. J., & Weikart, D. P. (1985). Evidence that good early childhood programs work. *Phi Delta Kappan, 66,* 545–551.

Shearer, M., & Shearer, D. (1972). The Portage project: A model for early childhood education. *Exceptional Children, 36,* 210–217.

Skeels, H. M. (1966). Adult status of children with contrasting early life experiences: A follow-up study. *Monographs of the Society for Research in Child Development, 31,* No. 3(Whole No. 105), 1–68.

Sontag, E. (1977). Introductory speech to 1977 BEH Project Directors' Conference, Arlington, VA.

Stebbins, L. B., St. Pierre, R. G., Proper, E. C., Anderson, R. B., & Cerva, T. R. (1977). *Education as experimentation: A planned variation model, Volume IV–A, An evaluation of Follow Through.* Cambridge, MA: Abt Associates.

U.S. Department of Education. (1984). *Sixth annual report to Congress on the implementation of Public Law 94–142: The Education for All Handicapped Children Act.* Washington, DC: U.S. Department of Education.

Vygotsky, L. S. (1978). *Mind in society: The development of higher psychological processes.* Cambridge, MA: Harvard University.

Wallace, G., & Kauffman, J. M. (1986). *Teaching children with learning problems* (3rd. ed.). Columbus, OH: Merrill.

White, B. L. (1975). *The first three years.* Englewood Cliffs, NJ: Prentice-Hall.

13

Adolescence and Adulthood

Sometimes what seems like success may be just the opposite. For instance, Gary, a high school student, was involved in our "transition" project. This program has attempted to help prepare students for various roles they must assume after formal schooling is over. At first glance, Gary looks like a success story. Not only did he complete high school but he began taking courses at one of the local community colleges. Things were going so well for him that he qualified for and received financial aid from the school. Here was a textbook example of how the transition process can work successfully. Unfortunately, this story turns a bit sour. Although Gary was fortunate enough to get financial assistance, he did not know how to handle this monetary windfall. Because as soon as he received his check, he left school and has not been seen since. Is this a case of being successful too quickly?

A high school girl was seeking competitive employment. What happened to her during one particular interview illustrates that general job-seeking skills can be more important than highly refined vocational skills.

This girl went to interview at a local fish cannery. She had been trained very well in the specific vocational skills needed for this job, exceeding the skill level as determined by industry standards. She was accompanied on this interview by one of her trainers. However, she picked her nose during the entire interview. Of course, she didn't get the job. Her lack of personal hygiene negated any advantage she might have had over less-qualified competitors. And when you think about it, it was good that she played her hand too soon, especially if you eat canned fish.

A citizen advocate captured the essence of the paradox that many disabled adults struggle against:

> It seems funny and ironic. . .that most people spend an exorbitant amount of time trying to distinguish themselves as unique and different while all that a handicapped person wants is to be just like everyone else. (Patton, Payne, & Beirne-Smith, 1986, p. 469)

Kevin, who is blind, went to the movies with a group of friends one evening. The person selling tickets became perplexed when Kevin stepped up to the window. The ticket person asked Kevin if he could see and the answer given was "No." As there was no recollection of ever issuing a ticket to a blind person, the employee thought carefully about what to do. There was a long line, the ticketer was under pressure, and realized that a decision had to be made. Without any further hesitation, he told Kevin that he would charge him half-price as Kevin was only going to hear the movie. Kevin readily accepted this offer and later confided that he'd take this deal anytime.

With the recent passage of PL 94–142, much attention was directed toward providing appropriate education to students in need of such. The thrust of these efforts was centered on a younger population even though this legislation mandated that concern be given to all individuals between the ages of 3 and 21. Parent groups were very concerned with this younger population as well. As a result, great changes were occurring in educating these children. However, the older student was still ignored to a great extent. As a matter of fact, when examining the literature, this group tended to be the most-overlooked age group (ERIC Clearinghouse on Handicapped and Gifted Children, 1981; Sherbenou & Holub, 1982).

Only recently has more professional attention and action been directed toward the needs of exceptional youth and adults. Some of this interest has been buttressed by the fact that the children to whom much attention was given over 10 years ago are now adolescents. Additional motivation has been provided by the realization that many handicapped students do not outgrow their problems. Years of frustration with a difficult and often unrewarding educational experience have taken their toll on some individuals.

As the termination of formal schooling approaches for these youth, there is much concern by parents, teachers, other school personnel, school board members, and the community at large as to what lies ahead. In relation to exceptional youth, the answer to this question is the interaction of many different variables, one of which is the functioning level of the individual. Certainly, the life choices for a severely mentally retarded person are appreciably different than for someone with a mild learning disability.

What are the life choices for most exceptional youth as they prepare to exit lower education? Patton and Polloway (1982) provide a cursory overview of some of the possible alternative life choices:

Work (full-time or part-time)

Further education or training (2- and 4-year colleges/universities, technical schools, trade schools, adult education, JTPA programs)

Military service

Volunteer work (community-based service, Peace Corps, etc.)

"Domestic engineering" (househusband/wife)

Absence of gainful employment or purposeful activity

This chapter will discuss these variables in the context of transition from adolescence to adulthood. Most of the discussion will focus on those exceptional adolescents and adults who are disabled; nevertheless, the issues and needs of gifted individuals will also be highlighted. We have also made an arbitrary distinction between "mildly" and "severely" disabled populations. This has been done for the sake of making the discussion clearer as many of the issues for these two groups are significantly different.

TRANSITION FROM SCHOOL TO COMMUNITY LIVING

The need to better bridge the transition from school to community living has recently enjoyed a wave of interest and activity. The Office of Special Education and Rehabilitative Services (OSERS) has identified this topic as a national priority. Accordingly, this office has funded a number of major transition projects. The need to better prepare disabled youth for various subsequent environments and to assist them in being placed in such has been recognized by local educational agency personnel, professionals in the field of special education, as well as parents of these youth.

The concept of transition links the two themes of adolescence and adulthood. The transition process can be broken into three phases:

1. School-related issues at the secondary level (e.g., curricula, IEP management, career development)
2. Transitional management (i.e., the linkage between school and community)
3. Community issues (e.g., postsecondary options, community adjustment)

The prospect of disabled youth adjusting to life after high school depends greatly on the cooperative efforts of local education personnel, vocational rehabilitation counselors, postsecondary education staff, adult service providers, and various other community agencies. Traditionally, there has been too little cooperation among these important groups.

If transitional planning is to be effective, then a number of concerns must be addressed within all three phases of the process. Some of these issues will be discussed in subsequent sections of this chapter. This whole process must be guided by the overriding goal of preparing disabled youth to adjust successfully to life after high school. The *major areas of transition* (Hawaii Transition Project, 1985) that relate to this goal include:

1. Continuing education or pre/nonvocational training
2. Vocational training, placement, and support

3. Living arrangements
4. Community leisure options
5. Transportation
6. Medical needs and insurance
7. Income and financial support
8. Guardianship/advocacy
9. Personal management needs

Certain disabled students may not need any specialized assistance in adjusting to adult life; however, for those who do, the schools must play an active role in helping them. This will necessitate systematic transitional planning as well as a re-examination of current practices (e.g., curriculum).

ADOLESCENCE

Although trying to define adolescence in a universally accepted fashion is not easy, this stage of life is clearly very important. It is in itself a transitional phase of moving from childhood to adulthood. It is a difficult time for everyone and may even be more trying for disabled youth. Smith, Price, and Marsh (1986) have summarized the major tasks of adolescence documented in the literature. These tasks have remained fairly constant over time and are relevant to today's youth·as well.

Creation of a sense of sexuality as part of a personal identity
Development of confidence in social interactions
Infusion of social values into a personal code of behavior
Acceptance of biological changes
Attainment of a sense of emotional independence
Contemplation of vocational interests
Identification of personal talents and interests
Awarness of personal weaknesses and strengths
Development of sexual interests with nonfamily members
Development of peer relationships
Completion of formal educational activities
Preparation for marriage, parenting, and adult relationships (p. 212)

The relevance of some of these tasks for specific exceptional adolescents will vary according to their level of functioning.

Issues

Mildly handicapped. *Mildly handicapped* adolescents include those individuals whose disabilities are problematic yet not so severe that they cannot participate in the mainstream of school or life. Categorically, this population often includes individuals with learning disabilities, mild behavior problems, and mild retardation. Some of the major issues affecting this population are described in the following paragraphs.

A group of researchers at the University of Kansas has conducted a series of epidemiological studies with learning disabled adolescents. Their findings, summarized by Schumaker, Deshler, Alley, and Warner (1983), provide a backdrop for examining problems common to many mildly handicapped youth. These researchers found that this population can be characterized in the following ways:

Low achievers—typically scoring below the tenth percentile in reading, written expression, and math

Generalized low performance in many academic areas

Plateau of basic skill development—little progress documented

Deficiencies in the study skill area (e.g., notetaking, error monitoring, test taking)

Problems in the ability to produce and implement various strategic behaviors necessary for successful problem solving

Deficiencies in social skill area

In addition to these areas, other concerns have been voiced about this susceptible group. An alarming number of secondary level students are not adequately prepared to deal with the demands of young adulthood. Knowles (1978) has identified *major life skills* needed for successful adjustment to various adult situations. These skill areas are presented in the listing on page 231.[1] These areas relate closely to the idea of transitional planning highlighted earlier in this chapter.

---

[1]*Note.* From *Adult Learner: A Neglected Species* (2nd ed., p. 146) by M. Knowles, 1978, Houston: Gulf Publishing. Copyright © 1978 by Gulf Publishing Co. Reprinted by permission.

Vocation and Career

Exploring career
  options
Choosing a career line
Getting a job
Being interviewed
Learning job skills
Getting along at work
Getting ahead at work
Getting job protection
  of military service
Getting vocational
  counseling
Changing jobs

Home and Family Living

Courting
Selecting a mate
Preparing for marriage
Family planning
Preparing for children
Raising children
Understanding children
Preparing children for
  school
Helping children in
  school
Solving marital
  problems
Using family
  counseling
Managing a home
Financial planning
Managing money
Buying goods and
  services
Making home repairs
Gardening

Personal Development

Improving your reading
  ability
Improving your writing
  ability
Improving your speak-
  ing ability
Improving your listen-
  ing ability
Continuing your
  general education
Developing your
  religious faith
Improving problem-
  solving skills
Making better decisions
Getting along with
  people
Understanding yourself
Finding your
  self-identity
Discovering your
  aptitudes
Clarifying your values
Understanding other
  people
Learning to be
  self-directing
Improving personal
  appearance
Establishing intimate
  relations
Dealing with conflict
Making use of personal
  counseling

Enjoyment of Leisure

Choosing hobbies
Finding new friends
Joining organizations
Planning your time
Buying equipment
Planning family
  recreation
Leading recreational
  activities

Health

Keeping fit
Planning diets
Finding and using
  health services
Preventing accidents
Using first aid
Understanding
  children's diseases
Understanding how the
  human body
  functions
Buying and using
  drugs and medicines
Developing a healthy
  life style
Recognizing the symp-
  toms of physical and
  mental illness

Community Living

Relating to school and
  teachers
Learning about com-
  munity resources
Learning how to get
  help
Learning how to exert
  influence
Preparing to vote
Developing leadership
  skills
Keeping up with the
  world
Taking action in the
  community
Organizing community
  activities for children
  and youth

Another issue that directly affects exceptional adolescents is the nature of secondary level programming provided to this group. Deshler, Lowrey, and Alley (1979) conducted a study of secondary level programs for learning disabled students and found that the following programming alternatives were being used: basic skills remediation model, functional curriculum model, tutorial model, work-study model, and learning strategies model. Masters and Mori (1986) have grouped these major orientations into three "programmatic thrusts": academic, life skill, and vocational. The most frequently used model found in the Deshler and colleagues study was the basic skills remediation model.

Many programs for mildly handicapped students still have a strong academic focus. This is due in part to the fact that a substantial number of these students are in diploma track programs. For certain students, an academic orientation is desirable. Some mildly handicapped students should be encouraged to pursue postsecondary educational opportunities and provided with a strong academic background. Other, less capable individuals may benefit from continued efforts to develop basic skills and remediate deficiencies as Polloway, Epstein, Polloway, Patton, and Ball (1986) have demonstrated. However, this focus on academics should be integrated with life skills and vocational preparation as well. Many professionals feel that a significant number of mildly handicapped students exit formal school with insufficient preparation for "the life after." This fact becomes more poignant when one realizes that these less capable individuals often do not perform well in postsecondary educational environments and that there are few other alternatives.

It is also true that many secondary programs offer a combination of programmatic orientations, thus preparing students for a range of possibilities. Exemplary secondary programs can be identified by their attempts to realistically assess and relate a student's abilities to the requisite demands of probable subsequent environments. At the same time, these programs teach the necessary life skills (see page 231).

Severely handicapped. The population referred to as *severely handicapped* can best be characterized as having "substantial functional limitations." Individuals in this group may have mental, physical, and/or emotional/behavioral problems of such a degree and nature that they require extensive special services.

The most important issues that involve this population during adolescence focus on the need to teach basic functional skills (e.g., self-care, daily living, communication, "functional" academics, socialization), leisure/recreational skills, and appropriate vocational skills. To be successful, teachers will need (a) to use a variety of training procedures, (b) to provide instruction in community-based settings, (c) to maintain skill acquisition by employing naturally occurring events, and (d) to program for generalization of skills. Furthermore, the importance of transitional planning with this group is obvious as all of the nine areas of transition must be carefully addressed.

Low incidence conditions. Youth with *low incidence conditions* include adolescents with vision, hearing, or physical/health problems. For this group, the major issues center on preparing them to function independently as adults. Specific training in the use of various adaptive equipment may be required. One of the most sensitive areas that needs careful attention is the acceptance of these individuals by others. We know how important peer acceptance is at this level of development and, for this reason, special effort might be required in ensuring that adolescents with vision, hearing, or physical disabilities are included and participate in school-related and extracurricular activities.

Giftedness. It is a tragic oversight to think that *gifted* adolescents do not need anything special in terms of intervention. It has been said that the special needs of this group may be just as unique and important as those of mentally retarded youth. This group of students who excel in specified ways (see Chapter 10 for a breakdown of the different distinctions of giftedness) typically requires unique forms of career education and preparation that match their diverse and accelerated needs. This group also requires programs that allow them to discover who they are (i.e., self examintaion) (Fleming, 1985). Gifted students can also benefit from well-designed and quality counseling services. The importance of this need is underscored by the amount of recent professional attention being given to this area.

Special problems of adolescence

In addition to the normal difficulties associated with adolescence, there are other problems. The exact relationship of these problems to exceptionality is not clearly understood; however, we do know that exceptional youth are just as susceptible to and maybe more at risk. The statistics that correspond with these special problems are staggering and sobering. While we will simply list the areas of concern here, the reader is encouraged to examine these areas more closely. Professionals who work with adolescents should be familiar with the following special problem areas:

Substance abuse (drugs and alcohol)

Teenage pregnancy

Teenage suicide

Runaways

Dropouts

Juvenile delinquency

These are problems to which teenagers are constantly being exposed and with which they must contend. These topics are serious and will not go away. We must be prepared to help adolescents address them.

ADULTHOOD

Nowhere has the principle of normalization (i.e., providing environments that are as normal as possible) been more evident than in various facets of adult living. In recent years, much effort has been directed towards the integration of all types of exceptional individuals into the mainstream of life. For many mildly handicapped persons, this has not been too difficult; for other, more severely handicapped people, it has been a challenge.

The demands placed on adults are many. As pointed out on page 231, a young adult needs to be proficient in a number of skill areas to deal adequately with community living. However, certain demands change over time and individuals must be able to adapt to these changes. As Polloway, Smith, and Patton (1984) suggested, it might be necessary to examine the experiences and resulting consequences of exceptional adults throughout their life span.

The question of what constitutes successful community adjustment still remains elusive. Even within the current professional excitement related to 'transition," no uniformity exists as to what successful transition actually is. Typical adjustment variables studied relate to living environments, employment, monetary status and management, marriage and children, sexuality issues, infrequency of antisocial behaviors and use of leisure time. While some consensus may be found to support the importance of most of these variables, we cannot help but be concerned about the value judgments implicit in some of them. For instance, people are no longer suspicious of any person or group that prefers a single lifestyle to being married and having children. Our responsibility is to help exceptional adults achieve to the best of their abilities and to accomplish what they want, not what we think that they want.

A cycle of frustration can arise as described in the following scenario:

> Having a job, a sweetheart or spouse, a room or home of their own, and personal possessions have become the hallmark of normalcy for many . . . persons and their major goal. Yet, even when these have been acquired, individuals may still feel that they risk exposure through daily blunders or failures, and remain caught in a whirlwind of stress—coping with frustrations of what they are, struggling to be what they are not. (Patton, Payne & Beirne-Smith, 1986, p. 470)

Although we still lack precision in defining the specifics of community adjustment, we do know that three major factors do play important roles in this process: *(a)* the characteristics and behaviors of the individual; *(b)* the demands placed upon the person to live and function adequately within the community setting—some of these demands are common to all adults while others are specific to a given environment; and *(c)* the interaction of these first two factors.

For the purposes of this chapter, we will consider the term *exceptional adults* to apply to people with characteristics that make them uniquely different and with needs that usually require special attention. In general, *disabled adults* can be described as manifesting significant functional limitations interfering with major life activities. Many exceptional adolescents might not necessarily become exceptional adults.

Characteristics of disabled adults

When discussing characteristics, there is always a danger of overgeneralization. So do not think that each of the findings listed in the following paragraphs will apply to every disabled adult.

In a hearing held by the U.S. Senate Subcommittee on the Handicapped, preliminary results of a study on disabled adults conducted by Louis Harris and Associates (Taylor, 1986) were presented. The study included 1,000 individuals, age 16 and above, representing the full range of severity levels. Some of the major preliminary findings of the Harris poll are as follows:

> Education: far less education—40% did not finish high school; only 29% have some college education

> Employment: two-thirds of this population are not working (yet many said that they want to); they lack marketable skills; they do not possess needed equipment or devices (e.g., communication)

> Financial status: 50% of this group have a household income of $15,000 or less; 32% report a household income of $7,500 or less; the greater the severity of the disability, the greater the poverty and the greater the probability that the individual was receiving benefits

> Mobility: 56% of this group report their disability interferes with their ability to get around in the community; lacks accessible or affordable transportation

Due to the method used for collecting this information and the number of individuals polled, the figures reported should be cautiously interpreted. Nevertheless, they do give us a ballpark idea of the status of disabled adults and corroborate other research findings that suggest high rates of unemployment and underemployment, low income levels, and inadequate preparation for adulthood.

Key areas of community living

Where do disabled adults work and live? What do they do with their time? How well do they get along in the community? To a great extent, the answers to these questions depend upon the abilities of the individual, the availability of appropriate community services, and community attitudes/behaviors. This section of the chapter will describe some important dimensions and options in employment, living arrangements, recreation and leisure, and mobility.

Employment. For those who are employed, there are a number of possible options. Many disabled adults are engaged in regular jobs and receive typical wages. Some people with disabilities have earned advanced graduate degrees and have become leaders in their fields. For most disabled adults who have been competitively employed, jobs are likely to be unskilled or semiskilled. Another option is transitional employment. This is an intermediate step between training and competitive employment allowing the individual to generalize skills learned to a real work site under supervision (e.g., job coaches). Sheltered workshops provide another alternative. These settings can serve either a transitional function (i.e., training clients for eventual competitive employment) and/or a long-term function (i.e., extended training or a permanent setting for clients who are not candidates for competitive jobs).

Living arrangements. A great number of disabled adults live very much like anyone else—with their parents, relatives, non-related persons, or alone. As with all of us, living arrangements are determined to a great extent by income level and financial status. For many disabled adults, their low levels of income limit the choices of where they can live. Consequently, we are reminded of the axiom which states: Where one lives greatly determines how one lives.

The continuum of living arrangements for the more moderately and severely disabled adult population includes:

Apartment programs: independent, residential, or apartment clusters

Protected settings: care, boarding, or companion homes

Group homes: family-like setting within a residential neighborhood

ICF-MR programs: (Intermediate Care Facilities for the Mentally Retarded) settings that provide 24-hour care (nursing, medical support, therapy, and training)

Institutions: residential facilities that tend to have the most severely and profoundly handicapped individuals

There has been a strong movement to establish living environments for all disabled adults in community residential facilities (CRF)s. Although this trend is in evidence, the availability of

CRFs is limited in some locations and the quality of services varies greatly.

Recreation and leisure. Disabled adults need recreational activities as much as anyone else to provide a change in daily routine and improve their overall physical conditioning. Unfortunately, many remain outside the mainstream of community life with regard to recreational activities and leisure time due to the nature of their disabilities and/or the inaccessibility of various community programs. A lack of community funds, trained personnel, and community awareness of disabled adults' needs have also contributed to this situation. However, therapeutic recreational programs designed for special populations do exist in many locales. And much recent attention has been given to the need to teach leisure skill activities.

Mobility. "The ability to travel about one's environment develops an awareness of other people and places and facilitates a sense of personal control over the environment" (Patton, Payne & Beirne-Smith, 1986, p. 464). As found in the Harris poll, this area of community living is problematic for many disabled adults. Public transportation systems may be inaccessible or inefficient. However, some cities have developed special transportation services for disabled populations. These services are usually only available during certain hours of the day, not operational on weekends, and can become costly.

Issues related to adulthood

For adults with various forms of disability, other issues are very important. The following discusses some of these issues.

Continuing education. As we all are finding these days, there is a real need to be lifelong learners. Disabled adults—perhaps more than nondisabled adults—require systematic efforts to assure their skills match the demands placed on them.

Friendship. Relationships are a very important part of most people's lives. They provide a sense of belonging, a feeling of being accepted, and an attitude of personal worth. A significant number of disabled adults are often denied opportunities to form relationships, perhaps due to their isolation or lack of appropriate interpersonal skills.

Sexuality. The areas of sexuality, marriage, and parenthood are of great concern for many disabled adults. It can be controversial when considering mentally retarded persons and involves unique problems for individuals with physical disabilities. Nevertheless, there is a verifiable need to deal with *(a)* the reality of sexuality, *(b)* sex education, and *(c)* issues related to marriage and parenthood.

Old age. Little professional attention has been directed toward the needs of disabled people as they age. However, interest has grown in the needs of the elderly in general. We know that as people age, they tend to acquire various disabilities (e.g., visual and other health problems). As a result, persons who were never considered disabled become so, thus having more in common with their long-term disabled peers.

CONCLUSIONS

It becomes clear that we must broaden our interests and professional efforts to take notice of older disabled populations. Many mildly disabled people will not need much assistance; others may require a full range of appropriate services. If we are to achieve the successful transition from adolescence into adulthood, we will need to prepare disabled persons for such. Furthermore, we must also recognize the major problems they will face as adults, appreciate the complex nature of these problems, and be ready to formulate ways to address them.

SUGGESTIONS FOR WORKING WITH EXCEPTIONAL ADOLESCENTS AND ADULTS

Adolescents

1. Consider likely postsecondary settings when deciding what curricular orientation to follow.
2. Educators should be prepared to spend as much time counseling as teaching students.
3. Ensure that transitional planning occurs; involve parents as much as possible.
4. Know what postsecondary services and agencies exist and how they can be accessed.

5. Be perceptive of subtle "at risk" signs (e.g., depression) that can have tragic consequences.

6. Encourage disabled youth to get involved in extracurricular activities.

Adults

1. In general, be aware of the individual's life situation and personal wants and interests.

2. Realize that exceptional persons need to be lifelong learners and as a result, provide mechanisms for giving them the necessary skills and knowledge to deal with an ever-changing, complex society.

3. For more severely disabled adults, provide situations (e.g., living arrangements, work settings) that are as normal as possible.

PONDER THESE

What are the advantages and disadvantages of each of the following program orientations as the sole thrust of a secondary level special education curriculum?

Academic

Functional/life skills

Vocational

In reference to the table on page 231, what other demands could be added to what Knowles has already presented?

How will technology benefit exceptional adults in the year 2000?

How would you react if you found out that a group home for mentally retarded adults was going to be established next door to your house? What concerns would you have? Are they justified?

REFERENCES

Deshler, D. D., Lowrey, N., & Alley, G. R. (1979). Programming alternatives for learning disabled adolescents: A national survey. *Academic Therapy, 14,* 389–397.

ERIC Clearinghouse on Handicapped and Gifted Children. (1981). *State of the art and future trends in special education 1980.* Reston, VA: Council for Exceptional Children.

Fleming, E. S. (1985). Career preparation. In R. H. Swassing (Ed.), *Teaching gifted children and adolescents* (pp. 340–374). Columbus, OH: Merrill.

Hawaii Transition Project. (1984). Honolulu: University of Hawaii, Department of Special Education.

Knowles, M. (1978). *The adult learner: A neglected species* (2nd ed.). Houston: Gulf.

Masters, L. F., & Mori, A. A. (1986). *Teaching secondary students with mild learning and behavior problems: Methods, materials, strategies.* Rockville, MD: Aspen.

Patton, J. R., Payne, J. S., & Beirne-Smith, M. (1986). *Mental retardation.* Columbus, OH: Merrill.

Patton, J. R., & Polloway, E. A. (1982). The learning disabled: The adult years. *Topics in Learning and Learning Disabilities, 2*(3), 79–88.

Polloway, E. A., Epstein, M. H., Polloway, C. H., Patton, J. R., & Ball, D. W. 1986. Corrective Reading Program: An analysis of effectiveness with learning disabled and mildly retarded students. *Remedial and Special Education 7*(4), 41–47.

Polloway, E. A., Smith, J. D., & Patton, J. R. (1984). Learning disabilities: An adult development perspective. *Learning Disability Quarterly, 7,* 179–186.

Schumaker, J. B., Deshler, D. D., Alley, G. R., & Warner, M. W. (1983). Toward the development of an intervention model for learning disabled adolescents: The University of Kansas Institute. *Exceptional Education Quarterly, 4*(1), 45–74.

Sherbenou, R. J., & Holub, S. (1982). The learning disabled adolescent: Ages 12 to 15. *Topics in Learning and Learning Disabilities, 2*(3), 40–54.

Smith, T. E. C., Price, B. J., & Marsh, G. E. (1986). *Mildly handicapped children and adults.* St. Paul, MN: West.

Taylor, H. (1986). *Harris poll on the disabled.*

14

Yesterday, Today, and Tomorrow

When I started teaching [mentally retarded children] in Lexington, I had little information about my students—no confidential folders, only one psychological assessment (five years old and showing that the child had a full-scale IQ of 93!), no educational assessments, no minutes of staffing or eligibility meetings, no data to tell me who had declared these children eligible for special education or why. After laborious digging through files I discovered that 10 of my 12 students had been retained in grade at least once. They had all been behavior problems. One comment from a classroom teacher was, "John is impotent in the classroom." I wondered if he was potent outside the class, until it dawned on me that the teacher had meant "impudent." IEP's hadn't been invented yet. Special education for the mentally retarded was still a waste basket for all the misfits—ill-behaved and otherwise difficult children who were considered the garbage of the schools. No one expected you to teach them anything, just make them happy. Some of my colleagues of the 1970s were hired for special education because they were music or art teachers. You were expected to cut, paste, sing, but not teach reading or math skills. I thought these children deserved more. . . .

Probably the biggest changes [in special education] are

243

those brought about by the law. I complain bitterly about the overwhelming paper work involved in complying with PL 94–142. And sometimes I do not agree with the placement of a child. But I do at least know who was responsible for the placement and why the decision was made, and I know whether or not the parents agreed with the placement. Even more important, I know the procedures for having a child reevaluated and for considering a change in placement. I am relieved that children can no longer be placed in special education classes or removed from them by merely trading cumulative folders in the office file cabinet. (P. L. Pullen, in Hallahan & Kauffman, 1986, pp. 68–69).

Many students now beginning their study of special education have difficulty understanding the changes that have taken place in the field just within the past decade. Practices that we take for granted today were mandated by federal law only about 10 years ago. Many people have the mistaken notion that special education is a discipline of twentieth-century vintage. Actually, the profession dates back to the late eighteenth and early nineteenth centuries. Many people also think that the issues facing special education today are new. But if you read the historical literature you will see that today's issues and problems are remarkably similar to those of long ago. Issues, problems, and ideas arise, flower, go to seed, and reappear when the conditions are again right for their growth. We'll give you a couple of examples.

Public Law 94–142, the Education for All Handicapped Children Act of 1975, is hailed by many as a landmark piece of legislation. It is, but a lot of the ideas it puts forward are not really new. For instance, the law says that every child must have an IEP, an Individual Education Program. Individualization is not a new idea for special educators, however. It is an idea forcefully described by Dr. Edouard Seguin in 1866:

> But before entering farther into the generalities of the training, the individuality of the children is to be secured: for respect of individuality is the first test of the fitness of a teacher. At first sight all children look much alike; at the second their countless differences appear like insurmountable obstacles; but better viewed, these differences resolve themselves into groups easily understood,

and not unmanageable. We find congenital or acquired anomalies of function which need to be suppressed, or to be given a better employment; deficiencies to be supplied; feebleness to be strengthened; peculiarities to be watched; eccentricities to be guarded against; propensities needing a genial object; mental aptness, or organic fitness requiring specific openings. This much, at least, and more if possible, will secure the sanctity of true originality against the violent sameness of that most considerable part of education, the general training. (Seguin, 1866, p. 33)

In 1968, Drs. Thomas, Chess, and Birch published a book entitled *Temperament and Behavior Disorders in Children.* They said that every child is born with a distinctive behavioral style and that the interaction of this behavioral style or temperament with how the child is managed determines whether or not the child will become disturbed. In their words:

Neither in theory nor in fact would we expect a one-to-one relation to exist between a specific pattern of temperament and the emergence of a behavior problem; temperament, in and of itself, does not produce a behavior disorder. We would anticipate that in any given group of children with a particular patterning of temperamental organization, certain of these children would develop behavior disorders and others would not. Hopefully, this variability in consequence could be identified as deriving from differences in the patterns of care and other environmental circumstances to which the children were exposed. However, we also would anticipate that given a uniform environment and set of stresses, certain patternings of temperament are more likely to result in behavior disorders than are others. We are therefore concerned with the identification of both the differential likelihoods for the development of disturbances that attach to different temperamental patterns, and the specific environmental factors that interact with each temperamental type to result in a pathologic consequence. (p. 9)

In 1807, Dr. James Parkinson of London, in his book *Observations on the Excessive Indulgence of Children, Particularly*

Intended to Show its Injurious Effects on their Health, and the Difficulties it Occasions in their Treatment During Sickness, made this point:

> That children are born with various dispositions is undoubtedly true; but it is also true, that by due management, these may be so changed and meliorated by the attention of a parent, that not only little blemishes may be smoothed away, but even those circumstances which more offensively distinguish the child, may, by proper management become the characteristic ornaments of the man. . .On the treatment the child receives from his parents, during the infantine stage of his life, will, perhaps, depend much of the misery or happiness he may experience, not only in his passage through this, but through the other stages of his existence. (Hunter & Macalpine, 1963, p. 616)

In the nineteenth century, professionals working with the insane (today called emotionally disturbed or mentally ill) wanted only the highest calibre of attendants. They realized that attendants, who worked hour-to-hour and day-to-day with children and adults, were probably the most important staff members. In 1852, Dr. Issac Ray described the ideal attendants:

> They must manifest patience under the most trying emergencies, control of temper under the strongest provocations, and a steady perseverance in the performance of duty, disagreeable and repulsive as it oftentimes is. They must be kind and considerate, ever ready to sacrifice their own comfort to the welfare of their charge, cleanly in all their ways, and unsaving of any pains necessary to render their charge so also. In all respects, their deportment and demeanor must be precisely such as refined and cultivated persons have indicated as most appropriate to the management of the insane. In short, they are expected to possess a combination of virtues which, in ordinary walks of life, would render their possessor one of the shining ornaments of the race. (pp. 52–53)

In 1966, Dr. Nicholas Hobbs said that the ideal teacher-counselor, a person trained to work in residential institutions for disturbed children, could be described as follows:

> But most of all a teacher-counselor is a decent adult; educated, well trained; able to give and receive affection, to live relaxed, and to be firm; a person with private resources for the nourishment and refreshment of his own life; not an itinerant worker but a professional through and through; a person with a sense of the significance of time, of the usefulness of today and the promise of tomorrow; a person of hope, quiet confidence, and joy; one who has committed himself to children and to the proposition that children who are emotionally disturbed can be helped by the process of re-education. (pp. 1106–1107)

With these examples in mind, we hope you will read the rest of this chapter looking for the historical continuity of issues and concepts while also trying to understand how social forces have shaped the field of special education.

Exceptional individuals have been found in every society and correspondingly, societies have always had covert and overt social attitudes toward these individuals. By studying the prevalent attitudes toward and treatment of exceptional people over the course of time, we can observe the historical development of the field of special education.

Two major benefits can be gleaned from studying the historical developments related to exceptional people. First, we can better understand the events responsible for our present state of affairs. Second, we can gain a perspective for our future endeavors (Mesibov, 1976). Ultimately, the rationale for studying history must be to make improvements for the future by analyzing the past, planning appropriate action, and actualizing these ideas. Blatt (1975) summarizes this ongoing process as follows: "History is the basic science. From history flows more than knowledge, more than prescription, more than how it was— how we might try to make it become" (p. 402). We must be aware of this "becoming" in order to maximize the lives of exceptional individuals.

To study the history of exceptional individuals, we will focus on important events, notable individuals, and the sociopolitical factors of a given time. Our discussion of the development of the field of special education partitions history into a chronological sequence of periods, each indicating the general social attitude of that time. The reader should be aware that the suggested time intervals of these periods are arbitrary and that clean divisions do not exist. Moreover, different societies show different attitudes. Our discussion here focuses on attitudes of Western societies, particularly those found in the U.S.

Historically, the evolving attitudes toward exceptional individuals can be conceptualized by the following periods: abuse, neglect, ignorance, benign acceptance, awareness, optimism, skepticism, alarm, limited progress, renewed interest, renewed optimism, and reexamination.

THE DEVELOPMENT OF A FIELD

Period of abuse, neglect, ignorance, and benign acceptance: prior to 1700

Societal recognition of exceptional individuals can be traced back to the ancient Greeks, Romans, and Chinese. While most mildly handicapped persons probably went unnoticed, cases of exceptionality referred to within these societies must have been rather severely handicapped. The ancient Greeks are recorded to have abandoned any deviant infant on a hillside to perish. While this action was rather cold and inhumane by our standards, it was nonetheless a very direct intervention program. Often the Romans employed the deviant individual as a buffoon for entertainment purposes: Augustus Caesar maintained a personal "jester" named Gabba during part of his reign as emperor (Kanner, 1964). In China as early as 500 B.C., Confucius stressed a philosophy of responsibility toward other people that included a responsibility toward exceptional people (L'Abate & Curtis, 1975). As Christianity developed, spreading the idea that everyone is a "child of God," more humane treatment was displayed. As a result, exceptional individuals were likely to be cared for in monasteries and asylums.

Often, the explanation of such exceptional individuals was given to misinterpretation and superstition. Martin Luther (1483–1546) taught that certain retarded persons were "possessed" by the devil, and the reknowned Danish astronomer,

Tycho Brahe (1546–1601), believed that his *imbecilic*[1] companion uttered divine revelations. In many uncivilized societies,
the exceptional individual was considered an "infant of the good
God," and, as a result, this person was granted certain privileges
that allowed him to move about the society freely and
undisturbed.

Prior to the eighteenth century, no systematic programs for
the education and training of exceptional individuals existed. At
best, there might be facilities that would provide care for certain
deviant people. In the middle of the eighteenth century, the first
attempts to work with exceptional individuals were initiated.
Typically, throughout the historical development of the field of
special education, the deaf and the blind were the first exceptionalities to receive attention.

Period of awareness and optimism: 1740–1860

Many historical documents attest to the fact that an age of
optimism accompanied by effective education emerged in the
first half of the nineteenth century. Recall the example of Charles
Emile described on pages 71–72. Charles was very-severely retarded and disturbed, but given a thoughtful and efficient education by nineteenth-century special educators, he made remarkable changes, changes that compare very favorably to those produced in similar children today:

> This same poor idiot boy is now docile in his manners,
> decent in his habits, and capable, though not without
> some visible effort, of directing his vague senses and
> wandering attention, so as to have developed his mem-
> ory, to have acquired a limited instruction concerning
> various objects, and to have become affectionately con-
> scious of the presence of his instructors and friends. His
> general appearance is still that of an idiot. His counten-
> ance, his mode of walking, all that he does, declares his
> very limited faculties. Nature has placed limits to the
> exercise of his powers which no art can remove. But he
> is redeemed from the constant dominion of the lowest

---

[1]Many terms used in the past to describe handicapped individuals (e.g., imbecile,
idiot, feebleminded, moron, etc.) seem harsh and offensive today. Social attitudes
and connotations of these terms have changed over the years. Terms in vogue
today may have offensive connotations 50 years from now.

animal propensities; several of his intellectual faculties are cultivated, some have even been called into life, and his better feelings have acquired some objects and some exercise. In such a case as this we are not so much to regard what is merely accomplished for the individual. A great principle is established by it in favor of thousands of defective organizations. After witnessing the general efforts of this school of the most imbecile human beings, and hearing the particulars of Charles Emile's history, it was really affecting to see him come forward when called, and essay to sing a little solo when requested; his attempt at first not being quite successful, but amended by his attention being more roused to it. His copy-book was then shown to me, and his writing was steady, and as good as that of most youths of his station in life. The schoolmaster, who seemed to take great pleasure in the improvement of the poor fellow, then showed us how he had taught Charles to count, by means of marbles and small pieces of wood, or marks made on a board, arranged in lines, the first containing an 0, the second 00, and the third 000, and so on. Charles was sometimes out in his first calculations, but then made an effort and rectified himself. He distinguished one figure from another, naming their value. Large pieces of strong card, of various shapes, were placed in succession in his hands; and he named the figure of each as square, triangle, etc., and afterward drew their outlines with chalk on a black board, and, according to the desire of M. Seguin, drew a perpendicular, or horizontal, or oblique line; so effectually attending to what he was doing, that if any line was drawn incorrectly he rubbed it out and began anew. He also wrote several words on the board, and the name of the director of the Bicetre, without the name being spoken to him. (*American Journal of Insanity*, 1845, *1*, 337–338)

In an era of drastic world change, the French and American Revolutions of the eighteenth century gave credence to the tenets of egalitarianism. With this new spirit of humanism spreading throughout Europe and the United States, social conditions were opportune for new ways of thinking about exceptional individuals. By the late eighteenth century, events occurring in Europe gave birth to the field of special education.

Many historical reviews of special education choose Jean Marc Itard (1774–1838) and his systematic work between 1799 and 1804 with Victor, the "Wild Boy of Aveyron," as the beginning of the field. However, in the mid- to late eighteenth century, the individual efforts of Pedro Ponce de Leon and Jacob Periere with the deaf and the work of Valentine Hauy with the blind are clearly significant. In addition to their achievements with the various exceptional individuals, these leaders established the foundation for the field. It is not surprising that these early efforts were directed at the deaf and the blind.

Jean Itard's work with Victor is significant because Itard, a physician, an authority on the diseases of the ear, and an educator of the deaf, shifted gears to tackle the challenge of educating and training a boy who was not deaf but rather lacked early stimulation and education. For the first time, an intensive program was initiated to educate an individual who was "retarded," deprived, and behaviorally handicapped rather than deaf or blind. Itard believed that sensory stimulation was paramount to Victor's development progress and blamed the absence of this sensory input as instrumental in his retardation. As explained in Chapter 4, after 5 years of intensive work with Victor, a dejected Itard terminated the educational program. Itard considered his efforts a failure; however, the professional community at that time did acknowledge his contributions. More importantly for the field of special education, however, was the precedent set by Itard and his systematic work with Victor and the influence that he had on other key figures who were to follow.

Edouard Seguin (1812–1880), a student of Itard, based many of his ideas and actions on those of his mentor. Seguin was responsible for developing teaching methods related to the physiological and moral education of retarded individuals, more commonly referred to during this period as *idiots.* In the late 1830s, Seguin began focusing on their needs and education. In 1848 Seguin moved to the United States; he brought with him the experience of one of the true pioneers of a developing field. A great contribution to the field was his book, *Idiocy and Its Treatment by the Physiological Method,* published in 1866.

Equally significant to the continuing evolution of services for handicapped people was the inauguration of residential settings that provided bona fide training and education to the resident. Such an institution was the Abendberg, established in Switzerland by Johann Guggenbuhl (1816–1863) in the 1840s. This institution was important because of the influence it had on the many prominent visitors it attracted (Kanner, 1964). Although later forced to close due to poor conditions, the Abendberg was, nonetheless, the precursor of formal institutional care and training of retarded individuals. By this time in both Europe and the United States, institutions dedicated to the education and training of the deaf and the blind had already been established.

While the birth of formal special education programs occurred in Europe, systematic efforts in the United States were soon to follow the European example. In colonial times, mildly to moderately handicapped individuals blended into society. Often these persons passed as normal because the culture made few demands that they could not meet. That is, a premium was put on physical abilities rather than on mental or academic abilities. Thus, the mildly handicapped coped until society began to demand more complex skills. Because the industrial revolution, which began in England in the late eighteenth century, accelerated the need for better educated citizens, it was not long before there was a more identifiable group of exceptional individuals. The recognition of more mildly handicapped children was further increased by legislative action mandating compulsory education. Regardless of these changes, the lives of the more severely retarded were basically unaffected because these new changes did not necessarily increase the noticeability of individuals who had always been visibly different.

In the United States, an individual who became very concerned with the conditions of exceptional people was Samuel Gridley Howe (1801–1876). Howe, a physician initially concerned with the problems of the blind, was instrumental in the founding of the Perkins School for the Blind located in Watertown, Massachusetts. In 1848, Howe extended his efforts to retarded individuals by establishing the first school for "idiotic" and "feebleminded" youth in Massachusetts.

Prior to Howe's accomplishments, two other familiar names were already at work in their respective fields. In 1817, the Reverend T. H. Gallaudet (1787–1851) founded the first American residential school for the deaf, the American Asylum for the Deaf and Dumb, in Hartford, Connecticut. In the following year, a small number of retarded individuals also received services at this institution. In 1829, Louis Braille (1809–1852) published his raised dot system *(braille)*, which allowed blind persons to read and write.

From the pioneering work of Howe, Gallaudet, and other early professionals, an interest in providing services for exceptional people in the United States was definitely emerging. In addition, during the 1840s, a crusade for better treatment of the insane, championed by the zealous Dorothea Dix, gained much attention. Similar notice was attained by Samuel Howe's vociferous confrontation with the governor of Massachusetts over a threatened veto of funds designated for exceptional persons. There was a hope and optimism that the more severely handicapped could be educated and reintegrated into society. During this time, many promises were made concerning handicapped people's ability to learn and the possibility that they would eventually assume productive roles in the community. The optimistic spirit created by the early achievement of individuals such as Itard, Seguin, Guggenbühl, and Howe was soon to give way to sharp criticism that would drastically affect the field of special education for many years.

Period of skepticism: 1860–1900

By the late nineteenth century, unfulfilled promises made by the enthusiastic pioneers in the field drew strong criticism. While these educators believed that many members of the severely handicapped population could regain a normal status in society through appropriate education and training in residential facilities, many critics were stressing that no "curing" had occurred as promised. Although the notion that these individuals could be "cured" was false, it was, nonetheless, an important factor in the growing criticism of training handicapped people in this country.

The general attitude toward integrating exceptional individuals into society was changing to one of segregation. Residential institutions now began to function as protecting agents for society by isolating handicapped individuals within their walls. By adopting this custodial philosophy, these institutions gave little attention to the education and training of their charges. The custodial care of the late nineteenth century was different from the care afforded handicapped individuals in the earlier era of the monastic asylum (pre-1700s). Naivete could not now explain the failure to provide services as it could prior to the eighteenth century. There is a difference between the benign acceptance that existed before 1700 due to the lack of adequate knowledge and the termination of educational services in the late 1800s due to skepticism.

Certain characteristics of the next period (referred to as "the period of alarm") that marks the opening of the twentieth century, were also beginning to evolve at this time. Because the social attitude in the late 1800s associated feeblemindedness with criminal behavior, poverty, incorrigibility, and disease, the efforts to segregate the feebleminded from society were enhanced. In 1869, Sir Francis Galton published a book entitled *Hereditary Genius* that extended the evolutionary ideas of his cousin, Charles Darwin, to include mental characteristics. The eugenics movement, whose aim was to control hereditary qualities through selective breeding, was to mature in the early 1900s and would utilize many of Galton's ideas.

Prior to the Civil War in the 1860s, American society was basically agrarian, but, after the war, urbanization commenced at a rapid pace. The complications of urbanization were exacerbated by the influx of immigrants from Europe and the continuing consequences of the industrial revolution. These factors were significant in establishing compulsory education laws.

The period of skepticism was not without its achievements. In 1869, the first day class for the blind was established in Boston, Massachusetts, and the first day class for the mentally retarded was founded in Providence, Rhode Island. And in 1871, the first ungraded class for children with behavioral problems was initiated in New Haven, Connecticut.

By the latter part of the nineteenth century, the societal position of optimism and enthusiasm had metamorphosed into one of criticism and skepticism, which finally culminated in a state of alarm by the early part of the twentieth century. Although services for exceptional individuals were continuing for the deaf and for the blind, they were regressing for the retarded population. Provoked by a few events that began in the late 1800s, the period of alarm came to a climax in the early 1900s.

Period of alarm: 1900–1920

The early 1900s were paradoxical when one considers that, despite the legislative advances made on behalf of exceptional individuals, an attitude of paranoia was developing. This state of alarm flourished at the height of the eugenics scare, which was catalyzed in part by the discovery of Gregor Mendel's laws of inheritance and by the advent of intelligence testing.

The eugenics movement, finding strong support in Mendel's work, espoused the idea that not only were the "feebleminded" a direct threat to this and future societies, but also that this handicap could be inherited. In 1912, H. H. Goddard gave fuel to the fire when he published his study of the Kallikak family in which he ostensibly documented the genetic transmission of feeblemindedness through five generations (see Smith, 1985).

In 1905, Alfred Binet and Theodore Simon provided French society with an instrument that would have significant worldwide implications throughout this century. The mental scale or intelligence test that Binet and Simon developed would now identify many handicapped individuals who previously had gone unnoticed. And this development gave the eugenics faction within the emerging social sciences a means of furthering their philosophy. In 1916, Louis Terman and his colleagues developed Binet's instrument into a workable scale for use in the United States.

It did not take long for the effects of the eugenics movement to be felt everywhere in the United States. In 1907, Indiana passed the first sterilization law in this country. And by 1930, 30 states would enact similar legislation. Apparently, the eugenics proponents were being heard! As the social attitude toward the mentally retarded before the turn of the century had evolved into one of caution, now the attitude was becoming one that considered these individuals as burdens to society rather than contributing citizens.

In spite of the alarmist atmosphere during the second decade of the twentieth century, the United States passed legislation that increased services to the handicapped. New Jersey passed mandatory education for the handicapped on a statewide basis in 1911. Ohio passed similar legislation in 1919. By 1918, all the states had enacted compulsory education laws for all children. Since all children were now required to attend school, children with mild handicaps became more apparent.

World War I affected the treatment of handicapped people in a number of ways. National attention was certainly focused on the events transpiring in Europe, and, as a result, the alarmist period decelerated. Even though World War I was more a killing than a maiming war, the need for federal assistance to disabled veterans was answered in the form of the Federal Civilian

Rehabilitation Act of 1920. The fear of the severely handicapped individual prevalent in the early 1900s subsided, perhaps influenced by the many disabled husbands and sons now returning from the ravages of war. World War I not only pacified the eugenics scare but also ushered in a new period that was characterized by a partial lull in the evolution of special education.

Period of limited progress: 1920–1946

As the nation tried to regain a stable posture after the war, the field of special education was put on hold. There were, however, some laudable events that occurred during the 1920s. In 1921, the National Society for Crippled Children was established. A year later, the Council for Exceptional Children (CEC), a national organization for professionals concerned with handicapped people, was established in New York, with Elizabeth Farrell chosen as the first president. Although not immediately apparent, the establishment of CEC was quite significant because, for the first time, organization was brought to a field that did not previously have any unifying structure.

Because of the compulsory education laws and the increasing use of mental tests, public educators were becoming acutely aware of the need for special educational services. Also at this time, many new psychological and social concepts were being hypothesized, a trend that can be exemplified by J. B. Watson's book *Behaviorism* published in 1919. Although the 1920s did not encourage a general optimism, worse yet was the stock market crash of 1929 that brought widespread financial catastrophe to the nation. Consequently, economic constraints were now operating nationwide.

However, special education did benefit from a few prominent events that occurred during the 1930s. Herbert Hoover brought national attention to the needs of the handicapped in a White House conference on youth and children that he sponsored in 1930. In 1939, Kurt Goldstein published *The Organism*, a book resulting from his work with brain-injured soldiers of World War I. Many authorities consider Goldstein's endeavors to be a major early factor in the eventual creation of the area of learning disabilities.

In the latter part of the 1930s, the field of special education in the U.S. was greatly aided by many talented and important individuals who fled to the United States when the Nazis gained control of Germany. Marianne Frostig, Alfred Strauss, and Heinz Werner all immigrated to this country, established various programs for exceptional individuals, and had a powerful influence on other professionals in the field (Hallahan & Kauffman, 1976).

The world in the early 1940s once again experienced the tragedy of war, and the "holding pattern" on special education continued. Yet, some advancement during this period can be observed in certain efforts that involved behaviorally disordered children. Efforts to service behaviorally disordered individuals were reflected by programs such as Bruno Bettelheim's Orthogenic School (founded in Chicago in 1944) and New York City's "600" schools for behavior disordered children (begun in 1946). World War II, just as World War I, terminated one period of development and initiated another. In this case, a period of limited progress was concluded and a period of renewed interest was created. World War II and the Korean conflict were characteristically maiming wars, and, as a result, the human reminders of these wars were quite visible. The national attitude became even more favorable and supportive of rehabilitation programs because many families experienced the cruelties of war. As a result, a more progressive social attitude toward handicapped individuals was also extended to other forms of exceptionality and induced a new interest in the exceptional person.

Period of renewed interest: 1946–1960

While the latter part of the 1940s was devoted to recovering from another world war, a new social attitude and the culmination of years of work by various professionals inspired further developments. In 1947, Alfred Strauss and Laura Lehtinen published their book *Psychopathology and Education of the Brain-Injured Child* based on many years of work at the Wayne County Training School in Northville, Michigan. While at this school, Alfred Strauss, Heinz Werner, and their associates were responsible for directly influencing many future leaders in special education such as Newell Kephart, William Cruickshank, and Samuel Kirk. Much of the work accomplished at Wayne County Training School formed the basis for the later development in the area of special education we now call learning disabilities.

State-level legislative advancements continued so that, by 1948, 41 of the 48 states required local school systems to provide special education for at least one exceptionality. Although there was still much room for improvement, this was certainly progress in the right direction. In 1954, federal legislation created a foundation for cooperative research in education; however, this action was not funded until 1958 with the enactment of the Cooperative Research Act. Thus, a provision for financial backing of special education was established through the efforts of advocacy groups and, later, the influence of political leaders such as John F. Kennedy and Hubert H. Humphrey, who had handicapped relatives.

Although the United States was involved in Korea in the early 1950s, it was not as economically demanding as the two world wars, and the development of special education was not stymied. The decade of the fifties was truly a turning point for special education. This decade saw the emergence of perhaps two of the most important forces responsible for the current state of special education services: parent organizations and litigation.

In 1950, the National Association for Retarded Children (NARC), a parent group that espoused the needs of mentally retarded children, was created. The importance of this parent group rested in the collective nature of its efforts. The establishment of similar parent groups for the other areas of special education followed. Hallahan and Kauffman (1986) summarize the important role that parent organizations serve:

> (1) providing an informal group for parents who understand one another's problems and needs and help one another deal with anxieties and frustrations; (2) providing information regarding services and potential resources; and (3) providing the structure for obtaining needed services for their children. (p. 25)

In 1954, the landmark *Brown v. Board of Education* decision handed down by the Supreme Court declared that racial segregation was unconstitutional. The implications of this decision for special education and exceptional individuals would arrive years later, but more importantly a legal precedent guaranteeing certain rights had been set. Eventually, the rights of exceptional individuals would be affirmed through other legal decisions in the early 1970s.

The field of learning disabilities, still in utero, came closer to parturition in 1957 when William Cruickshank published his research with cerebral palsied children. This research was important because Cruickshank had extended the early work done with brain-injured mentally retarded children to children with neurological damage who also displayed normal intelligence.

By the end of the 1950s, the field of special education was ready for the exponential growth that was soon to follow in the 1960s. This predisposition was shaped by a rekindled interest in exceptional individuals and by the need for technological advancement due to the Sputnik scare of 1958. It did not take long for a virtual renaissance to occur in the services for exceptional individuals.

Period of renewed optimism: 1960–1970

Not since the optimism of the first half of the nineteenth century had there been such enthusiasm for the education and training of special people as existed in the 1960s. This activism was engendered by the Kennedy administration. In 1962, John F. Kennedy established a presidential panel on mental retardation that was commissioned to construct a plan to combat mental retardation in the next decade.

One method of gauging the progress of special education during this time is inspection of the quantity and quality of the legislation that was passed. During the 1960s a number of significant laws was enacted. Because the country was supportive of special education, it was willing to pour a sizeable amount of money into the field. Passage of the Elementary and Secondary Education Act in 1965 provided services to the handicapped (Title I of this Act). Two amendments to this Act, PL 89–313 and PL 89–750, extended the coverage of the original act to include exceptional individuals. In 1965, PL 89–313 assured that exceptional children in state-operated schools or hospitals would be provided with federally supported educational services. The effects of PL 89–750, passed in 1966, were threefold: *(a)* to provide a prototype program for the education of the handicapped, *(b)* to furnish a grant program that would benefit the handicapped, and *(c)* to create the Bureau of Education for the Handicapped (BEH).

Programs for the handicapped were greatly expanded during this period. A closely related project, started in 1965, was the Head Start Program. This program evolved from research studies concerning early intervention and from President Lyndon Johnson's War on Poverty. Head Start went through the familiar cycle of optimism, skepticism, and refinement (Payne, Mercer, & Epstein, 1974). At the core of many special education programs, the basic philosophy of early intervention remains a fundamental concept.

During the early 1960s, the field of learning disabilities became an identifiable branch of special education. In 1963, Samuel Kirk named the field in an address at a meeting of parents held in Chicago. The Association for Children and Adults with Learning Disabilities (ACLD), the parent organization specifically concerned with the problems of the learning disabled, was formed during this same time. The early work of Goldstein, Strauss, and Werner and the later work of Kephart, Cruickshank, and Kirk are considered to be responsible for the evolution of learning disabilities as a distinct field. Two books that served as guides for teachers of special education in the 1960s were Kephart's *The Slow Learner in the Classroom* (1960) and Cruickshank's *A Teaching Method for Brain-Injured and Hyperactive Children* (1962). The development of the *Illinois Test of Psycholinguistic Abilities* (Kirk, 1961) must also be considered to have had a major impact on the field of special education.

The 1960s also witnessed many developments in the area of childhood behavioral and emotional problems (Kauffman, 1985). Nicholas Hobbs and his associates began their ecologically based Project Re-ED in Tennessee and North Carolina in 1961. The concept of an engineered classroom was introduced by Frank Hewett in his book *The Emotionally Disturbed Child in the Classroom* (1968).

While the field of special education was generally in a controlled, euphoric state with regard to its own status during the latter part of the sixties, certain key questions were beginning to be asked. In 1968, Lloyd Dunn published an article challenging the efficacy of placing children in self-contained special education classes. Other concerned people were becoming alarmed at the number of children from minority and low socioeconomic groups who were placed in special classes; many observers were similarly shocked at the inordinate number of mildly retarded individuals in institutions. A detectable change of attitude seemed to be occurring in professional circles; while many people maintained their enthusiasm into the seventies, other dedicated individuals were starting to reappraise various aspects of special education. Perhaps things weren't as great as most people thought!

Today it is wishful thinking to conclude that we have the available techniques to change children as we'd like, regardless of the handicaps they have. Although advances have been made, there is still a long way to go. For example, in dealing with psychotic children, the work of Lovaas and his colleagues has been remarkably effective. Using behavior modification techniques, he and his coworkers have vastly improved the condition of numerous autistic, schizophrenic, and retarded children. But are his techniques always successful? In every child he's worked with, his research reports document how he has produced some improvement. In some cases, the improvement has been extreme—the formerly psychotic child now appears very normal (Lovaas, 1982). In other cases the improvement has been painfully slow. Remember the case of Jose on page 73? His is not a smashing success story, and there are many cases like his today:

> We probably made slower progress with Jose than with any of the other children. At discharge, his gains in language were minimal. He would obey some commands; his vocabulary included a number of common nouns, some names, and a few verbs. He would use these words to label objects or express a desire for something, but never for commenting. He would attempt to imitate new words spontaneously on occasion. His greatest improvements were social. His social quotient of 74 reflected increases in smiling, laughing, and self-help skills. He was partially toilet trained. He was testable on the Stanford Binet Intelligence Scale (IQ–47).
>
> At present, Jose uses only a few words spontaneously (e.g., "car," "go to school," etc.), and what he has retained of his speech training is negligible. He can take care of himself at dinner, and is fully toilet trained. His greatest gains at home have been in his play, which has become elaborate and creative, enabling him to entertain himself. He appears indifferent to people. While at intake he appeared unaware of ("blind" and "deaf" to) social contact, it now looks more as if he does not care whether anyone is there or not. He has to be watched constantly. Otherwise, he runs away from home, going nowhere in particular. His parents fear he will be killed because he is unaware of many common dangers. His parents plan to place him in a nearby state hospital. He will be able to come home on weekends and short vaca-

tions. We concur in these plans. (Lovaas, Koegel, Simmons, & Long, 1973, p. 158)

Period of reexamination: 1970–present

Various controversial issues of the 1960s continued to be the concern of special education during the 1970s. Issues such as intelligence testing, labeling, placement, prevention, fundamental rights, mainstreaming, and deinstitutionalization, have come under the discussion of competent, intelligent individuals who actively support their own position in these controversies. Consequently, we find ourselves in an era when professionals in the field are reevaluating their efforts as well as the efforts of others. For example, programs favoring perceptual-motor and process training have been called into question because there is currently a paucity of sound studies that validate such programs. In order to expedite resolution of these and other questions, we need to develop rigorous research projects, encourage replication of previous research, and, perhaps most importantly, cultivate creative thinking.

Growth and change in the last few years have been accomplished primarily through legal and legislative action. Actually, our national attitude has been reflected by the actions of each branch of our government. Events such as Hoover's White House Conference, Kennedy's activism, and Johnson's War on Poverty definitely exemplify the executive branch's efforts. Before 1970, legislative accomplishments established laws mandating compulsory education, rehabilitative services, and variable services for the handicapped. Only recently, however, has the judicial branch become an active, integral part of the development of special education.

During the early 1970s, four major legal decisions helped shape the current state of special education. The right to education for mentally retarded individuals, regardless of the degree of impairment, was guaranteed in 1972 when the Pennsylvania Association for Retarded Children won their suit (*PARC v. Commonwealth of Pennsylvania*). Also in that year, the same right was extended to all exceptional children (*Mills v. Board of Education of the District of Columbia*). In 1971 the right to treatment for institutionalized retarded persons was guaranteed in an Alabama court of law (*Wyatt v. Stickney*). And in 1970, the issue of misplacement was addressed in a California suit (*Diana v. State Board of Education*). Although settled out of court, this legal battle was responsible for issuing mandates regarding placement that were to be followed in the future. Even though these and other court cases have had an impact on special education, the mandates issued in the rulings have not always been followed because of the difficulty in implementing them.

Apparently, more legal suits will continue to be initiated; however, MacMillan (1982) warns that a new twist could occur in future legal proceedings:

> A potential problem that may someday concern you is that lawsuits on behalf of mentally retarded individuals may begin to name specific professionals as defendants and sue for damages. (p. 324)

Significant legislative events have also occurred during the 1970s that have provided a legal basis for services to the handicapped. Late in 1973, President Nixon signed into law, after two previous vetoes, the revised amendments to the Vocational Rehabilitation Act (PL 93–112). Section 504 of this law has been considered the "Bill of Rights for the Handicapped." Thus, the stage was set for the passage of the Educational Amendments of 1974 (PL 93–380) that increased basic aid to states and guaranteed the legal rights of exceptional children and their parents (La Vor, 1977). In November of 1975, these previous legislative actions were significantly expanded when President Ford signed into law the Education for All Handicapped Children Act (PL 94–142).

Public Law 94–142 was a landmark event in the history of special education. As the culmination of years of previous legislative and legal decisions, this Act, which has no expiration date, authorized substantial increases in aid to special education through federal funding to states. In addition, the Act reaffirmed the guarantees and legal rights of exceptional individuals to a free, appropriate, public education. Never before has federal legislative action in the education of handicapped students had the singular impact of PL 94–142.

Implementation of PL 94–142 has met with some problems. Not only have some of the mandated procedures (e.g., integration of students into regular classes or identification of students as handicapped) been difficult to carry out, but some of the basic concepts of the law (e.g., appropriate education and least restrictive environment) have not been clearly defined. Moreover, Congress has never appropriated the monies originally authorized. Kauffman (1981) even wonders if the legal and bureaucratic structure now established will not eventually work to the disadvantage of handicapped people.

WHERE ARE WE HEADED?

Without a doubt we live in times characterized by terms such as austerity, budget cuts, fiscal restraint—terms that never have implied good times for people who require or prosper from various social services. Yet many very important issues still confront us. For example, a few years ago the Association for Retarded Citizens (ARC) produced a document entitled *Issues Related to Services for Mentally Retarded Persons* (1981). ARC is attempting to receive feedback on the issues contained in this document. We have listed these issues as a way of highlighting the type of concerns that must be addressed in the future.

1. What are the implications of the developmental model for retarded persons of different ages and functional levels?
2. To what degree should the normalization principle be applied?
3. How should the principle of least restriction be interpreted and applied?
4. Is integration an appropriate means and/or goal for all retarded persons?
5. Are individual program plans necessary and meaningful?
6. Should all retarded persons participate in work- and employment-related activities?
7. Are we overutilizing and/or misusing behavior modification procedures in programs for retarded persons?
8. Should aversive approaches be used in behavior management programs?
9. Do institutions with self-contained comprehensive programs have a legitimate role to play in the array of residential services?

10. If it is desirable to phase down (or totally phase out) traditional institutions, how rapid should the process be? Should phase down/out be applied to private facilities?

11. Is overall size a critical variable in residential programs?

12. What relative weight should be given to the rights of parents vis-à-vis the rights of their retarded offspring?

13. Are we placing undue restrictions on guardians?

14. Should mentally retarded people have special rights over and above those enjoyed by nonretarded citizens?

15. Are we placing too much emphasis on monitoring and accountability?

Although some of the statements are applicable to areas other than mental retardation, they very much relate to this one area of exceptionality. Nevertheless, the importance of these issues exemplifies the type of questions that professionals in all areas of exceptionality face.

Times like these require that we all take action as suggested in the following admonition:

> The future in many ways can be influenced by what we do or, at the very least, try to do today. The times are such that we can no longer remain passive observers, but must become active participants in the problems and needs of all handicapped people. Our attention should be focused not only on handicapped persons but also on the public, because the key to the future rests there. Without positive public sentiment toward those who are different, nurtured by what happens today and reflected in financial support for our efforts, the future outlook for the handicapped is not favorable. It thus becomes evident that our foremost goals should incorporate the elements of social acceptance of handicapped people, active participation on the behalf of all advocates, and the continued search for new knowledge. (Adapted from Patton, Payne, & Berne-Smith, 1986, p. 514.)

Without doubt we also live in times when the *possibilities* for helping exceptional individuals reach their fullest potential are more exciting than ever. Advances in medical technology, computers, and other electronic devices are revolutionizing our ideas. Reconstructive surgery, transplants, artificial body parts, and microcomputer programs for controlling devices that allow the handicapped to communicate or move more effectively are becoming more readily available each year (see Stowitschek, 1984).

We tend to think of technology as something very cold, perhaps even frightening. But the application of technology to the solution of everyday problems of the handicapped typically calls forth very warm and touching human responses. Consider, for example, the case of Lois, a 50-year-old woman who is severely physically disabled by cerebral palsy. She had never been able to communicate with anyone through words until Howard F. Batie demonstrated his computerized communication system. What was her first response when she could finally send a verbal message to another human being? "Thanks," repeated over and over. And what was her first connected sentence in 50 years, addressed to her mother? "Dear Mother: Thank you for all the patient love I have received all my life" (Myers, 1982, p. 39).

The technological revolution in special education is well under way and gaining speed. Teachers of the exceptional will need to be armed with knowledge of instructional technology and the technological advances most pertinent to the types of children they teach. Advances will also affect the training of special education teachers. In the near future, a common part of learning to be a teacher of the handicapped may involve teaching "simulated" children created by a microcomputer (Kauffman, Strang, & Loper, 1985).

CONCLUSIONS

To understand the history of services to exceptional individuals, we must ultimately look behind the laws, the lawsuits, and the programs. We must realize that the advances made are indices of the prevailing social climate. Unless an acceptable social atmosphere exists to support the recent legal and legislative actions, these achievements will only masquerade as being effective and will eventually collapse under the pressure of criticism. Without the proper social attitude, court decisions and legislation can become little more than political displays.

Over a century and a half ago, the field of special education emerged through the early efforts of a few devoted individuals.

Since that time, the people of the United States have witnessed changes in their attitude toward exceptionality. Many issues in special education that were debated in the past continue to be argued today. We can see this recycling phenomenon in issues such as individualized instruction, mainstreaming, and various teaching philosophies. Commensurate with the changes in national attitude and the reemergence of certain issues over time, the concept of exceptionality has changed too. The attitude of society emphasizes the specific concerns predicated by the various social dynamics of a given time period.

Through the perspective of an historical study of special education, we can improve our understanding of how we got where we are today to plan accordingly for the future. Having a perspective on the development of the field of special education, we might possibly avoid many pitfalls of the past.

As a final word, it seems appropriate for the reader to ponder the following prophetic words of the National Advisory Committee on the Handicapped (1976) in their annual report:

> The crucial central issue goes far beyond optimum pedagogical practices or research or funding or the mechanics of moving youngsters into different settings. The overriding issue in this and all other provisions affecting the handicapped is the matter of attitudes.
>
> The progress of the past 200 years, and the last ten in particular, will in fact remain essentially meaningless until handicapped people win their appropriate place not just in "regular" classrooms but in the "regular society," there to be judged not on the basis of their disabilities but on the basis of their worth as human beings. (p.3)

PONDER THESE

Should individual teachers be held legally responsible when their students fail to learn?

Technological advances make it possible for us to do a better job of early detection and prevention of handicapping conditions. What handicapping conditions should we be most concerned about reducing or preventing? Is prevention *always* justified? For example, would we be justified in not allowing parents whose babies carry a very high risk of defects to have children? Can abortion of handicapped fetuses be justified?

Many technological advances find their way into our everyday lives, but our society does not seem to have enough money to provide them for the handicapped. For example, many grocery stores now have computers that read the prices on items by laser scanner and *tell* you the price of the item, the total due, and the amount of your change using highly realistic voice synthesizers. But voice synthesizers of this quality are seldom available for handicapped people who could use them for communication. How can our society make sure that its best technology is accessible to its handicapped citizens?

REFERENCES

Blatt, B. (1975). Toward an understanding of people with special needs. In J. M. Kauffman & J. S. Payne (Eds.), *Mental Retardation: Introduction and personal perspectives* (pp. 388–426). Columbus, OH: Merrill.

Hallahan, D. P., & Kauffman, J. M. (1976). *Introduction to learning disabilities: A psycho-behavioral approach.* Englewood Cliffs, NJ: Prentice-Hall.

Hallahan, D. P. & Kauffman, J. M. (1986) *Exceptional children: Introduction to special education* (3rd ed.). Englewood Cliffs, NJ: Prentice-Hall.

Hobbs, N. (1966). Helping the disturbed child: Psychological and ecological strategies. *American Psychologist, 21,* 1105–1115.

Hunter R., & Macalpine, I. (Eds.). (1963). *Three hundred years of psychiatry, 1535–1860: A history in selected English texts.* London: Oxford University (1981).

Issues related to services for mentally retarded persons. (1981). Arlington, TX: Association for Retarded Citizens.

Kanner, L. (1964). *A history of the care and study of the mentally retarded.* Springfield, IL: Charles C. Thomas, 1964.

Kauffman, J. M. (1981). Historical trends and contemporary issues in special education in the United States. In J. M. Kauffman & D. P. Hallahan (Eds.), *Handbook of special education* (pp. 3–23). Englewood Cliffs, NJ: Prentice-Hall.

Kauffman, J. M. (1985). *Characteristics of children's behavior disorders* (3rd ed.). Columbus, OH: Merrill.

Kauffman, J. M., Strang, H. R., & Loper, A. B. (1985). Using microcomputers to train teachers of handicapped. *Remedial and Special Education, 6* (5), 13–17.

La Vor, M. L. (1977). Federal legislation for exceptional children: Implications and a view of the field. In R. D. Kneedler & S. G. Tarver (Eds.), *Changing perspectives in special education* (pp. 245–270). Columbus, OH: Merrill.

L'Abate, L., & Curtis, L. T. (1975). *Teaching the exceptional child.* Philadelphia: Saunders.

Lovaas, O. I. (1982, September). *An overview of the Young Autism Project.* Paper presented at the annual convention of the American Psychological Association, Washington, DC.

Lovaas, O. I., Koegel, R. L., Simmons, J. O., & Long, J. S. (1973). Some generalization and follow-up measures on autistic children in behavior therapy. *Journal of Applied Behavior Analysis, 6,* 131–165.

MacMillan, D. L. (1982). *Mental retardation in school and society* (2nd ed.). Boston: Little, Brown.

Mesibov, G. B. (1976). Mentally retarded people: 200 years in America. *Journal of Clinical Child Psychology, 5* (3), 25–29.

Myers, W. (1982). Personal computers aid the handicapped. *IEEE Micro, 2* (1), 26–40.

National Advisory Committee on the Handicapped. (1976). *Annual report.* Washington, DC: U.S. Office of Education.

Patton, J. R., Payne, J. S., & Berne-Smith, M. (1986). *Mental retardation.* Columbus, OH: Merrill.

Payne, J. S., Mercer, C. D., & Epstein, M. H. (1974). *Education and rehabilitation techniques.* New York: Behavioral Publications.

Ray, I. (1852). On the best methods of saving our hospitals for the insane from the odium and scandal to which such institutions are liable, and maintaining their place in the popular estimation; including the consideration of the question, how far is the community to be allowed access to such hospitals? Paper presented at a meeting of the Association of Medical Superintendents of American Institutions for the Insane, New York, May 18, 1852. (Reprinted in *American Journal of Insanity, 9,* 36–65.)

Seguin, E. (1866). *Idiocy and its treatment by the physiological method.* New York: Lea & Blanchard.

Smith, J. D. (1985). *Minds made feeble: The myth and legacy of the Kallikaks.* Rockville, MD: Aspen.

Stowitschek, J. J. (1984). (Ed.) Technological advances in special education. *Exceptional Education Quarterly, 4*(4).

Thomas, A., Chess, S., & Birch, H. G. (1968). *Temperament and behavior disorders in children.* New York: New York University.